PORTRAIT OF CAMBRIDGE

BY C. R. BENSTEAD

RETREAT, A STORY OF 1918   ATLANTIC FERRY
SHALLOW WATERS   H.M.S. RODNEY AT SEA
THE WEATHER EYE   A LANDSMAN'S GUIDE TO SEA LORE

In Lighter Vein, with Illustrations by Edgar Norfield

HIC, HAEC, HOCK!   ALMA MATER
STEADY, BOYS, STEADY!   MOTHER OF PARLIAMENTS

Translations from the French

MEN OF THE SEA   OUTWARD BOUND FROM LIVERPOOL

OTHER *PORTRAIT* BOOKS

Portrait of the Broads
J. Wentworth Day
Portrait of the Burns Country
Hugh Douglas
Portrait of the Chilterns
Annan Dickson
Portrait of Cornwall
Claude Berry
Portrait of the Cotswolds
Edith Brill
Portrait of Dartmoor
Vian Smith
Portrait of Devon
St. Leger-Gordon
Portrait of Dorset
Ralph Wightman
Portrait of County Durham
Peter A. White
Portrait of Gloucestershire
T. A. Ryder
Portrait of the Highlands
W. Douglas Simpson
Portrait of the Isle of Man
E. H. Stenning
Portrait of the Isle of Wight
Lawrence Wilson
Portrait of the Isles of Scilly
Clive Mumford

Portrait of the Lakes
Norman Nicholson
Portrait of Lancashire
Jessica Lofthouse
Portrait of the New Forest
Brian Vesey-Fitzgerald
Portrait of Northumberland
Nancy Ridley
Portrait of Peakland
Crichton Porteous
Portrait of the Quantocks
Vincent Waite
Portrait of the Scott Country
Marion Lochhead
Portrait of the Shires
Bernard Newman
Portrait of Skye and the Outer Hebrides
W. Douglas Simpson
Portrait of Snowdonia
Cledwyn Hughes
Portrait of the Thames
J. H. B. Peel
Portrait of the Trent
Peter Lord
Portrait of Yorkshire
Harry J. Scott

Portrait of
CAMBRIDGE

C. R. BENSTEAD

ILLUSTRATED
AND WITH MAPS

ROBERT HALE · LONDON

© C. R. Benstead 1968
First published in Great Britain 1968

SBN 7091 0112 0

Robert Hale Limited
63 Old Brompton Road
London, S.W.7

PRINTED IN GREAT BRITAIN
BY EBENEZER BAYLIS AND SON LIMITED
THE TRINITY PRESS, WORCESTER, AND LONDON

CONTENTS

Bibliography and Acknowledgements — 9

Preface — 11

I   'The Little Place in the Fens' — 13

II   A College is Born — 32

III   The Colleges Take Root — 42

IV   Southern Approach — 55

V   'Our Henry's Holy Shade' — 72

VI   The Wind of Change — 83

VII   The Family Grows — 98

VIII   'Lady Maggie' — 113

IX   Beyond the Ditch — 126

X   'Maudlin' — 137

XI   'Noble and Magnificent' — 146

XII   South-Eastern Approach — 162

XIII   The Learning of the Clerks — 180

XIV   Late Comers — 191

XV   Wider Still and Wider — 207

Index — 217

ILLUSTRATIONS

facing page

1   The Senate House and the Old Schools   32
2   The Bridge of Sighs, St John's College   33
3   Clare College and King's Chapel from the river   48
4a   The 'Leper Chapel' at Sturbridge (*circa* 1150)   49
4b   Along the Backs: Clare College Gate   49
5   Great St Mary's Church, the historic centre of Cambridge   64
6a, 6b   Half a mile from Great St Mary's today: Coe Fen; Midsummer Common   65
7   The Fitzwilliam Museum   80
8   Clare College Court   81
9   The Round Church, seen from St John's College   96
10a   Wren's Chapel, Emmanuel College   97
10b   The Gate of Virtue, Gonville and Caius   97
11   King's College Chapel and Gateway   112
12a   Emmanuel College Garden   113
12b   The single-span wooden bridge at Queens'   113
13   Queens' College: The President's Gallery   128
14a, 14b   The Backs: Spring; Autumn   129
15   St John's Gatehouse   144
16a, 16b   Winter on the Cam: 'The Wedding Cake', St John's; Trinity College Bridge   145
17   Trinity Great Court   160
18a   St John's College from the river   161
18b   Summer on the river by Trinity bridge   161
19   The University Library   176
20a   The Woolfson Library, Churchill College   177
20b   The History Faculty, Arts Precinct   177

21 Downing College   192
22 New Hall   193
23 Fitzwilliam College   208
24 Churchill College   209

MAPS

Cambridge   16–17
Elizabethan Cambridge   100–01

ACKNOWLEDGEMENTS

The above illustrations are reproduced from copy-
right photographs provided by the following:
Cambridge News (6a, 6b, 14a, 14b, 20b); Ramsay
and Muspratt (7, 9 and 18a); the remainder,
Edward Leigh. The map of Elizabethan Cambridge is reproduced by permission of the British
Museum. The quotation from "The Scholars" by
Rudyard Kipling on page 49 is included by permission of Mrs George Bambridge.

BIBLIOGRAPHY and ACKNOWLEDGEMENTS

The bibliography of Cambridge is immense. Apart from studies of the University itself and particular periods of its existence, there are histories of the colleges and a ceaseless flow of memoirs from old members once resident in them. In addition, there are illustrated guide-books, some of them excellent; a local antiquarian society whose 'proceedings' are invaluable; and, not least, an evening paper, the *Cambridge News,* that completely covers University affairs and, not long ago, won the prize for being the best newspaper of its kind in the country.

The University was some four-hundred-years-old when the great, if querulous, Dr Caius started a notable sequence with *Historiae Cantebrigiensis Academiae ab urbe condita* in 1574, and prominent among the many historians and commentators on the local scene during the centuries that followed are Thomas Fuller with his lively approach to *The History of the University of Cambridge* in 1655; Edmund Carter, using the same title in 1753; George Dyer adding 'colleges' to it in 1814; Henry Gunning, in 1854, relating his *Reminiscences of Cambridge* over a period of seventy years; and James Bass Mullinger producing the first of three volumes bluntly entitled *The University of Cambridge* in 1873, with the others in 1884 and 1911. Also in that year, 1911, came Mayor's *Cambridge under Queen Anne* with its translation of Uffenbach's critical account of college libraries in 1710. Edward Conybeare's *Highways and Byways in Cambridge and Ely* first appeared in 1910, and Arthur Gray's 'Episodical History' of the University in 1912. Its companion, *The Town of Cambridge,* followed in 1925. Moreover, there is a range of literature, less serious though still informative within its self-imposed limits, of which *Sketches of Cantabs* by John Smith (of Smith Hall) Gent, will suffice for an example. According to the old *Morning Post,* in 1850, it drew attention to 'some obvious betterings much to be desired in the tone and manners of a too gent-ridden portion of the new generation of Cambridge lads'.

Architecture is a subject in itself—comprehensively dealt with, in 1886, by Willis and Clark in the four volumes entitled *The Architectural History of the University of Cambridge,* and later, in 1959, given worthy recognition in the two-volume report of the Royal Commission on Ancient Monuments. Bryan Little, in his *Cambridge Discovered,* published in 1960, happily develops the University scene through its architectural phases. Then there are the maps of Lyne in 1574, Braun in 1575, Hamond in 1592, hardly accurate but revealing nevertheless, and the collection, *Old Plans of Cambridge,* published by Clark and Gray in 1921. There are, too, pictorial records dating from Loggan's *Cantabrigia Illustrata* in 1688 to Le Keux's *Memorials of Cambridge* in 1841, and although Ackermann makes the modest dome of the Gate of Honour peep over the lofty roof of the Senate House, and Loggan fails as a prophet by giving one college a non-existent frontal range, these old pictures are often revealing and some are undoubtedly attractive.

But in a class by themselves are the four volumes of Cooper's *Annals of Cambridge,* published over the ten years from 1842, for they are virtually a reproduction of the local archives, so complete and revealing that Cooper himself—Town Clerk from 1848 to 1866—earns the gratitude of anyone who writes about the Cambridge of long ago. I am also indebted to Miss Mary Blamire Young for allowing me to quote from the letters of her great-grandfather, whose life she describes in her book, soon to be published, *Richard Wilton, A Forgotten Victorian.* Some of these letters, from a future Canon of York in residence at Cambridge, are of unusual interest since they were written on the eve of the great reconciliation between Town and Gown, and during a period when the University itself was at last throwing off its medieval shackles.

Cambridge, 1967   C.R.B.

PREFACE

It can be accepted, I think, that wherever English is spoken by responsible adults, mention of Cambridge at once calls to mind a great University. Nor can it be doubted that to the visitors who pour in by coach and car during the Long Vacation, making it possible to walk along King's Parade for appreciable distances without hearing a word of English, Cambridge is still the splendid survival of a medieval University with a small town adjoining. That time and, particularly, the Cambridge Award Act of 1856 have largely reversed the emphasis is not at once apparent. Today, the city of Cambridge embraces a population of nearly one hundred thousand, and exists in its own right as a market town with industry such as Pye and the cement works on the perimeter. Its good fortune, as well as its glory, is the presence of the University that bears its name.

But Cambridge is rapidly changing. Soon after Hitler's war when I added my name to an unbroken roll of University Proctors dating back to the fourteenth century, and walked at night with my constables, the Park Street area was still a warren of dim-lit passages and mysterious alleys, so fascinating that on one occasion an American photographer insisted on posing us for a flashlight record of the scene. Now a multi-storied carpark dominates a broad approach. Elsewhere a sprawl of housing estates carries the city to villages that are themselves dormitories for those who add to the traffic congestion; extensive 're-development' threatens the commercial centre; relief roads are planned with the purposeful thrust of the Romans whose Via Devana virtually marks the main road through the city today; and there is little doubt that before long the older colleges and University buildings, with a few churches and possibly a Victorian railway station remarkable for what is said to be the longest platform in the country, will be all that remains to tell of a more solid if less material age. For the sight-seeing visitor, Cambridge must ever be a square miles or so of antiquity, and—happily—it is inviolate.

Any portrait of Cambridge is therefore one of a University that down the centuries has adjusted itself without betraying its heritage. Today, in the Senate House, when undergraduates take their B.A. degrees, the Vice-Chancellor pronounces the same unchanging Latin formula:

> *Auctoriate mihi commissa admitto te ad gradum Baccalaurei*
> *in Artibus in nomine Patris et Filii et Spiritus Sancti.*

—and if such ritual is noted in its context, rather does one see a gracious old lady, wise in the years she carries, loved and respected by thousands as their Alma Mater.

It is about her that this book is for the most part written.

C.R.B.

I

'THE LITTLE PLACE IN THE FENS'

ANYONE entering Cambridge today from the north-west, along the Via Devana, descends to the river from the only high ground truly in the city—Castle Hill. It is a modest eminence with an attractive Shire Hall and well-kept lawns but no trace of the Norman castle built when Ely was overcome, and little to remind one of the earlier Roman camp or 'chester' from which Chesterton takes its name and probable seniority as the oldest part of Cambridge. One cannot be sure that a settlement existed on the other bank during this period. The Romans left Britain in A.D. 411, and not until the seventh or eighth century did the Saxons build the Great Bridge, commemorated since 1575 in the Arms of the City:

Gules, a bridge, in chief a flower de luce gold between two roses silver on a point wave three boats sable . . .

That the Saxon bridge replaced a Roman is an attractive supposition though unsupported.

It seems that the advantages of its geographical position were reason enough for the new settlement. The Via Devana linked Colchester with Leicester and, it is thought, Chester as well; Akeman Street ran from the Norfolk coast near Hunstanton to the Severn; and not only was the settlement near their intersection in an era when Roman roads provided the only means of speedy travel: it also lay at the head of a waterway navigable from the sea at Lynn. The river was then tidal as far as Waterbeach, a few miles downstream. Ely, with its great abbey founded in 673, was an island of alluvial deposit, easily accessible; and so conveniently was the settlement placed that, even as late as the seventeenth century, a condition imposed on Cornelius Vermuyden in his task of draining the fens compelled him to preserve the waterway. Nor was the site without merit in itself. St Andrew's Hill, Peas Hill and Market Hill pass unnoticed as rising ground today, but their names disclose the existence of dry areas suitable for habitation a thousand years ago. Uncertainty of detail there may be, but in conjunction these several factors do reveal a settlement known as Grantanbrycge in Saxon times, Grantebrigge in the Domesday Book, as Cantebrigge to Chaucer, and, by way of such variants as Cauntbrigge and Cawnbrigge, finally as Cambridge. Moreover, it lay on the edge of the fens rather than in them, as Oxford lightly suggests when referring to her sister university as 'The Little Place in the Fens'.*

Should one pause on top of Castle Hill and climb the mound—itself a hillock attributed by some to the Ancient Britons—the reward is the only worthwhile panorama of Cambridge. To the west, Madingley Hill is not high enough to offset the intervening distance, though a splendid site for the American War Cemetery, and to the south-east the Gog Magog Hills, by the chalk pits, do little more than overlook a sprawl of modern houses backed by a flour mill. But this view from the Castle mound not only takes in that square mile or so of antiquity: it reveals in side elevation the most widely-known building in Cambridge, the cliff-like wall of buttressed stone with its lofty pinnacles that is King's College Chapel. Thousands of people come to see it every year. Millions, at one time and another, must have heard the Festival of Nine Lessons and Carols which is televised and broadcast at Christmas. And the King was Henry the Sixth. He founded his college in 1441, with the royal command that the chapel which he had in mind should be 'clene and substancial, setting a parte superfluite to too gret curious werkes of entaille and besy molding', and it is probable that in contemporary judgment these instructions were not exceeded. Only Ruskin, burning his lamps

* No less affable, Cambridge sees Oxford as the Latin Quarter of Cowley.

of Truth and Beauty, has seen the chapel as 'a piece of architectural juggling', like a 'table upside down with its four legs in the air'.

Castle Hill, the Cam, Bridge Street—they are significant names in local history. Red-bricked Magdalene, the earliest of the transpontine colleges, lends a mellow charm to the river's western bank by today's descendent of the Great Bridge. Though adequate within the bounds set by a narrow street, and soberly cast in iron, it is hardly 'great' by any standard, but it does mark a key point in Cambridge history and provide a convenient diving board from which intrepid undergraduates, in the cause of charity, can hurl themselves blazing into the river. Of more enduring interest, however, are Quayside at the foot of the bridge, the last of the many hithes that once made the city an inland port, and Bridge Street itself, for that is the old Via Devana. Some years ago, back in the last century, excavations uncovered the square-cut wooden beams resting on piles as the Romans had laid them, a method of construction used, less solidly, in the rough plank roads that enabled men to cross Passchendaele's mud nearly two thousand years later.

Wordsworth rode this way, down the hill and over the bridge, and 'at the Hoop alighted, famous inn', when coming into residence at St John's in 1787. Today the Hoop is no more, demolished and forgotten like so many of the coaching inns, and a recent extension of his college borders the Bridge Street artery. The horse, too, has almost disappeared, and even the academic gown is far less frequently worn. Yet this corner of the old town still leaves much the same impression as it did when Wordsworth wrote:

> I was the Dreamer, they the Dream; I roamed
> Delighted through the motley spectacle;
> Gowns grave, or gaudy, doctors, students, streets,
> Courts, cloisters, flocks of churches, gateways, towers.
> Migration strange for a stripling of the hills,
> A northern villager.

—about a year younger than today's undergraduate.

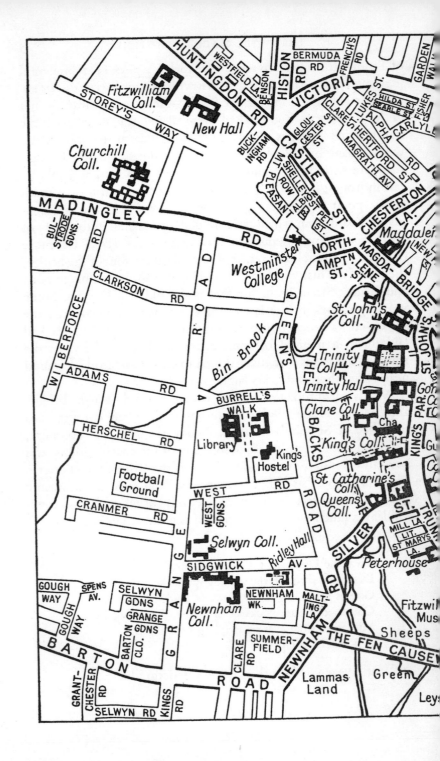

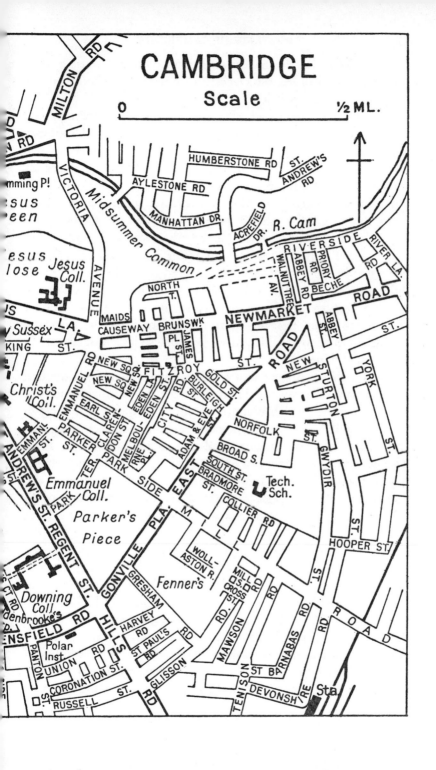

How, then, did this Saxon settlement come to house a great university? What led the clerks, the wandering scholars of the time, to descend upon it?

That Grantebrigge had prospered is certain. It was paying 'geld' to the King for a hundred hides of land in its Domesday rating. But its progress had not been smooth. The Danes had occupied it for a whole year in 875, annexed it to Denmark by the Treaty of Wedmore three years later, and finally burnt it in 1010. Further harried by the Normans, it suffered particularly from the predatory Sheriff Picot who not only filched land belonging to St Etheldreda's Church: he then denied all knowledge of that important lady 'who began the minster of Ely'; and generally its lot was that of the underdog while the country's differences were settled at the level of Church and State. There is nothing here to suggest an embryonic university town. Yet the clerks who came pouring in from Oxford after the riots and bloodshed in 1209 would hardly have done so if facilities for study had been lacking.

It is possible that the educational seed was sown when the first of the many religious orders arrived—the Augustinian canons of St Giles whom Picot had endowed after the apparent miracle of his ailing wife's recovery. They settled by the castle towards the end of the eleventh century, and moved to Barnwell in 1112. The Benedictine nunnery of St Rhadegund, which has now made way for Jesus College, followed some twenty years later, as did the Augustinian hospital that stood on the present site of St John's; and the small stone chapel of St Mary Magdalene's 'leper hospital' survives at Barnwell today. It is significant, too, that the clerks themselves enjoyed benefit of clergy—apparently on the grounds that, like the clergy, they could read—and that some of the earliest teaching took place in St Benet's, the oldest church in Cambridge, and St Mary's-by-the-Market, soon to be known as Great St Mary's, the University Church. Of this educational slant the Oxford clerks must have been aware, and it is not straining credulity to see in their arrival one reason for the further influx of religious orders that quickly followed—the Franciscans or Grey Friars, the Carmelite or White, and among others the Friars of the Sack who appropriately enjoyed a reputation for scholarship as well as for humble clothing.

Before the coming of the clerks, Cambridge appears to have been a normal medieval town of some two thousand inhabitants, locally important by reason of its geographical position and rising status, but that was all, and the 'university' resembled a student-guild of growing repute. It was therefore inevitable that the sudden influx of a horde of quarrelsome students, armed with bows and arrows and the daggers of their day, should set a problem far less welcome to the townsmen who had to find them living-space, than to the guild which merely had to teach. That it quietly assumed the rights of a *universitas* while thus engaged was no more than a corollary to its rising importance in the town. In 1246 there is reference to a Chancellor's Court, duly christened 'The Townsmen's Scourge', for by exercising the right of 'conusance' and trying all cases involving its students, it became a refuge for them against which the townsmen had no redress. One Chancellor excommunicated the Mayor. So, in 1318 when Pope John XXII, at the request of Edward the Second, not only issued the Bull that formally recognized the hitherto 'unofficial university' as a *studium generale* with its 'Masters and Scholars' enjoying the rights of a *universitas,* but also released them from the jurisdiction of the Bishop of Ely, Cambridge University emerged as an extremely powerful institution.

Whatever the legal niceties in the relationship between Town and Gown, there is no doubt that, in looking after its own interests, the University clashed incessantly with local authority, re-presented by the Mayor. It licensed ale-houses. It measured the coal and grain landed at Quayside. It controlled the market. (On ceremonial occasions one of the Junior Proctor's constables still carries a butter-measure used when butter was sold by the yard.) Then, as time went on, it sought to prevent such levity as bear-baiting in sermon-time, and its own enforced celibacy no doubt led it to cast an almost puritanical eye on the local women. Nothing, however, angered the townsmen more than the University's right of entry into private houses, and, on one occasion, provided the Mayor with so splendid an opportunity for obstruction. As the event is recorded: 'In the time of the Sturbridge Fair, the Proctors upon great complaint made to them, going their rounds one night, had taken certain evil persons in houses of sin, and had brought them to the tolbooth, in order to the commitment of them there. But having sent to the Mayor for the keys, he resolutely refused to part with them. So they were fain to carry their prisoners to the castle, where they left them in custody. But the Mayor's son, after an hour or so, let them all out, to return, if they pleased, to their former lewdness, to the breach of the law and the affront of the magistrate.'

That was in 1547, and the Mayor had to explain his conduct to Archbishop Cranmer.

The office of Mayor was indeed no civic reward in those far-off days. Rather was it a period of frustration and peril, well illustrated by the experience of one Mayor who, 'going about to repress misdemeanours offered by divers young men of the University, was assaulted and evil intreated by three or four scholars, and his gown rent and spoiled, and some used lewd speeches to him, and he put in danger of his life. And the scholars being complained upon, answer was made by some University officers that they could not amend it, for so it hath been and so it will be still.'

Small wonder that Town-and-Gown riots, with bloodshed attendant, were common until the University abrogated most of its privileges in the Award Act of 1856.*

To the clerks who straggled down Castle Hill and crossed the Great Bridge in 1209, nothing could have suggested the academic upheaval that was to follow their arrival. There were no colleges then, flanking the river upstream to the King's Mill where the 'small bridges' carried what is now Silver Street to Newnham: only hithes, built on the eastern bank with Milne Street behind

---

* Although this abrogation was extensive and seemingly put University residents on the same footing as ordinary citizens, it appears that a few quaint survivals were overlooked. Calling attention to one at a reunion dinner, the late Master of Trinity Hall, Sir Ivor Jennings, offered to sell his St Catharine hosts any marriage licences they might require.

them and, beyond the river, a swamp drained by nature's channels which today encircle college gardens and create the Cambridge Backs. First crocuses, daffodils to follow, lining avenues of burgeoning trees, with gracious buildings from another age scattered along the river bank—one must wander carefree through this one-time swamp to know the glory of Cambridge in the spring.

But this transformation lay centuries ahead of the early clerks. They knew only a medieval town, essentially rural, with all the crowding and squalor then accepted as normal. Dwellings of stone were few—the rich, and the religious orders, alone could afford them—and it is the antiquarian's good fortune that one survives today as the School of Pythagoras although the name suggests a University link that finds no historical support. When the Dunning family lived there, the town was the size of a housing estate; for the river ceased to be its western boundary at the King's Mill and the King's Ditch took over, heading east from the millpool up Langrithe Lane (later to be Pembroke Street), skirting the nominal eminence of St Andrew's Hill (once the Hog Market) and turning north through the site of Sidney Sussex, a college yet unborn, to run down Park Street (at one time Garlic Fair Lane) and rejoin the river just below the Great Bridge. Medieval Cambridge was therefore shaped like a crude ellipse, some six hundred yards at its greatest width and a mere half mile along its major axis—about one hundred acres, that is; four times the area of Parker's Piece, and less than half the total acreage of recreation grounds and open spaces in the modern city.

The King's Ditch became prominent in the Cambridge story during the reign of Henry the Third when he brought his army to the town, in 1268, to quell the marauding islanders from Ely, and ordered a moat to be dug. It is probable that the conscripted townsmen, denied even a rest on saints' days, did no more than hastily repair the one that King John had inspired at the turn of the century before he gave the borough its freedom. For additional defence, Henry the Third also directed that gates should bar the road to Trumpington at the bottom of Pembroke Street, and the main road through the town between Petty Cury and what is now Christ's College in, that is, the very heart of the city one knows today. They were called the Trumpington and Barnwell gates, and had not the King returned with his army to London, they would doubtless have proved their worth. As it was, the islanders promptly burnt them, along with some of the better dwellings, while the townsmen looked on from afar. Although restored, the gates inevitably lost their usefulness as the town grew larger, and they quietly fade out of the story. But not the Ditch. That became a dumping place for every kind of filth, virtually an open sewer, and it started a row between the Mayor and the University lasting some three hundred years, a long period even in University history. During it, as many as sixteen colleges were founded, ten of them within the bounds of river and Ditch, and of the others, two were on the bank of the Ditch and one just over the river. Cambridge was therefore taking the shape that one knows today—a core of antiquity surrounded by modern expansion.

At the start of the wrangle one must picture a small medieval town of some local importance but no distinction apart from that bestowed upon it by a growing University, low-lying and surrounded by river and moat. Lesser ditches traversed it, stagnant and polluted, their seepage adding to the wells that gave the community its drinking water. Ague was endemic. Soon the Black Death was to ravage the town almost out of existence, claiming the Mayor as a victim, and such was the 'sad mortality proceeding from the infection of the air and that caused by the unclean keeping of the streets', Henry the Sixth declined to lay the first stone of King's College Chapel, his own foundation, and sent 'thidder our cousin, the Marquess of Suffolk', instead. Nor was this caution ill-founded. Sanitation, as the word is understood today, did not exist. Dung and household refuse lay in the streets and market place until rain washed it into a ditch, and it is on record that, in 1393, masters and scholars were overcome merely by walking along Foul Lane—now Trinity Lane between Trinity College and Caius—so noisome was the stench.

Meanwhile the Ditch lay stagnant, devoid of purpose, its existence a symbol as well as a menace.

Nearly fifty years of deadlock drifted by before the University, in 1330, sought the aid of Parliament with a formal complaint that the Mayor and bailiffs neglected to keep the Ditch and the streets clear of filth, and another eighteen before Edward the Third appointed a commission to enquire. But the Black Death intervened, and when, in 1351, the University again petitioned Parliament, there was the Peasants' Rising with far more urgent problems. In short, Cambridge was left to look after its own sanitation, and although in 1402 the Town went so far as to direct that all dung should be taken away within a week and not left lying about indefinitely, a whole century had to pass before, in 1503, it undertook to clear 'the common sege' once every three years. Nevertheless, the undertaking does suggest the dawn of reason, and when, in 1574, the Vice-Chancellor proposed and the Mayor agreed that water should be channelled into Cambridge from Trumpington ford, and the infamous Ditch made tolerable that way, there was the promise—if only the promise—of real co-operation. Another thirty-six years slipped by before the plan was given effect, and the cleansing water flowed as a 'new river' from the Nine Wells at Shelford. Then one notes, with not unamused suspicion, that Dr James Montagu, the Vice-Chancellor in office at this belated consummation, was none other than the first Master of Sidney Sussex on the very banks of the Ditch.

The apparently sudden introduction of a Vice-Chancellor as the University's champion is explained by an adjustment in duties performed. At first the Chancellor was the active head of the University and held office for only a year or two, but since 1504 the practice has been to elect a distinguished non-resident for life. His duties are therefore intermittent and mainly cere-monial. The active head is the Vice-Chancellor who is chosen from the 'Heads of Houses', as those who reign in the colleges are known, and his year of office is usually extended to a second.

The Vice-Chancellor who made the first suggestion of flushing the Ditch was Dr Andrew Perne, vividly described as 'a founder of novelties' and, among much else, 'a morning book-worm and afternoon malt-worm, a right juggler, as full of his sleights, wiles, fetches, casts of leger-de-main, toys to mock apes withal, odd shifts and knavish practises as his skin can hold'. Also his conduct during the difficult years of the Reformation suggests an affinity with the Vicar of Bray. But no one will quarrel with 'a founder of novelties', for so successful was the scheme, and so obviously capable of beneficial extension, that in 1614 a new conduit brought the fresh spring water to a Jacobean fountain which the University and Town united to build on Market Hill. Hobson the carrier—he of the 'choice'—left money for its maintenance when he died in 1631, and probably met some of the earlier costs.*

Today that water still flows. It provides, along its banks, a short yet picturesque country walk within the modern city's boundary, and the no less attractive little canal by the Trumpington Road where it approaches the ancient borough. Here, in its early days, it ran down the middle of Trumpington Street, and it survives in the runnels that take the place of normal gutters—of great interest to sight-seeing tourists but only annoyance to motorists. Until a few years ago the water also rippled along St Andrew's Street, up to the site of the old Barnwell gate, but traffic and bus stops have taken precedence, and the water merely provides a swift and not unpleasant way of freshening the gutters when required. As for the Ditch, in so far as it exists at all, it lurks in the culverts and drains of underground obscurity.

It is said that some three thousand clerks left Oxford in 1209— a mass protest after three of their number had been hanged in spite of the Church's jurisdiction over them, and on no other evidence than that they had lived in the same house as an alleged murderer. It is also known that they spread themselves for the most part between Cambridge, Reading and Maidstone, but how many chose Cambridge is uncertain. Had a third done so, the population would have jumped by fifty per cent, and half that number would still have created an ugly situation, apart from overcrowding, for these youths were hardly what is understood today as 'gentlemen *in statu pupillari*': rather were they hooligans living 'under no discipline, having no tutor, saving him who teacheth all mischief'.

* The conduit head now stands where the canal ends and the water goes underground by the junction of Lensfield Road and Trumpington Street.

One can therefore accept without astonishment that, until the breed was extinct, the town was the scene of 'strifes, fights, spoilings, breaking open of houses, woundings and murder between the burgesses and scholars of Cambridge, and that in the very Lent, that with the holy time holy persons might also be violated'. Nor was their passing the end, for tradition once established does not die overnight. The University, as the years slipped by, undoubtedly moved towards the shape that is known today, but the men of Cambridge still resented its dominance. As late as 1848, with the Award Act only eight years ahead, a future Canon of York wrote to his mother on being allowed rooms in college: 'It is a great advantage being so near Chapel and Hall as there is a town-and-gown row at present raging every night in the streets, and I have no danger of having my head broken by the vulgar rabble. It is a serious thing when a quarrel of this kind commences: it may require weeks to end it. The Proctors have a sad time. . . .'

The Proctors, indeed, owe their existence to the early and riotous clerks, though not as disciplinary officers. They were the representatives of the Boreales and Australes, the northern and southern 'nations' into which universities then divided their scholars, and Cambridge had to take shape as a growing federation of colleges before the Proctors, as disciplinary officers of the University, rode the streets on their white horses with their constables mounted on black. (On ceremonial occasions their constables still wear horse-cloaks, carefully rolled and tucked under the left arm.) But even as *procuratores* they shouldered heavy responsibility, for if the two 'nations' were not fighting the townsmen, they were no less bloodily fighting each other.

In 1261 the townsmen joined the Australes in a particularly vicious riot involving the Boreales, and the outcome provides an interesting light on the privileged status of the scholar at the time, for the King directed his judges to examine the Boreales' complaint not with a view 'to the hanging and mutilating of the clerks, but that they be chastened in some other way by the counsel of the University'. Of the sixteen townsmen and twenty-eight scholars found guilty, only the townsmen were hanged.

The scholars were pardoned. That the Boreales, the aggrieved party from the start, should thereupon set off to Northampton, exactly as the Oxford clerks had migrated in 1209, was a form of protest helping to give the wandering scholar his name. On this occasion, however, satisfaction was short-lived. Before long, migrants from both Oxford and Cambridge were lining the walls of Northampton against the King's army, and it does not seem unreasonable that, in 1265, the King should dissolve Northampton's embryonic university. The mere existence of these wandering students is evidence that Cambridge in its formative years was a loosely knit community, and with this lack of cohesion, discipline could not fail to go by the board. The King's writ, enforced by the Sheriff, alone maintained order, but in those early days even the Sheriff could not imprison or expel an offending clerk except on the Bishop of Ely's order and at the Chancellor's discretion.

In so far as thirteenth-century Cambridge bore any resemblance at all to a modern university, it was a non-residential one. Its clerk's either lodged with the local burgesses—and it is significant that two Masters of Arts and 'two good and lawful men of the town' were appointed to control the rents and check extortion, rather as the University Lodging House Syndicate licenses and supervises lodging-houses today—or they crowded into hostels which were usually dwellings rented by the Masters who taught them. Finding a Master to teach him was, in fact, the wandering scholar's sole preliminary to entering the University—a criterion of scholarship in strange contrast with the 'Little-Go', or entrance examination of later years with its Latin and Greek and Paley's *Evidences of Christianity,* and the assorted A-levels of today. An early regulation that gave him a fortnight in which to complete his search, and threatened imprisonment if he failed and did not resume his wandering, was no more than a spur to the lazy and a bar to the mendicant.

Nor did the scholar invariably pursue his studies when he had found a Master, preferring, it seems from the Mayor's complaint, to set up as a taverner or tradesman, buying and selling to the hurt of the townsmen. Not until the college system came into being did the University begin to exert an effective authority over its members, and hostels overlapped until the sixteenth century. Some became attached to colleges—forerunners of the splendid residential blocks which colleges erect beyond their precincts in this overcrowded age. Others grew as big as a college —without its discipline—and replaced the strife of the Australes and Boreales with their own. The part that the Proctors played as disciplinary officers on these occasions is revealed in their expense accounts, one item of which reads:

> For keeping the peace when the controversy was between St Clement's Hostel and the other Hostel on the day of St William—6s. 8d.

St Clement's was a lawyers' hostel in Bridge Street, and the last to disappear.

These expenses also reveal the University's history from a clearly unobstructed if unusual point of view, and they undoubtedly suggest a wide field of activity.

> For carrying the cross at the time of the King's coming—4d.
> For wine and confections for the Pope's nuncio—8½d.
> For wine and ale when the fire was at Gunwell Hall—1s. 9d.
> For drink and other expenses about the burning of the books of Martin Luther—2s.
> For the scribe in the proceedings against Sygar Nicholson for heresy —8s.

So one sees the *universitas scholarium*, this guild of scholars that received the royal blessing and the accolade of papal recognition, if not playing cuckoo in its Cambridge nest to the extent of ejecting the Mayor and burgesses, doing little more than tolerating their presence and then as servants. One finds, too, in the nest itself, no suggestion of that 'brooding peace and cloistered calm' which is commonly supposed to hall-mark an old university town. Churches there were in plenty to tell of Wordsworth's 'flocks', among them the 'round' twelfth-century Church of the Holy Sepulchre, but memorials such as Trinity College with its antechapel where—

                                             the statue stood
On Newton with his prism and silent face,
The marble index of a mind for ever
Voyaging through strange seas of Thought, alone.

—these were then undreamed of; and the idea that a magician
named Rutherford would one day experiment with things too
small to see in a devil's workshop almost on the bank of the King's
Ditch, would, if conceived, surely have been heretical. As late as
1764, when he was appointed Professor of Chemistry, a future
Regius Professor of Divinity and Bishop of Llandaff, named
Richard Watson, exposed the neglect of Science with his confession that 'he knew nothing at all of Chemistry, had never read
a syllable of the subject, nor seen a single experiment in it', and
another hundred years had to pass before undergraduates could
study Experimental Science, apart from Physics. The early
curriculum favoured a culture of the finer arts.

    Perhaps the most remarkable achievement of the University
itself in these early days was that, virtually penniless, with neither
buildings of its own nor effective control of its students, it
steadily increased in authority and repute. But the age at which
some of the students entered leads one to see it as a school and
university combined. Fourteen was not unusual. Bacon was only
twelve when he came into residence at Trinity in 1573, and in
1676 William Wotton entered St Catharine's before he was ten,
having at the age of six demonstrated that he could read and
correctly translate Hebrew, Latin and Greek. At thirteen he was
second in the *Ordo Senioritatis,* and at twenty-one a Fellow of the
Royal Society. Referring to the Scholars of the King's Hall,
founded by Edward the Second in the fourteenth century, the
King himself mentions 'his beloved John de Baggehote and
twelve other children of his chapel in the University of Cambridge', thereby revealing that he then maintained at Cambridge
a school for the further education of his choristers. This foundation, moreover, gave its name to King's Childer Lane.

    The period of residence also reflects the youthfulness of these
early students, for the B.A. degree that they knew was no more

than a step towards the essential M.A., whereas the B.A. is now all-important and the M.A. demands no examination or further period of residence—merely a cheque at the end of a short qualifying period. But the B.A. course is still one of only three years although much of the ground it covers was unheard of in the days of the old *trivium,* a three-fold study of Latin Grammar, Rhetoric and Logic covering the same period. Only if the candidate survived his oral 'disputation' could he proceed as a 'commencing' bachelor to the *quadrivium* of Arithmetic, Geometry, Astronomy and Music. Success in that, a four-year course, qualified him as a Master of Arts, entitled to lecture himself. So the pattern was established, and although the broadening horizon of scholarship very soon allowed a choice between Theology, Medicine and Law, both Canon and Civil, for another eight years of study by the M.A. seeking a doctorate, a trace of the old 'disputation' lingered well into the last century before it was completely overshadowed by the written test. Today, in the name of research, a professor nonchalantly listens to stellar voices raised when the Earth was probably molten, and the age of undergraduates coming into residence laden with A-levels is about eighteen.

Affording a glimpse of medieval education from an unusual angle is the presence of those intending to be grammar-school teachers. They were the Glomerels, studying Glomery, a corruption of gramarye which, in this context, meant Latin, and it is possible that their school was older than the University, for the Archdeacon of Ely appointed the Master of Glomery who looked after them, and the Chancellor's authority was restricted. Their quarters, known as the Gramerscole or Glomery Hall, stood at the south-west corner of what are now the Old Schools, and they were officially part of the University. But they were hardly accepted as such. Their bedell was not allowed to carry his mace with the University bedells in front of the Chancellor, and the Master of Glomery himself was forbidden to attend certain funerals officially. Only when the University conferred the degree of Master in Grammar did the Glomerels receive full recognition. As the stage directions out it:

Whan the Father hath arguyde as shall plese the Proctour, the Bedyll in Arte shall bring the Master of Gramer to the Vice chauncelar, delyvering hym a palmer wyth a Rodde, whych the Vyce chauncelar shall gyve to the seyde Master in Gramer, and so create hym Master. Than shall the Bedell purvay for every master in Gramer a shrewde Boy, whom the master in Gramer shall bete openlye in the Scolys, and the master in Gramer shall give the Boye a Grote for hys Labour, and another Grote to hym that provydeth the Rode and the Palmer.

Perhaps to posterity's loss, by mid-sixteenth century the Glomerels had dropped out of the Cambridge scene.

In the medieval town, compressed into its hundred acres between the river and the King's Ditch, there were two arterial roads—Bridge Street, cutting across the north-east corner to the Barnwell gate a mere quarter-mile away, and the High Street, branching off to the right some two hundred yards from the Great Bridge and heading south for half a mile to the Trumpington gate. Yet, within that short distance, bordering the High Street or close at hand, were nine churches, central among them being St Mary's-by-the-Market, and seven are still there. Only 'All Halowes-in-the Jury' and the Church of St John Zachary have made way for progress. So it is not idle to say that this old church by the market, probably dating from the twelfth century and largely rebuilt at the University's expense in the sixteenth, marks the centre of Cambridge for both City and the University. The first milestone out of Cambridge along the Trumpington Road, where the Trumpington ford used to be, gives the distance from Great St Mary's, but the High Street is now successively St John's Street, Trinity Street and King's Parade after the colleges it passes, and, for its last hundred yards, Trumpington Street.

As Great St Mary's had long been the University's meeting place, no doubt because of its position, there is good reason for thinking that the Chancellor bore this in mind when he chose, and hired in 1309, the house of Nicholas the Barber as the first of the University's lecture-rooms, for it stood between the Church and the Gramerscole, and time was to show that he could not have chosen a better centre for the University's administration and ceremonial. Soon there were hired 'schools' all along what is now Senate House Passage, but two centuries had to pass before increasing revenue and benefactions enabled this makeshift accommodation to be exchanged for the quadrangular building that stands today between King's College Chapel and Senate House Passage, still bearing the name of the Old Schools although its purpose—and its appearance—has long been altered. For some time the upper room of the Theological School, on the eastern side of the quadrangle, provided a chapel for the University and a meeting place for the regents or teaching officers, but Great St Mary's, facing it across the lawn of the Senate House Yard, once the clutter of old houses had been swept away, continued to be the University Church.

Today, during term, the University Sermon is preached there every Sunday, attended by large congregations and the Vice-Chancellor in procession, although the strict conformity which marked the University's earlier religious attitude has long since vanished with the unseemly incidents connected with it. Not for many years has a Proctor created a riot by preaching a heretical sermon, and the other day even the Vice-Chancellor's consternation was little more than momentary when the Senior Proctor —reading the Litany as he does every Ash Wednesday, one likes to think in expiation of that earlier lapse—introduced an entirely new concept into theology by inadvertently omitting the critical adjective *false* and seeking deliverance from *all* doctrine.

To that extent the University has moved with the times. Agnosticism is not unknown, and recently a number of under-graduates, calling themselves Humanist, advocated that college chapels should be turned into libraries. But the University does not forget the circumstances of its own foundation.

II

A COLLEGE IS BORN

TODAY, when visitors throng the 'High Street' in the summer, they come to see the colleges, not the University, and they could hardly do otherwise, for *universitas* itself means an organized body of students, not the place where they meet. The Senate House, the Old Schools, the splendid new library . . . these are merely centres of specific activity. There is no building to which one can point and say: 'That is the University.' The colleges, in contrast, are definite and visible in themselves. Loosely, therefore, it can be said that the University is a collection of colleges, and so the idea persists, reinforced by the close interlocking of the two. Not long ago, the colleges virtually provided the University's teaching staff, in addition to the Vice-Chancellor and its officers. Eminent teachers from elsewhere brought in by the University could then be readily absorbed. But the years since the war have been years of expansion. More undergraduates require more teachers, and the influx of migrants has become so great that, apart from any limitations imposed by statutes, space alone has left a number without an academic home, and the University with the problem of finding one. It is not easy. Speaking of his own experience at a dinner of fellow Oxonian exiles, the late A. E. Housman confessed that he found Cambridge an asylum in both senses of the word.

Legally, the University is a corporation with the additional rights of conferring degrees and taking disciplinary action against its erring members, but no longer that of returning two

representatives to Parliament. The colleges, too, are sovereign independent states, ruled in accordance with their statutes. For this reason the Proctors, being University disciplinary officers, have no authority inside a college. The division, however, does call for tactful observance at times. So much a Proctor discovered late one night when he came upon an undergraduate climbing head first out of his college through a ground-floor window which had been partly forced open, an activity that all colleges frown upon; and there he lay, half in, half out, and over the street itself, gownless—an offence the University then punished with a fine of 6s. 8d. No doubt recalling Solomon, the Proctor politely informed the college authorities that he thought justice would be done if he fined the top half 3s. 4d., and left them to do what they liked with the rest.

This independence of the colleges also means that a young man 'going up to Cambridge' must first be accepted by one before he is admitted to the University—a task of some magnitude for college tutors until the establishment of new universities and a central control of candidates for admission between them reduced the pressure. Moreover, the University again does the teaching— its age-old function which to a large extent passed into college hands after the Reformation. Colleges now supervise and accommodate, and this division between their functions and that of the University is also inevitable: in modern science alone the richest college could never by itself provide the facilities demanded. The University does that with Treasury help through the University Grants Committee. Colleges, mindful of their independence, have no Government assistance—except indirectly through the fees paid by undergraduates who are themselves assisted from public funds—and the tendency for them to lapse into mere halls of residence would be real indeed but for the supervision by which, in effect, the undergraduate is privately coached, if not by someone in his own college qualified to do so, then by an authority his Director of Studies arranges for him in another. That supervision is invaluable.

Undoubtedly the visible change in the University since it came into being is tremendous, not least in stature, but the fundamental

3

The Bridge of Sighs, St John's College

structure has not altered. One can still detect in the modern University and the colleges the old student-guild that taught and the hostels that accommodated. Heredity, too, is more obvious in the older colleges, born as small foundations and differing fundamentally from the hostels only in their discipline and endowment. The fifteenth century had nearly run its course when the *pensionarii* appeared—undergraduates, that is, who paid for their keep and their instruction. *Socii,* or Fellows, men of some maturity, also replaced the youthful scholars of early foundations, and by the eighteenth century wealthy men were entering their sons as fellow-commoners who dined with the Fellows at High Table. At the same time poor students were admitted as sizars or part-time servants who fed on the crumbs that fell from it. Today the title of fellow-commoner, where it survives, is honorary and without blemish, as, indeed, is that of sizar which is still in use although it has long since lost its old significance.

With Hugh de Balsham, the Bishop of Ely, lies the distinction of introducing the first college into Cambridge, even if unwittingly. He did not see it take shape as one. In 1280, with the royal approval, he had set out to alleviate the misery of some apparently worthy clerks by arranging free board and lodging for them in the Augustinian Hospital of St John, but the experiment lasted only four years. Lacking the discipline enforced on the brethren, the clerks proved just as unruly in the Hospital as in their hovels, and both parties sought relief. The Bishop, however, was not a man easily deflected from his purpose. The King's refusal to confirm his nomination to the episcopal see in 1257 he had met by mounting his horse and riding to Rome for the papal, and superior, blessing, and he dealt with this upheaval in the Hospital of St John by transferring the clerks to fresh quarters— two houses next to St Peter's Church, now St Mary's-the-Less, just outside the Trumpington gate. Here, by letters patent granted in 1284, they were to live as 'scholars studying in the University of Cambridge' and—importantly—follow the rule of 'the Oxford scholars of Merton'.

This reference to an Oxford prototype is itself interesting

because the preliminary thought behind it might have included one at Cambridge where Walter de Merton, in due course Bishop of Rochester, had purchased the Dunnings' 'stone house' seemingly with college endowment in view, and fundamentally it was this endowment that distinguished the early college from the hostel. 'The House of the Scholars of Merton', which he had founded in 1264, was the first of the Oxford colleges, and the statutes governing the scholars' everyday life, which he had drawn up, were destined to set the pattern of collegiate life in Cambridge. Scholars in 'The House of Peter' therefore had to be poor, and the House itself endowed—a hurdle that Hugh de Balsham cleared with tithes and altar-dues, and, on his death only two years later, a benefaction of 300 marks. But it is doubtful whether the idea that he was founding a college occurred to him—or anyone else. Simon Montagu, another Bishop of Ely, gave Peterhouse its statutes in 1338.

Inevitably the way of life revealed in these statutes is strikingly different from what it is today, for the change since the last war has been iconoclastic. To older Cambridge men it seems but yesterday since 'chapel' was compulsory, perhaps three times during the week and twice on Sunday, with surplices worn on saints' days as well as Sundays, and except on the tennis court and hockey pitch, the chaperon was a young woman's shadow. Now, with the vast increase in undergraduate population, few colleges could accommodate anything like a compulsory congregation, and since 1948, when the women of Newnham and Girton achieved full membership of the University on the same footing as the men, the barriers have been down. Moreover, not only has the academic 'square' disappeared from the undergraduate's uniform: he is no longer required to wear his gown in the streets after dark. The wonder is therefore not that the Peterhouse statutes of Bishop Montagu appear so quaintly out of date, but that, in underlying principle, they continued pertinent for so long.

Not the least interesting feature of the statutes is that, in a period when religious emphasis was inescapable, there was no suggestion of a theological college about the new Peterhouse. Rather was the touch monastic. The Master alone enjoyed real freedom. He was allowed to keep a horse at college expense, and had a bedroom to himself. Others had to share, a senior scholar with a junior 'so that the younger be stirred on by the elder to learning and good manners'. It was, however, stipulated that the Master should be 'a man of circumspection in both spiritual and temporal matters', and 'sufficiently well educated'; also that his salary should be forty shillings a year.

Although they were not required to take Holy Orders, the young men had to receive the clerical tonsure—a deprivation in startling contrast with today's luxuriant hair-style—and they had to attend both services at normal canonical hours and the weekly masses for the souls of their benefactors. They wore, too, the clerical habit, forerunner of the academic gown which distinguishes between the colleges as well as the various degrees. But women were not barred outright. They could be 'interviewed', if only in the college hall and the presence of an accredited male chaperon. As for entering a student's room, not even washerwomen were allowed to do that, 'especially young ones'. Authority also frowned on the pleasures of what is commonly known as pub-crawling, and the student was forbidden to carry arms, play at dice, sleep out of college and keep a dog inside it— a prohibition still generally observed among colleges although it is not unknown for a Master's dog to be registered as a cat. Byron managed to keep a tame bear in his rooms at Trinity on the pretext of running it for a fellowship because it reminded him of the dons —only it was better mannered.

The essentials of an early college are simply stated: a lodging for the Master; a chapel in which to pray; a library in which to study; a hall in which to eat, and quarters where the scholars could sleep, the whole backed by a generous endowment; and apart from adjusting themselves to evolution, so they continue. That adjustment, however, is considerable, and even statutes have to be brought up to date. Today it is not unknown for a college to dispense with a chapel, and the influx of paying undergraduates has long since swamped the idea of a small foundation. At Peterhouse, the 'fourteen scholars', if not the Master, were to pass their

time 'studiously engaged in the pursuit of literature', and a
scholar could then be anything from a schoolboy to a commencing bachelor. As late as 1573 the University's new charter
required all students over the age of sixteen to acknowledge the
Thirty-Nine Articles and the Royal Supremacy. In contrast, a
scholar is now a young man holding a scholarship, and the
running of a college with several hundred undergraduates and
research students lies with 'The Master and Fellows' who are
M.A.'s or Doctors, all men of distinction in their subjects. They
are the dons.

But a college must start with available accommodation, adequate or not, and build to specification afterwards, a sequence
that in Peterhouse meant the speedy use of the founder's benefaction for building 'a very beautiful hall'. Part of its south wall
survives today among the oldest masonry in Cambridge. Meanwhile the Church of St Peter served as its chapel—the scholars
being segregated in the chancel, away from the normal congregation—and so for nearly 350 years the arrangement continued,
apart from the hiatus caused by the collapse of the Church itself
in 1340, after which it was rebuilt and consecrated as the Church
of St Mary-the-Less. Not until 1632 was the present chapel
completed, and the college given the unusual but quite charming
front which the visitor sees when arriving in the city by the
Trumpington Road today; for the chapel with its flanking
galleries and arcades beneath, centrally placed on the site of Hugh
de Balsham's two 'ostles', is close to the street and makes the
eastern side of what would otherwise have been an open or
three-sided court. It is also the first college that the visitor sees,
and the only thirteen-century one in Cambridge.

Matthew Wren, Master of Peterhouse at the time and uncle of
Sir Christopher Wren who built so much of Cambridge, takes a
well-deserved place with the many other masters of character and
determination whom the colleges have produced. In the course of
a long and varied career, he was also Master of Pembroke and
Bishop of Ely, and having fallen foul of Parliament, he spent
eighteen years imprisoned in the Tower. He was eighty-two when
he died. Of his work in Peterhouse it is written that he 'built great

Part of the College from the Ground, rescued their Writings and Records from Dust and Worms, and by indefatigable industry digested them with a good Method and Order'. Laxity, however, appears to have crept in with his departure, if one is to believe Zacharias Conrad von Uffenbach, the German bibliographer who visited Cambridge on a tour of inspection in 1710 and found the manuscripts not only 'sorry stuff', but so buried in dust that he had to wear a pinafore while the librarian used a towel.

The impression that a college chapel makes on the ordinary visitor is naturally a first and personal response to what he sees as a whole and not to detail that is often scattered and difficult to appreciate, especially by anybody coming straight out of strong sunlight. It is therefore derived from the general unless the particular is dominating, and in Peterhouse chapel the particular is. For that reason the architectural style—described as a fusion of Gothic tracery and Classic moulding—may pass, if not unnoticed, at least with no more than a secondary glance in the presence of the striking Münich glass of the nineteenth century that fills the side windows. Like most colleges, Peterhouse did not escape the fanatical attentions of William Dowsing in 1643, when he bore down on Cambridge charged with the task of destroying 'monuments of superstition'. The Fellows had wisely buried the glass of their east window, but even so Dowsing found much to engage his attention, and before he strode off to Pembroke across the road and broke a mere ten cherubim, he had 'pulled down two mightie great Angells with wings and divers other Angells, and the four Evangelists, and Peter with his Keies over the Chappell Dore, and about 100 cherubims'.

If Dowsing took offence at the priceless glass at King's, posterity can rejoice that, as some believe, his ladders were not long enough to reach it. But the friendship of Cromwell and Milton cannot be overlooked. The Chapel with its—

> storied windows richly dight
> casting a dim religious light

—had meant enough to Milton to ensure his tolerance of the Laudian revival, and it is difficult to believe that so desirable a target could have been spared without Cromwell's connivance. On the whole, the Puritans did far less damage than they might have done.

All colleges have their famous *alumni*. In the last century Peterhouse acquired an immense reputation for producing mathematicians who applied their talent with distinction, among them William Thomson, a second wrangler who became Lord Kelvin; Peter Tait, senior wrangler and physicist; and not least, Edward Routh who, as a mathematical coach, produced as many as twenty-seven senior wranglers in this yearly Tripos. On the proud roll of English poets, however, there is only Thomas Gray, although a claim might be made for Richard Crashaw, the religious poet a full century his senior, who was a Fellow of the college for eight years. Nor was Peterhouse the college of Gray's own choice. That was Pembroke, to which he came as a pensioner in 1734. But he soon switched to Peterhouse as a fellow-commoner, and there he might have passed the rest of his days, had not the incident of 1756 sent him back to Pembroke in disgust.

There is no doubt that Gray as a man commanded less respect than he did as a poet. His friend, Horace Walpole, with whom he made the grand tour of the period, said 'he never was a boy'. Dr Johnson called him 'a dull man in every way'. Others, more harshly, described him as 'a solitary fly', and he saw himself as 'a captive linnet'. Nothing of the University's basic study was even tolerable. 'Must I plunge into metaphysics?' he wrote, after two years at Cambridge. 'Alas, I cannot see in the dark: nature has not furnished me with the optics of a cat. Must I pore upon mathematics? Alas, I cannot see in too much light: I am no eagle. It is very possible that two and two make four, but I would not give two farthings to demonstrate this ever so clearly; and if this be the profits of life, give me the amusements of it. The people I behold all around me, it seems, know all this and more, and yet I do not know one of them who inspires me with any ambition to be like him. Surely it is of this place, now Cambridge, but formerly known by the name of Babylon, that the prophet spoke when he said the wild beasts of the desert shall dwell there, and their houses shall be full of doleful creatures, and owls shall build there, and satyrs shall dance there: their forts and towers shall be a den for ever, a joy of wild asses.'

It is also evident that the 'wild asses' gathered in Peterhouse terrified him. His rooms, in 1756, were noisy, the 'people of the house dirty'; and in their 'wines' they not only roused him at midnight: worse still, they ever threatened to burn down the college. Incautiously he said so. There is, too, no doubt that he wrote to a friend begging him 'to bespeake for me a rope ladder, for my neighbours everyday make great progress in drunkenness', and that not long afterwards he took himself in high dudgeon to Pembroke where he was at least welcomed 'civilly'. But the happenings meanwhile are not so certain although it seems inevitable that his neighbours should falsely raise the alarm of 'Fire!' in the night, and that the wretched Gray should hasten down the rope into the tub of cold water carefully placed to receive him.

So this melancholy poet found a haven, though not one entirely free from distraction. To watch 'that old rascal', Roger Long, the Master of Pembroke, riding a primitive water-cycle about the garden-pond was amusing enough, and to study Icelandic and Celtic verse was a preliminary to his Eddaic poems in no way disturbing the calm of his later years. But his appointment, in 1768, to the professorship of Modern History by the Duke of Grafton, then Prime Minister, was an acute embarrassment, not only because he knew nothing about the subject and never gave a lecture—£400 a year has been mentioned—but also because it was his turn to write the customary ode when the Duke became Chancellor next year, an occasion on which 'the whole University was very owlish and tipsy', according to the victim. It was not the easiest panegyric to write:

> What is grandeur, what is power?
> Heavier toil, superior pain.
> What the bright reward we gain?
> The grateful memory of the good.
> Sweet is the breath of vernal shower,
> The bee's collected treasure sweet,

Sweet music's melting fall, but sweeter yet
The still small voice of gratitude.

But it did raise a smile.

Gray died in 1771, sixteen years before Wordsworth drove down Castle Hill and at the Hoop alighted in a less unhappy age.

III

THE COLLEGES TAKE ROOT

SOME forty years sufficed to bring Hugh de Balsham's 'endowed hostel' the flattery of imitation, and if numbers mean anything, it was sincere, for Clare Hall in 1326, Pembroke Hall in 1347, Gonville Hall in 1348, Trinity Hall in 1350 and the House of Corpus Christi in 1352, with Michaelhouse in 1324 and King's Hall in 1337, both destined to form part of Trinity College, were all founded in the next twenty-nine years. It is interesting, too, that there is no college among them—only 'halls' and 'houses', derived from *aula* and *domus*. Trinity Hall survives as 'The Hall of the Holy Trinity of Norwich' to avoid confusion with Trinity, 'The College of the Holy and Undivided Trinity' with which Henry the Eighth sought to eclipse every other foundation, not excluding King's.

This early expansion is the more remarkable when it is seen against the open antagonism of the townsmen and the misery of their surroundings. The town might prosper as a fish-mart for the district, as well as an inland port at a time when road traffic offered small challenge, and also, the University would say, batten on the scholars through accommodation hired, but only by medieval standards was that accommodation fit for habitation. The Black Death swept away three successive Masters of the Hospital of St John, and sixteen of the forty scholars of King's Hall which adjoined it. Fire alone was the cleanser. The pinky-cream Ketton stone from Rutland was then a rarity. Even substantial buildings, including the early colleges, had to rely on clunch, the tough Cambridgeshire clay, and apart from the houses of the religious orders and local families of wealth, such as the Dunnings, most dwellings were of wood. In 1385 fire destroyed over a hundred, a lot for the acreage within the bounds of river and Ditch. The plight of the teeming clerks was therefore intolerable, and it remained for the benevolent to offer the haven of the 'endowed hostel'.

If the merging of Michaelhouse and King's Hall with Trinity is counted as one, fifteen colleges received their statutes as such during the next three hundred years, six of them—Clare, Pembroke, Queens', Christ's, St John's and Sidney Sussex—being founded by women, and five—King's, Trinity, Queen's, Christ's and St John's—by royalty although a reigning monarch was concerned with only two. Queens' is a double foundation, as the position of the apostrophe indicates, and Margaret of Anjou made the first. (Even when involved with the founding of King's College, Henry the Sixth apparently could not resist such a plea as: 'Besecheth mekely Margaret quene of England your humble wyf.') But the Wars of the Roses intervened disastrously, and Elizabeth Woodville, consort of Edward the Fourth and at one time Margaret's lady-in-waiting, had to refound the college virtually as its foster-mother. Lady Margaret Beaufort, mother of Henry the Seventh, founded Christ's and St John's.

Although, after forty years, Hugh de Balsham's innovation had clearly come to stay, it was still no more than a signpost pointing to the unknown where the modern colleges stand, centuries distant, when Hervey de Stanton, Chancellor of the Exchequer to Edward the Second, founded Michaelhouse. In finding suitable quarters off Foul Lane and reserving the chancel of St Michael's Church in the High Street, at the end of the Lane, he followed Balsham's procedure exactly, although it did necessitate rebuilding the Church, but after that he gave wing to his own ideas. His establishment was entirely for graduates already in Holy Orders, and the statutory provision of six priests confined to the study of Theology, none below the degree of B.A. and one of them acting as Master with no extra stipend or amenity, was far too restricted to allow development. The 'poor scholar' found no place.

So, in spite of the high ceremony of the priestly induction which even the Mayor attended, 'The House of the Scholars of St Michael' is best described as still-born. If Hervey de Stanton had founded anything at all, it was a restricted theological college, and neither the addition of a library about 1400, nor the later building of a hall among the largest in the colleges—it was seventy feet long—could make it otherwise. But it was not wasted. The great merger was at hand. With the adjoining buttery and kitchen it met the needs of Trinity until 1605, and its oriel window continued to grace the south-west corner of the Great Court until 1772.

Yet Michaelhouse has left behind a name of rare distinction. That was John Fisher, donor of the £500 without which Henry the Eighth would have had no temporary hall while his splendid college took shape. Chaplain to Lady Margaret Beaufort; Master of Michaelhouse; President of Queens'; first Lady Margaret Professor of Theology; Chancellor of the University a year later, and finally victim of the Reformation—such was the man who denied the legality of Henry the Eighth's divorce and trod the melancholy path to Tower Hill and the block.

He was canonized in 1935.

The exact status of Edward the Second's Scholars of King's Hall is impossible to define. What evidence there is suggests a private arrangement by the King, the expenses of which the Sheriff met from his revenues, and to that extent King's Hall seems to have crept into Cambridge, hardly by accident but with no statement of intent to class it as a foundation. Had there been one, Edward the Third would not have found it necessary to start again, in 1337, with letters patent for an entirely new foundation —the Hall of the King's Scholars, to the number of thirty-two with a warden in charge, appointed by the Crown. Although the Sheriff continued as paymaster for the first year, substantial endowment followed in the second, and in the revelation of the royal bounty, this new foundation clearly surpassed any of its predecessors, apart from being the largest. But there was nothing to suggest the ultimate crescendo that produced King's and Trinity, to the great advantage of Cambridge itself as a tourist attraction. Also, the scholars were no more than schoolboys, and the rules governing their conduct still referred to them as children. Not until 1380 did Richard the Second decree that boys on admission should be over fourteen, and that they should study logic and anything else the warden considered suitable. To that extent they resembled the Glomerels, and such a foundation could never last in a University expanding in thought as well as material status.

At first the Scholars of King's Hall dwelt in the large timber-framed house of their predecessors in King's Childer Lane, parallel with Foul Lane and linking the High Street with the river, and for their religious observance Edward the Third assigned the Church of St Mary-by-the-Market, the nearest available. Expansion waited for the century's turn, and then it reflected the royal bounty. It began with a stone-built hall; a small cloister court soon followed; and before Henry the Eighth's plan for Trinity pronounced its doom, a vaulted four-turret gateway led on to King's Childer Lane, and another on to the High Street. The plan might engulf the site, but here was early college architecture at its best—far too good for the hammer and pick. So today, behind Trinity Chapel, one range of that fifteenth-century cloister court survives almost as it was built, and to reach it the visitor goes through a splendid gateway that once led on to a lane, re-sited now at the Chapel's western end. Even more famous, the other stands proudly as the Great Gate of Trinity College itself, though not quite the same as it was when built. The arms of Edward the Third remain to tell of its origin, but pride of place now goes to the statue of Henry the Eighth, a Jacobean addition, and of late years a charming mixture of dignity and impudence, for a close look reveals that he clutches, not the royal sceptre, but the leg of a kitchen chair. Undergraduate whim placed it there, and undergraduate determination restores it when authority rebels.

Not the least pertinent, if oblique, comment on this astonishingly successful incorporation of two colleges in the formation of a third, is found in Thomas Fuller's *History of the University of Cambridge,* written in 1655, for there he tells of stone taken from the Norman castle and used in the building down the years, and referring to the castle, adds: 'That stately structure, anciently the ornament of Cambridge, is at this moment reduced next to nothing.'

There is, too, Uffenbach adding almost as a corollary that, apart from the colleges, Cambridge is 'one of the sorriest places in the world'.

In deciding to found a college of its own, the University may well have been influenced by Oxford's success with 'the great University Hall' which had clearly taken root during the last sixty years, and as, in 1326, Richard de Badew, the Chancellor, made a start with the purchase of two houses in Milne Street, next to St John Zachary's Church and near the Gramerscole, the University College of Cambridge at least had the advantage of a good site. But little is known of the foundation itself apart from its fiery end twelve years later, and its Phoenix-like rejuvenation as Clare House. (It became Clare Hall in 1346 and Clare College in 1856.) Nor does one know what approach the Chancellor made to Elizabeth, Countess of Clare, unexpectedly enriched by a third of her brother's estates on his death at Bannockburn. There is, however, no doubt that the Chancellor ceded all his rights to her, and out of this tragedy on a distant battlefield came ideas that still survive in a modern college.

That her statutes were 'to last for all time' suggests hyperbole rather than prescience, but there is again no doubt that she had the advice of a University itself growing wise with experience. Already the Chancellor's Court was a hundred years old. Also one can accept as felicitous preamble her stated belief that 'under the protection of a more solid peace and the blessing of harmony', her scholars would be enabled 'to devote themselves more freely to study', and justify her hope that they would long continue to be 'docile, proper and respectable'. More significant is the distinction drawn between Fellows and scholars. For the first time *Socii* appear, and Clare House was to have not only a Master

and nineteen Fellows, but ten poor scholars as well. They were to
be taught singing, grammar and logic. Nor does the mention of
Master and Fellows lose anything of its modern ring when one
learns that the Fellows were to elect the Master and any of their
own number as vacancies occurred, and that the Fellows themselves could be of any nationality and from any university.
Finally, as if to ensure that the Fellows could speak with some
authority, they were to include three regents and one canonist,
and any who were not already B.A.s had to be on the point of
'commencing'. Only six were required to be in Holy Orders. So
the horizon broadened, not much though perceptibly, and so,
too, one gets the first whiff of what, in these days of teeming
faculties, must surely rank as the commonest question in the
University—'What is your subject?'

In those far-sighted statutes, religious observance was alone in
keeping with the period. Every day one of the chaplains celebrated
before the scholars set off to the schools, and until its own chapel
could be built, Clare did as other colleges have done, and made
use of a nearby church. After St John Zachary's had been pulled
down to make room for King's, both Clare and Trinity Hall had
to attend St Edward's on Peas Hill. Each added a small chapel.

Meanwhile the new college started to fashion itself on what
were soon to be traditional lines, beginning with a low clunch-
built court that in turn made way for a Carolian transformation
sufficiently impressive to satisfy the exacting Uffenbach—approval
that extended to the foreign books in the library. There is, indeed,
a note of quiet purpose about Clare, and even frugality, for rich
though Lady Elizabeth might be, and far-seeing when pointing
the way for others, her benefactions hardly encouraged extravagance. In early days, it seems, the college possessed only two
chairs, one valued at a shilling for the Master and the other,
valued at 1s. 4d., for distinguished visitors. The rest sat on forms.
Also, if the inventory is correct, one jug and two basins sufficed
for everyone. There is, too, an entry in the accounts that, in
default of explanation, rouses the gravest suspicion: 'Expenses
incurred in obtaining the favour of the Lord Protector—10s.'

Today one enters Clare from a lane that the modern world of

noise and bustle has passed completely by—a fragment of Milne Street converted to academic calm. Gone are the hithes and the tenements, the old clunch buildings and the squalor. Clare now extends to the river and far beyond. Its Renaissance court is described as 'more like a palace than a college', and framed by King's Chapel and Grumbold's seventeeth-century stone bridge in its setting of trees, all mirrored in the Cam, it is one of the sights of Cambridge—such is the transformation within the triangle formed by the old High Street, the river and Small Bridges (now Silver) Street, with the Great Bridge at its apex. Apart from a slender façade of shops in places, the whole area is filled with college and University buildings. The Senate House and the Old Schools flank King's Chapel; St John's, Trinity, Trinity Hall, Clare, King's and Queens' all go down to the river, and only Trinity Hall, which does not reach beyond, is without a bridge. But St John's has two, and Queens' proudly claims the last wooden survivor, first built in 1749 and crossing with a single span. Then, filling the triangle, there are Gonville and Caius—to give this double foundation its full name—which neatly occupies the space between the old Foul Lane and Senate House Passage, apart from engulfing St Michael's Church across the road; and, to complete the transformation, there is St Catharine's which at birth faced Queens' across Milne Street, but now turns its back, preferring frontal access to Trumpington Street.

So, in turbulent centuries long ago, the University and the colleges between them acquired about half the moated town, an encroachment that did little to mollify an already ancient borough, but nobody could foresee a 'string of Tudor palaces whose broad lawns and well-nurtured gardens mark the lazy passage of the Cam'—certainly not a breakdown in Monasticism that would help in providing the colleges. Yet, of the eight endowed in the period covered by the royal foundations of King's in 1441 and Trinity in 1546, only one failed to benefit from the spoliation of religious houses, and as four of the others joined Trinity Hall and Clare on the river bank, it might be argued that seldom were the proceeds of robbery better expended. For here, in great part, is the Cambridge that visitors know today and pause to admire, the

Clare College and King's Chapel from the river

Cambridge of which Rudyard Kipling wrote when the Navy sent its young officers there after the Kaiser's war:

Hallowed River, most gracious Trees, Chapel beyond compare,
Here be gentlemen sick of the seas—take them into your care.

A sense of peace, an escape from tumult to tranquillity—these are terms that belong to the Backs when the courts are free of trippers and the walks are dappled with shade. Nor, it seems, does distance fail to enhance the view of St John's transpontine block from Trinity bridge, half-veiled by majestic willows on a sunlit day, for the whole effect is delightful. Nothing suggests a 'dreadful building' dismissed in contempt as a 'wedding cake'. And having gone upstream to Clare's magnificent bridge, few will deplore a defacement so discreetly achieved that to thousands it passes unnoticed. Many years ago the explanation hinged on a bet—an undergraduate having asserted that there were not fourteen stone balls on the parapets, as everyone thought. Nor were there, after he had taken a neat slice out of one and reduced the number to about thirteen-point-nine. On another occasion in those gayer though not very distant days, a Johnian raiding party managed to push most of the fourteen into the river, where, in the mud, one of them remains.*

Rebuilding was a necessity that overtook most of the early colleges after a few centuries, Clare in the reign of Charles the First. Not until the end of the eighteenth century was the work completed. Then the college graduated as one of the most perfect examples of Carolian style in the country. There is, too, a story, less graceful but indicative of donnish eccentricity, that tells of a disgruntled Fellow who delighted in a particular set of rooms, the windows of which enabled him to spit on the Master as he entered and left the college.

That Clare should develop down the centuries and produce its

---

* Statues and suchlike carry their own special hazards in Cambridge. One night, since the war, a group of young men ingeniously contrived to make the front entrance of their laboratory resemble that of a cinema, to the pained astonishment of their professor who arrived in the morning to find himself billed as the star of a witty though hardly flattering film.

4

The 'Leper Chapel' at Sturbridge (circa 1150)
Along the Backs: Clare College Gate

great men—among them Hugh Latimer—was inevitable. Every college did so as the hostels died and the few 'poor scholars' gave way to an undergraduate population. Nor was it likely that the young men of Clare would be any less free with their shafts of wit. But no other college has moved the Mayor to seek the Privy Council's protection.

As long ago as 1386, Michaelhouse hired six vizors and six beards for a 'comedy' or masquerade, and down the ages until play-acting acquired an aura of respectability, the attitude of authority might be described as sternly parental. Only within college walls was it tolerated, and then to encourage the practice in declamation and classical speech that it provided. Elizabeth made this point clear in her statutes for Queens' when she directed that two competent dons should receive 6s. 8d. each for producing two comedies or tragedies at Christmas every year 'lest our youths should remain rude and unpolished in pronunciation and gestures'. Authority's objection was to 'drolls, joggulers and tumblers' who, with inn-yard actors, were able 'to draw the students from their books', and it disliked most of all itinerants who chose the hostile territory of Chesterton, 'which town doth continually annoy our University'. It mattered not that in 1575 the Privy Council empowered the University to ban 'the attempts of unlawful, hurtful, pernicious and unhonest games' within five miles of Cambridge. Led by the Mayor, the townsmen refused to forego their simple pleasures, especially as the young men of the University gladly shared them, and there was high scandal when, in 1600, Dominus Pepper of Corpus was seen to perform at the Black Bear 'with an improper habit, having deformed long locks of unseemly sight and great breeches, undecent for a graduate or scholar of orderly carriage'. Retribution included a hair-cut with suspension from his B.A. degree.

The Clare incident that engaged the Privy Council's attention related to a skit performed by what would now be called the College Dramatic Society, and it was aimed at the Mayor and leading townsmen who were not only invited with their wives, but compelled to watch themselves being ridiculed. As Fuller wrote: 'A convenient place was assigned to the townsfolk, riveted in with scholars on all sides, where they might see and be seen. Here they did behold themselves in their own best clothes (which the scholars had borrowed) so lively personated, their habits, gestures, language, lieger-jests and expressions, that it was hard to decide which was the true townsman, whether he that sat by, or he who acted on the stage. Sit still they could not for chafing, go out they could not for crowding, but impatiently patient were fain to attend till dismissed at the end of the comedy.'

Significantly, the skit was entitled *Club Law*, and the Mayor sought redress from the Privy Council with the plea that 'the Mayor's mace could not be played with but that the sceptre itself is touched therein'. It was a neat point, promising a salve for the mayoral dignity. Nevertheless, even at this level the cards were stacked against him, for, says Fuller: 'Though such the gravity of the Lords as they must maintain magistracy, and not behold it abused; yet such their goodness, they would not with too great severity punish wit, though waggishly employed; and therefore sent some slight and private check to the principal actors therein.'

But the Lord Chief Justice had not even that small consolation when, a few years later in 1615, Clare excelled itself with *Ignoramus,* for James the First was present at this satire on lawyers, and not only 'laughed exceedingly'—whereas the Lord Chief Justice 'glanced at the scholars with much bitterness'—but insisted on returning to Cambridge to see a second performance.

To what extent Clare's neighbour, Trinity Hall, sympathized with the Lord Chief Justice in his distress is not recorded, but it is reasonable to suppose that its young men laughed with less abandon at what was, after all, virtually their own profession; for at the foundation of Trinity Hall in 1350 William Bateman, although Bishop of Norwich, had decreed that as many as seventeen of its twenty Fellows should be lawyers, and only seven of them canonists in Holy Orders. This legal emphasis is no more than a first and inevitable move towards the narrow professional studies which are accepted today when the urgent demand is for scientists, and it does not appear to have restricted the all-round activity of Trinity Hall men down the years. One of them—Lord

Howard of Effingham—commanded the English fleet against the Spanish Armada, and of the versatile Etonian, Thomas Tusser, Fuller wrote: 'Successively a musician, schoolmaster, serving man, husbandman, grazier, poet, more skilful in all than thriving in any vocation.' His book, *A Hundredth Good Pointes of Husbandrie*, published in 1557, gives a possible reason for his lack of success as a farmer, for there he says, among much else:

> Sowe peason and beans in the wane of the moon;
> Who soweth them sooner, he soweth too soon.

—and when it was enlarged to *Five Hundredth Pointes of Good Husbandrie* in 1573, with a metrical autobiography added, it scarcely enhanced his fame as a poet although it certainly testified to his love for Trinity Hall.

Four other names will suffice to indicate the contribution that 'The Hall' has made to Church and State—Gardiner, Bilney, Chesterfield and Bulwer Lytton. Stephen Gardiner had proceeded to his doctorate in both canon and civil law, been secretary to Wolsey and Master of Trinity Hall itself before he was enthroned as Bishop of Winchester and caught in the throes of Reformation. But he did live long enough to die of gout—an end, even so, less appalling than that of Thomas Bilney, burnt at the stake as a heretic. In Lord Chesterfield the college produced a politician who was also an intimate of Swift and Pope, with 'a turn for satire and contempt' of his own. For that he blamed the University at large. With Trinity Hall he found nothing wrong. It was 'infinitely the best in the whole University', being the smallest and 'filled with lawyers who have seen the world and know how to live'. They had only one attendant who was 'also the only drunkard in the college', and, he concludes: 'Whatever people may say of it, there is certainly very little debauching in this University, especially among men of standing, for the simple reason that one must have the tastes of a street porter to endure it here.' In contrast with Chesterfield, the politician in Lord Edward Bulwer Lytton came after the novelist, playwright and essayist. He was, too, a migrant from Trinity as plain Bulwer, and as such not only won the Chancellor's gold medal for a poem on 'Sculpture', but went on to achieve fame as a Union speaker in the days of the eloquent Praed and the argumentative Macaulay.

The Union Club began in 1815 as a University debating society, quartered in the Red Lion, a Petty Cury coaching inn. Now it is commonly said to be a training ground for Prime Ministers, and its spacious premises behind the Round Church are in mid-Victorian Waterhouse, a name that rouses anything from mirth to blasphemy in Cambridge. Also, its Praeds and Macaulays are imported for any momentous debate, and the oyster supper afterwards has long since been abandoned. Women, too, are now members. Yet even in these days of the 'new' undergraduate when changing interests are reflected in many club-memberships, it still prospers, though perhaps not so gaily as when Praed sang of Macaulay:

> Then the favourite comes,
> With his trumpet and drums,
> And his arms and his metaphors crossed.

When Bishop Bateman founded Trinity Hall, he had the good fortune to acquire a ready-made hostel, a long rectangular stone house built some thirty years earlier for the Benedictine student-monks of Ely. The usual court of clunch soon followed, and but for an unexpected hazard introduced by a lane running down to the river and giving access to the Cambridge Field, progress was uninterrupted. The northern range of the court, however, lined one side of the lane, and the tough hides of the jostling cattle and pigs wore away the clunch so alarmingly that a rubbing strake of hard brick had to be introduced.

The 1,200 acres of grazing and arable land to the north and west of Cambridge, with a similar expanse on the other side known as the Barnwell Field, formed what might be called the town's allotments, most of them tithed to the churches; and not far from the site of the old Norman castle, Pound Hill survives to remind one that beasts straying from the Cambridge Field were collected there. But that is the only reminder. Today the Field makes room for the University and college buildings and grounds that form so pleasant a fringe to the Cambridge Backs, and only a modified lane survives, its position slightly adjusted, to keep alive the name of Garret Hostel. The Barnwell Field, lying beneath housing estates and the threat of an airfield runway, has left not even a name.

Meanwhile Trinity Hall moved to the shape by which it is known today, and if Uffenbach was not impressed—he found the college 'very mean' with nothing of note among its books—few will agree when looking at the early Elizabethan library and the medieval windows that still open on the second court. Trinity Hall is unashamedly old, and its charm is that of the old world.

IV

SOUTHERN APPROACH

To enter Cambridge by the London road through Trumpington
is to acquaint oneself with a city-approach as fine as any, and also
to pass along a corridor of time. There is nothing mean about it,
nothing to suggest the eyesore known today as a housing estate.
But for its width as a motorway, it would be a magnificent avenue
from the village to the milestone where, curving left, it makes
for St Mary's-by-the-Market. There, too, at the milestone and the
site of the old Trumpington ford, it enters Cambridge history.

Back in the days of the King's Ditch, and starting from the
millpool, a belt of land half-circled Cambridge to the south,
revealing its nature in the names it bore—Coe Fen, Sheep's Green,
Coe Fen Leys, Swinecroft—and the last two extended from the
river to that part of the Via Devana which is now Hills Road. At
the turn of the eighteenth century it was still wild, for as Gunning
put it: 'Crossing the Leys you entered Cow Fen. This abounded
with snipes. Walking through the osier bed on the Trumpington
side of the brook you frequently met with a partridge and now
and then a pheasant.' But the years have not been unkind. Tamed
and friendly, Coe Fen and Sheep's Green are still there, the Leys
also, less the part enclosed by Act of Parliament in 1811 where
the school of that name now fronts on the Trumpington Road;
and although Swinecroft has gone, a belt of 'open land' still
reaches that eastern limit, starting at Hobson's Conduit, as the
canalized waters from the Nine Wells are usually called, and
providing the University with its Botanic Garden.

Like so much else in Cambridge, even this well-ordered amenity and educational necessity had its period of uncertainty at birth. Dr John Eachard, Master of St Catharine's and on two occasions Vice-Chancellor, conceived the idea of a 'Physic Garden', for as such it was then significantly known, but he died in 1697, and it remained for Richard Walker, a Vice-Master of Trinity, to carry out his plans in the belief, one gathers, that the wisdom of God was 'no more manifest than in the vegetable part of creation'. He therefore purchased, and gave to the University, a large part of the Augustinian Friary site bordering Free School Lane between St Benet's Church and St Botolph's, and the 'Physic Garden' started there. That the site now bears the name of Cavendish and is ever associated with Rutherford whose discoveries, some people insist, may split creation itself, is therefore yet another touch of local irony.

For the visitor entering by Trumpington Road, Cambridge begins at no boundary mark. It rises abruptly where water appears in the kerbside runnels to tell of that infamous Ditch, and the street itself rebukes the motor car. For here is the story of centuries, written in stone and brick, a story that tells of the nation, and one that still has to end. A glance to the left may perchance have revealed the new Engineering School fronting Fen Causeway— a title that speaks for itself—and one to the right, down Lensfield Road, if affording no more than a peep at the splendid new Chemical Laboratory, will have told of continued expansion, but the street is bordered with history, going back seven hundred years. The medley of Addenbrooke's tells of a great East Anglian hospital, founded in 1760 with money bequeathed by a St Catharine's doctor. Almost opposite, on the left, the magnificent Fitzwilliam Museum suggests at first sight a Grecian temple, built though it was a hundred years ago. Facing it stands the pleasant eighteenth-century red-brick dwelling of a prosperous brewer that, for many years, served to locate the non-collegiate Fitzwilliam House before it migrated to the heights of the Huntingdon Road and achieved full collegiate status. Left again there is Peterhouse, and a few yards further on, across the road and its runnels, Pembroke flanks the street, its Wren chapel reaching back to the pavement. So it goes on, first one side, then the other.

On the left is the imposing tower and frontage of the Pitt Press, once known as the Freshers' Church from the number of gullible freshmen sent there to hear the University Sermon, and on the right, St Botolph's Church with its fourteenth-century nave, huddling against Corpus Christi, the college founded by two Cambridge guilds. Opposite is St Catharine's, proud of the only three-sided court that shares its charm with the passer-by. Beyond lie King's and Great St Mary's, Gonville and Caius, and the Senate House. One should walk down Trumpington Street and along King's Parade.

Today Addenbrooke's is a household word in Cambridge, a symbol of the Welfare State to which it is tied for good or ill, but neither the parent building in Trumpington Street—soon to make way for University expansion—nor its lusty and dominating offshoot along the Hills Road, more than two miles from the city centre, improves the local scene; for one, at the moment, is mainly Victorian, and the other, still growing, resembles a cluster of factories straight from the Great West Road. Such is the 'small physical hospital' that Dr John Addenbrooke had in mind when, at his death in 1719, he left some £4,500 and preceded Ratcliffe's foundation of Oxford's famous infirmary by half a century. Historical, too, is the site of the Georgian house where, in 1766, the hospital first took shape. That recalls the thirteenth-century invasion of Friars soon after the founding of Peterhouse, when the Gilbertines established themselves and their own little college which perished at the dissolution.

Necessarily modest, the hospital began with only ten beds, and the Matron's salary was £10 a year, with 'a gratuity not exceeding £5 to be given her if she behaves well'. Use of the hospital baths was also strictly controlled, the regulations stating that 'if any Person, not a patient of this Hospital, go into the cold bath of the said Hospital, such person shall pay Three-pence every time; if into the warm bath, sixpence, unless the same is heated on purpose, in which case One Shilling and Sixpence shall be paid'. Furthermore, 'when patients are cured, they shall be enjoined to return public Thanks in their respective places of worship'.

Addenbrooke himself, a pensioner who became a Fellow in 1704 when the college statutes restricted his studies to Philosophy, Theology and the Arts, resigned on becoming a Doctor of Physics only seven years later. (Not until 1860 were the restrictions removed.) But he did not forget St Catharine's where his medical cabinet now stands in the library—one of the two survivals of its kind in Cambridge. 'Given to Dr Addenbrooke's man, for bringing ye materia medica presented by ye Dr his Master to ye Library—£oo. 5. o.' So the Steward's accounts record, and among the prophylactic resins and roots that shed some light on the period, the bark of cinchona, introduced from Peru in 1638, survives with coffee, then becoming a popular beverage.

The nurse who attended him in his declining years described him as 'a tall thin man skilled in necromancy', and asserted that he foretold the hour of his death to within five minutes. With more certainty, he lies today in St Catharine's Chapel, and his memorial is the hospital he founded. Noble, too, it is in conception, but in the tremendous, ugly blocks of the 'new' Addenbrooke's, with more to come, an eminent surgeon has already seen a not far distant day when no family will be without one of its members receiving treatment, and another gainfully employed attending the sick, if only by pushing a trolley.

In the pattern of the University as it is now, Pembroke follows Clare as third in seniority, and it was the first in that brief though troubled period, 1347 to 1352, which produced as many as four colleges. Like Clare, it was founded by a woman—Marie de Valence, the widowed Countess of Pembroke—and her chosen title, the Hall of Valence-Marie, remains the official one though seldom used. Like Peterhouse, it found a temporary home beyond the Trumpington gate, if only just, for the University sold the college its hostel by the Ditch, and when, in 1355, the Countess obtained the Pope's permission to build a private chapel, she further ensured that Pembroke became the first college to have one of its own. Until then, her Master, twenty-four Fellows and six scholars attended St Botolph's. Her statutes, also, were liberal according to the time. Though hardly a copy of Clare's, they did resemble them sufficiently to suggest that University advice had been taken. Theology and the Arts were compulsory studies—so much was inevitable—but only two Fellows were to be canonists, and one had to read Medicine. All were to be unmarried, and that, too, was a normal provision, celibacy being a condition of fellowship until removed by the Oxford and Cambridge Act of 1882. The Countess, however, was not opposed to formal meetings. She did enjoin her society by the Trumpington gate to be constant in their visits to Denny Abbey, the convent she had founded near Waterbeach.

Pembroke's adolescence proved happily free from the delays and frustrations that some colleges knew, not least King's with its royal founder. It grew up, one might say, as a small but model court that embodied everything a college then required, and as late as the sixteenth century there was still sufficient room to house the whole society. Not until 1663 did Matthew Wren—now Master of Pembroke—employ his nephew to build a new chapel and, by so doing, introduce Italian style to Cambridge; and 1874 had arrived when Alfred Waterhouse ran loose, replacing the splendid fourteenth-century hall of Marie de Valence and the Master's lodging, as well as a complete range from the Old Court, with his neo-Gothic disaster, described as 'terrible and better unseen'. Essentially modern in both method and ideas, he used dynamite for removing the ancient hall which he had considered to be in danger of falling down, an expedient prompting the suggestion that 'less drastic methods might avail to remove the building that now occupies the place of that fine old hall'. And the kindly Provost of King's, observing the Waterhouse library, was moved to the sad comment: 'It would only suffer by any description of it that I might write.' Today the old gateway into Trumpington Street, with the range running back behind it, is about all that survives of the medieval college, and if Pembroke has any consolation at all, it derives from the fate of others. Girton and Caius notably suffered from what has been described as 'the great artistic misfortune of Cambridge'.

Of Pembroke men who have left a name behind them, and there are many, one thinks first, perhaps, of Nicholas Ridley who died at the stake with Latimer, hard by Balliol, Oxford, but in the course of man's normal activity the crown must surely be shared by Spenser and Pitt, one poet, the other statesman, with two hundred years between them; one entered in 1569 as a menial sizar, the other in 1773, the second son of an earl, privileged to take his M.A. degree without examination three years later; one sixteen years of age, the other fourteen.

If the two had anything in common, it was precosity. Before he left the Merchant Taylors' School in London, Spenser had not only acquired a fluent knowledge of French and Italian, as well as the classical tongues, but also published his first poetical work, although anonymously. Furthermore, he had acquired an immense determination to escape from the 'thraldom and bindings' of Latin. For Latin was still a spoken language, the medium of learning, and as such it died hard. In 1592—by which time Shakespeare had arrived—Elizabeth's royal wish to be entertained at Cambridge with a comedy in English was countered by the University with the plea that college actors 'had no practice in the English vein', and very little in the Latin, Uffenbach would no doubt have added, mindful of his own difficulty in understanding Latin as Cambridge spoke it.*

Pitt, on the other hand, enjoyed a private tutor, and at the age of fourteen was too young, his father hoped, 'for the irregularities of a man' but old enough not 'to prove troublesome by the Puerile sallies of a Boy'. As Lord Chatham assured the college:

* Latin still survives in the University's Senate House ceremonial—at some length in the Public Orator's speech when an honorary degree is conferred—but, it is lightly said, the translation which is now printed alongside the speech in the order of proceedings at least tells the unlearned when to laugh. The use of Latin in the twentieth century, however, does carry its problems. Paying tribute to the Prime Minister of Malaya, *Tunku* Abdul Rahman Putra El-Haz, the Public Orator explained that the prowess of His Highness with a Riley motor car when an undergraduate at St Catharine's had led to the appointment of a *Procurator Extraordinarius vehiculorum igne interno propulsorum* to deal with motoring affairs.

'An ingenious mind and docility of temper will, I know, render him comfortable to your discipline, in all points.' More specific, his tutor wrote: 'Mr Pitt is not the child his years bespeak him to be. He has now all the understanding of a man, and is, and will be my steady friend for life. He will go to Pembroke, not a weak boy to be made a property of, but to be admired as a prodigy; not to hear lectures, but to spread light. His parts are most astonishing and universal. He will be fully qualified for a wrangler before he goes, and be an accomplished classic, mathematician, historian and poet.'

But the youthful Pitt sought no mathematical honour. Nor could he study political economy, a subject not introduced until 1816 and then unofficially. (Recognition came with the appointment of a Professor in 1863.) Instead, he acquired the great arts of rhetoric and invective demanded by his career in an age when the classical quotation was indispensable in argument. At one time he was the Member of Parliament for the University. Unlike Uffenbach who found the Pembroke library devoid of anything worthwhile, and the college itself 'neither large nor fine', the adolescent Pitt had no complaint. The Pembroke he knew was both 'sober and staid' with 'nothing but solid study', and, it would seem, in every way adequate. To what purpose he put his considerable talent is written in history, and out of the surplus money raised for the erection of his statue in London, rose the Pitt Press as a further memorial in Cambridge.

If it should be thought that a printing press is a curiously utilitarian memorial at any time, and one not usually dedicated to the memory of an eminent statesman, it should also be borne in mind that the Cambridge University Press, of which the Pitt Press is no more than a later extension, however worthy, has long been an important part of the University. As early as 1534—only a year before John Fisher, the University's Chancellor, was beheaded for refusing to accept the King's supremacy—Henry the Eighth had granted the University the right to print any books of which the Chancellor approved, and in 1662 when the Authorized Version of the Bible and the Prayer Book had to be printed, it shared the privilege of doing so with the Oxford

University Press and the King's Printer. Moreover, it continues to exercise this developing privilege.

In that five-year spurt of colleges wherein Pembroke led the way, the House of Corpus Christi and the Blessed Virgin was the last—founded in 1352—and, in the detail of its conception, the most remarkable of any of the earlier colleges. It owes its birth to townsmen—the united guilds of Corpus Christi and the Blessed Virgin. That townsmen should conceive the idea of founding a college for educating priests whose religious offices would include the singing of masses for the souls of departed guildsmen, though hardly free from personal advantage, did suggest a brotherly approach to the University, and to further the reconciliation implied, a guild-alderman went so far as to present the college with a drinking horn of quite outstanding splendour. But there were others who recalled the Black Death's devastation, and the exorbitant charges for masses sung by a still depleted clergy. Might it not be that this new college, with its Master and two Fellows already in Holy Orders and confined, as at Michaelhouse, to the study of Theology and Canon Law, merely ensured that departed guildsmen had their masses in perpetuity—for nothing? But the foundation went ahead. Brethren of the Guilds who lived in Free School Lane—then Luthburne or Lurthburgh—made over their tenements, and in the small area that was cleared, the House of Corpus Christi rose.

So this tiny college of 'scholar chaplains' came into being with a foot in each camp, as it were. For religious observance there was St Benet's Church next door, and there was a court to be built of Cambridgeshire clunch, but the omens were hardly good for a 'townsmen's college' when the town itself was touching the depths of misery. Only the University prospered, and that the townsmen hated. Yet, at the same time of the Peasants' Rising, twenty-nine years after its foundation, the House of Corpus Christi owned more property in the town than any of the other seven colleges— such was the patronage it had acquired—and that it should find both its feet in the University camp was inevitable. Nevertheless, although this smacked of betrayal and was bad enough, no other consequence angered the townsmen more than the payment of candle-rents—a charge on local houses for the supply of light to the Guilds—made over to the college at its foundation and now used for its own purposes. When, therefore, Wat Tyler's revolt spread to East Anglia, it was no less inevitable that the House of Corpus Christi should be the special object of the townsmen's wrath, with the University—represented by the Chancellor and Great St Mary's—a close second.

As the college owned farm land in Grantchester, it may be significant that the rioters found Thomas and James of Grantchester to lead them on that summer night when they assembled by the tolbooth and, having destroyed the house of a University bedell, seemingly by way of warming up for the major assault, advanced on their almost defenceless victim. 'Here', says Fuller, 'they brake open the College gates on the Saturday night (a good preparation for the Lord's Day following) and, as if the readiest way to pay their rent was to destroy their landlords, they violently fell on the Master and Fellows therein. From them they took all their charters, evidences, privileges and plate to the value of fourscore pounds. Hence they advanced to the house of the Chancellor, threatening him and the University with fire and sword . . . except they would instantly renounce their privilege, and bind themselves in a bond of three thousand pounds to subject themselves hereafter to the power of the townsmen, and free the townsmen from any actions, real or personal, which might arise from this occasion. This done, they went into the market-place, where with clubs they brake the seals of the University Charters, and then burnt them in the place. One, Margaret Sterr, a mad old woman, threw the ashes into the air, with these words: "Thus, thus let the learning of all scholars be confounded!" '

It was during this phase of the rioting, which continued over the Sunday, that the townsmen broke into Great St Mary's and rifled the University chest; and on the Monday, having assembled on Midsummer Common, they dealt with their other enemy, the Barnwell canons, against whom they alleged the enclosure of common land.

'From Cambridge', Fuller goes on, 'they went to Barnwell, doing many sacrilegious outrages to the Priory therein. Nor did their fury fall on men alone, even trees were made to taste of their cruelty. In their return they cut down a curious grove called Green's Croft, by the river's side (the ground now belonging to Jesus College), as if they bore such a hatred to all wood, they would not leave any to make a gallows thereof for thieves and murderers.'

It was a timely thought because at this point the 'warlike' Bishop of Norwich intervened with the episcopal archers and cavalry, killed some, captured others, and, as Fuller puts it, 'seasonably suppressed their madness'.

In the subsequent 'pacification' at law, the townsmen suffered badly. Against the Mayor, the Prior's claim alone included £2,000 for damage to property at Barnwell, and £400 for growing timber destroyed, preposterous sums to claim in 1381; and in the following year the unhappy man had to appear, with the bailiffs, and answer to Parliament for the deeds of emancipation which the Chancellor had been forced to sign—deeds held to be void because no one could believe that the Mayor himself had been acting under compulsion. Nor was the King without sympathy for the University in its claim for redress, and, with Parliament's approval, he took away all the townsmen's liberties. In effect, the townsmen were completely under the University's thumb, and although the King restored a number of their liberties in the following year, he still left the control and pricing of bread, wine and ale in the hands of the University, together with the survey of weights and measures and the punishment for infringements. 'Thus', Fuller comments, 'ill manners occasion good laws, as the handsome children of ugly parents', and the University increased its authority appreciably.

Corpus, too, having been awarded £80 in compensation for damage and theft, took the opportunity to discontinue the annual dinner on Corpus Christi Day at which the townsmen were entertained, and the drinking horn passed with the grave cere-monial of a loving cup. But, one learns, the townsmen 'still unfortunately demanded their dinner as due to them', and the

Great St Mary's Church, the historic centre of Cambridge

Mayor 'required it of the college in a commanding manner'.
Then, said the Master, sue me for it, and—stupidly—the Mayor
did.

In its material development, Corpus has been fortunate in
avoiding any architectural style comparable with that of Waterhouse, and in the outward preservation of the Old Court, backing
today on Free School Lane, it has achieved the oldest complete
medieval court in Cambridge—fourteenth century, and a gem of
its kind. Of necessity, towards the end of the sixteenth, buttresses
were added to support the weathering clunch, but they are not
destructive: the feel of antiquity survives. 'Lovably picturesque'
is one description applied to it. Not until the 1820s was New
Court created, with its Gothic façade symmetrical about a conventional gateway opening on to Trumpington Street, and
although, in this adjustment, the old Elizabethan chapel disappeared, its replacement so enchanted the designer, Wilkins, that
he expressed the wish to be buried there—a wish observed some
twenty years later. But New Court, like every addition to the
local scene, has its critics, and if one hears that the rather heavy
façade resembles a superior coastguard station, it should be borne
in mind that denigrating local architecture is a parlour game in
Cambridge.

As might be expected, Uffenbach had nothing good to say of
'Benet College' as a building in 1710, finding it 'one of the ugliest
colleges, lying among the houses, so that one cannot see it, and
must approach by mean entrance', and the library was not only
small but so dark that one had great difficulty in seeing what was
there. But the collection of manuscripts was the best of any, as
indeed it should have been, for today it ranks as one of the most
famous libraries in the world. Matthew Parker, Archbishop of
Canterbury and Master from 1544 to 1553, virtually saved it from
the rubbish heap, and among its treasures are St Augustine's
Gospel Book used in his missionary work among the English,
King Alfred's copy of the Anglo-Saxon Chronicle, the first draft
of the Forty-Two Articles of Religion annotated by Parker, and a
Psalter belonging to Becket. But a library of such richness is for
5

Half a mile from Great St Mary's today: Coe Fen
Midsummer Common

the few, and it is possible that this thought occurred to the love-sick couple—one of them the Master's daughter—who found there the solitude they sought. As the story is told: 'Mr Betts of Diss in Norfolk, a fellow-commoner, paid his addresses to the young lady, and when her father was abroad, she used to meet him privately in the college library, which communicated with the lodge. Being once surprised by his coming home unex-pectedly, she was put into such an affright that she never after recovered, and it was thought to have been the occasion of her death.' Sorrowfully, no doubt, Mr Betts returned to Diss.

In the happy way that the main streets of Cambridge change their names as they go along, the visitor leaving Corpus and heading for Great St Mary's finds himself almost at once on King's Parade, and not without reason for King's Chapel dominates this final stage of his journey. Appropriate, too, is the sense of finality that lingers on Senate House Hill, the flat little terminal 'square' which is flanked by the Senate House railings, with that 'silvery masterpiece in Portland stone' and the fine Old Schools beyond, Great St Mary's opposite, and jutting from Senate House Passage, the towering corner of Gonville and Caius in Waterhouse Gothic—privately called 'The Prudential'. Here, indeed, is the University centre, but it also suggests a sink, for the Trinity Street traffic all runs south to meet the north-bound stream from King's Parade head-on in a glorious swirl, most of which drains away down St Mary's Street on to Market Hill.

Caius, as 'The College of Gonville and Caius founded in honour of the Annunciation of Blessed Mary the Virgin' is known in ordinary conversation today, is the remaining one in that spurt of four during the period 1347 to 1352, and as the official title suggests, its early years were complicated. In 1348 Edmund Gonville, a parish priest in Norfolk, founded it as Gonville Hall on a site in Free School Lane which overlapped the burial ground of St Botolph's, and his Master and four Fellows were directed to study the Arts and Theology; but he died in 1351, and had not William Bateman, the Bishop of Norwich, adopted the puny orphan, already engaged in founding Trinity Hall though he was,

Gonville Hall might have passed away. As it was, Bateman gave the college a new site at the bottom of Foul Lane, opening on to Milne Street and reaching south to another parallel lane about half way to what is now Senate House Passage, and he virtually started afresh. Quite shamelessly, too, though not unexpectedly after the line he had taken with Trinity Hall, the statutes he gave to his foundling offered both Canon and Civil Law as substitutes for Theology; and so the foundation remained till the Doctor himself, the great John Caius, the Latinized form of Keys which he affected, came back to give his old college a third and quite different look.

Elected a Fellow at the age of twenty-three, this extraordinary man stayed on for six years before, in 1539, he took to the practice of medicine as a living, and another nineteen had slipped by when he came back as a London doctor of wide repute who, before his death, professionally attended Edward the Sixth, Mary and Elizabeth, and was honoured as President of the College of Physicians on as many as nine occasions. Also he was rich, and Trinity's rising splendour across the lane derided the little clunch court of his youth—a court now sordid and black with age, where cattle wandered at will. But he was an eccentric, with likes and dislikes far too strong to be adjusted, and if his election as Master was certain, so were the endless dissensions that followed. Only a cantankerous idealist would have refused to consider applicants who were 'deaf, dumb, deformed, lame, confirmed invalids or Welshmen'.

Yet Caius built well for his college—in Tudor Gothic—resolutely turning his back on Foul Lane, filling much of the space up to Senate House Passage, and setting the pattern one finds today. The Cambridge clunch he faced with stone from the ruined abbey at Ramsey, in the neighbouring county of Huntingdon, and to ensure that those who came to study did not forget their purpose, he arranged that, from the High Street, they entered by the Gate of Humility, passed through the Gate of Virtue—unexpectedly found in the centre of the new design—and emerged through the Gate of Honour which led to and hopefully symbolized the student's successful disputation in the schools. All three are still to be admired, but since the Waterhouse misfortune the Gate of Humility has hung its head in the Master's garden. Moreover, the court that enshrines the Gate of Honour is itself unusual, being 'open' by the passage though not to reveal the beauty of its architecture. Caius was ever the doctor, even in his statutes, and no building should shut off the southern side 'lest the air, from being confined within a narrow space, should become foul and dangerous'.

So Gonville Hall became Gonville and Caius, with a bias towards Medicine that has given the college a distinction all its own, but the statutes he gave to this third foundation were the rules of a fussy old man. No one should fasten a candle on the wall. No one should go on the roof except to repair it. All, in fact, were treated as children, and offenders were put in the stocks. Moreover, the college had moved towards Reformation whereas he had not. Already Bishop Nix of Norwich, with Bateman in mind, had approached the Archbishop of Canterbury, calling his attention to a 'college in Cambridge called Gunnel Hall, of the foundation of the Bishop of Norwich', and adding that 'no clerk that hath come out lately of that college but savoureth of the frying pan, though he speke never so holily'. It therefore comes as no surprise that a later Archbishop should learn of 'the preposterous government of Dr Caius and his wicked abuses in Gonville and Caius College'. 'He maintaineth within his College', the complaint said, 'copes, vestments, albs, crosses, tapers, with all massing abominations, and termeth them the College Treasures. He hath erected and set up of late a crucifix and idols with the image of a doctor kneeling before them.'

But the Archbishop did not have to intervene. In a raid on the Master's rooms, the offending articles were seized, and 'it was thought good by the whole consent of the Heads of Houses to burn the books and such other things as had served most for idolatrous abuses, and to cause the rest to be defaced; which was accomplished yesterday with the willing hearts, as appeared, of the whole company of that House'.

That was on the 13th of December 1572, and according to Caius himself: 'All the ornaments of the College were torn and

cut to shreds by the private authority of Thomas Bynge, the
Vice-Chancellor, as he himself has said. To him nothing was so
detestable as the name and image of Christ crucified, the Blessed
Mary and the Holy Trinity. Outrageously he treated them,
cutting them in pieces, casting them on the fire, and assailing them
with horrible names and epithets. . . . Present at the fire from
midday until three o'clock were the same Thomas Bynge, John
Whitegifte, Master of Trinity, and William Gode, Provost of
King's. Finally, what they could not burn they broke and defaced
with hammers.'

Six months after this curious acknowledgment of his bounty,
Caius surrendered, worn out and disillusioned by thirteen years
of troubled mastership; and the end was near. In a final effort
at prolonging life, he sought his nourishment from nursing
mothers, but the experiment was not a success although it did
revive suggestions of infancy—one day 'tractable, docile and of
amiable countenance', and the next, 'froward, peevish and full of
frets'.

He died in 1573, and was buried in the college he loved.

Until Caius returned to give his college a unique distinction, in
the University itself Medicine was little more than a nominal
'school', Anatomy not even that; and his work in arousing these
dormant studies—which involved laying on an adequate supply
of dead felons for dissection—together with his own immense
renown in wider fields, suffice to place him at the head of the
college roll of outstanding *alumni,* with William Harvey following. He, too, studied at Padua after leaving by the famous
Gate in 1597, and he was Lumleian Lecturer at the College of
Physicians when, in 1628, he published his revolutionary treatise
on the circulation of the blood, and took his place with
Caius.

Moreover, where unusual distinctions are concerned, Gonville
and Caius also has a two-thirds share with St John's in the only
Cambridge man deemed eligible to appear in Seccombe's
anthology, *The Lives of Twelve Bad Men.* As Titus Oates in due
course took Holy Orders, he stands in almost startling contrast

with Jeremy Taylor, Caius' other eminent divine who, incidentally, 'had no rival in lofty and impassioned prose save Milton'. That Oates himself could also speak with passion, his tutor at St John's has testified, for after Caius had 'spewed him out', the record states: 'He stole from and cheated his tailor of a gown, which he denied with horrid imprecations, and afterwards, at a communion, being admonished and advised by his tutor, confessed to the fact.' In the opinion of St John's, 'he was a liar from the beginning' and 'a great dunce', and as he ran into debt, he was 'sent away for want of money and never took a degree'.

Of Oates's extraordinary life, let it be said that he was the son of a parson, a 'dipper' who enticed women into the local river, often at night and at ten shillings per head, and that his own evangelical career was marred by his expulsion from every curacy he held, and even from the hard-bitten Navy in which he served as a chaplain. Of his infamous 'plot' in which the Catholics were going to massacre the Protestants, burn London and murder the King while a French army invaded Ireland, it is sufficient to record that, from the hysteria of the day, he acquired an apartment in Whitehall and a pension of £480; and that although he was subsequently fined the impossible sum of £100,000 for saying the Duke of York was a traitor, cast into prison and, when the truth of the 'plot' came out, stripped of his canonicals, pilloried, flogged and given a life sentence, yet, such was his astonishing buoyancy, he was released after the revolution with a pension of £300—from a presumably grateful government.

One can readily sympathize with his Johnian contemporary who declared that Oates and the plague both visited Cambridge in the same year.

Five years after the death of Titus Oates, it was the turn of Gonville and Caius to suffer Uffenbach in his quest for manuscripts, on this occasion in 'a miserable garret under the roof, which could have been very little or not at all visited', for the top step was buried in pigeons' dung. That was bad enough, but inside the garret the precious manuscripts 'lay thick with dust on the floor and elsewhere', in such disorder that even with the aid of a catalogue he could find 'nothing at all'. As he mournfully explained, it was doubtful whether he could have handled anything for the dust, especially in his black clothes, although he would gladly have searched for one or two.

V

'OUR HENRY'S HOLY SHADE'

TODAY one accepts the glory of the Backs and the architectural charm of the older colleges as part of the Cambridge scene. They grew with the city; and the plight of the townsmen as their liberties and livelihood, and even the town itself, were steadily taken from them by a medieval University, is seldom given a thought. Yet they deserve at least a word of sympathy, for if the close of the fourteenth century found their lot appalling, the dawn of the fifteenth held only the promise of worse to come. Their abortive rising had done no more than strengthen the University. Now there were colleges adding themselves to the plethora of religious orders whose buildings and grounds had so far been the best in the town, and still the plague of students remained. Craftsmen owning houses of the better sort had them virtually commandeered as hostels. Even as late as 1574, by which year fourteen colleges had been founded, Lyne's map of Cambridge shows a dozen hostels between the river and Ditch. Meanwhile the resentful townsmen, with pestilence as a further affliction, simmered in what remained of their town and in a squalor that increased by comparison as the colleges blossomed to a splendour exceeding the monastic houses themselves before their dissolution. Not without reason did Uffenbach call the town one of the sorriest places on earth. And he was not alone. A few years earlier another visitor described its streets as 'abominably dirty', most of them being so narrow that, should two wheelbarrows meet in the largest, 'they are enough to make a stop for half an hour before they can well clear themselves of one another to make room for passengers'. There were no pavements; overhanging gables and gutterless roofs spilled their water on to passers-by and filled the central drain in the street; and 'the buildings in many parts of the town were so little that they looked more like huts for pigmies than houses for men'.

On this scene—more primitive still in the first half of the fifteenth century, one would suppose—Henry the Sixth cast his 'holy shade' and, among much else, plans for a chapel 288 feet long, 40 feet wide, and 90 feet high. His age was then nineteen.

It seems likely that William Waynflete, the founder of Magdalen, Oxford, did much to foster the idea of a royal college at Cambridge, and the King's design for a campanile conveys the royal idea of magnificence; but whatever the inspiration, the founding of the King's College of Our Lady and St Nicholas in 1441, a year after its sister foundation at Eton, meant the complete disruption of the townsmen's way of life; for when the other colleges followed King's to the river bank—and over—as they surely would, Cambridge itself would cease to exist as an inland port, and subservience to the University would be inevitable. As it was, the broad strip of land requisitioned for the new college reached from the river almost to the High Street, cutting a section out of Milne Street—part of the chapel would stand on that—and swallowing two lanes that led from the river to Market Hill, the busiest part of the town. Moreover, in those early days, the town still huddled between the river and Ditch, and the chapel alone would cover a sixth of the distance between them—the complete site about a third.

Apart from the townsmen's humble property, St John Zachary's Church had to go, and, saddest of all, the puny infant of God's House. This, a college for schoolmasters, a London schoolmaster had hopefully founded in 1442 after travelling extensively in the midlands, but 'no further north than Ripon', and finding 'seventy schools void, or more, that were occupied within fifty years past, because there is so great a scarcity in masters of grammar'. Now God's House stood in the way of the chapel, and to a plot of land by the Barnwell gate the cradle was swiftly transferred. Soon, therefore, the tatty fringe of the High Street backed on what looked like a vast open space while a chapel grew slowly in its north-east corner, and with tempers frayed as they were, it is probably fortunate that the townsmen of the fifteenth century were not to know that for nearly three hundred years cattle and sheep would graze within call of Market Hill and Great St Mary's before the college began to assume the shape that the world today comes to admire. As it was, in the June riots of 1454, according to Cooper, the townsmen knew enough to make King's 'an especial object of attack' and to provide 'guns and habiliments of war against the college'.

Oddly, in view of its ultimate dominance, the new college roused little dismay when it was first mooted, for the young King—no doubt on the advice of his chaplain, John Langton, who was also Master of Pembroke and, in 1441, Chancellor of the University—limited his ideas to one so modest, however magnificent its chapel, that the small plot of land opposite Clare, between Milne Street and the Schools, sufficed to hold its court. Stone came from the castle. A splendid gateway appeared, opening on Milne Street, as it does to this day. But the founder's ideas were expanding, rapidly, and the court was never completed although, roughly made habitable, the hall was used as such until the reign of George the Fourth. Two years sufficed for these second thoughts, and by 1443 the college he had in mind not only allowed for a Provost and seventy Fellows: it was also tied to Eton. This meant that only Etonians could come up to King's. No other source was eligible. Eton scholars, moreover, could proceed to fellowships as a right; the University had no authority over them, a concession, unwillingly granted, that the college interpreted as permission for Kingsmen to take their degrees without the University's normal examination; and except that their founder's statutes required them to forswear the monstrous heresies of John Wycliffe and Reginald Pecock, it seems that they could do very much as they liked.

The extent to which the ideas of the young King grew with contemplation reflects his own unhappy state of mind, for he planned not so much a college chapel as a cathedral, and his

conception of the college itself—apart from being a finishing
school for Eton—most nearly resembled a wealthy religious
foundation hiding itself from the sinful world behind its battle-
mented walls. But the passing centuries ensured that such privacy
was never achieved, to the great enhancement of the local scene
and the delight of thousands of visitors who, by courtesy of the
college, sun themselves on the grassy slope to the river, and no
one recalls the wretched townsmen of long ago who saw their
dwellings and livelihood swept away.

Whatever Ruskin had to say about the design and deformities
of King's Chapel, there seems to be little doubt that opinion, no
less responsible, ranks its vast interior among the finest in the
world, 'breath-taking in its beauty'; and if some small enquiring
wonder should intrude, there is Wordsworth to advise:

> Tax not the royal Saint with vain expense,
> With ill-matched aims the Architect who planned—
> Albeit labouring for a scanty band
> Of white-robed Scholars only—this immense
> And glorious work.

That work began in 1446 with limestone, in part, from the
quarries that the college owned near Tadcaster in Yorkshire—
brought by sea to Lynn, thence up the river to Cambridge—and
Reginald Ely, master mason at the time, must take an honoured
place among those humble citizens who contributed so much by
their skill. But soon there was civil war in the land, with years of
uncertainty and fitful labour on the site. For over twenty, until
Henry the Seventh bestowed his blessing in the last year of his
life, there was none at all, and it remained for Henry the Eighth to
ensure that completion was possible. Then another name was
added to the roll of master masons, the name of him who replaced
the temporary wooden roof with the most exquisite of all ceiling
design, the great fan-vault which is the glory of King's today:
George Washtell—

> the man who fashioned for the sense
> These lofty pillars, spread that branching roof
> Self-poised, and scooped into ten thousand cells,

Where light and shade repose, where music dwells
Lingering—and wandering on as loth to die;
Like thoughts whose very sweetness yieldeth proof
That they were born for immortality.

There are many superlatives applied to King's College Chapel.
By 1515 the roof was complete. Within the next sixteen years
Flemish glaziers had provided what has been described as 'the
finest series in the world of glass on a large scale', and five years
later Henry the Eighth presented the stalls and screen, the carving
of which is said to rank with the best in Europe. That Henry the
Eighth should also have left his private mark in heraldic decoration, quite at variance with the founder's dislike of 'curious
werkes of entaille and besy molding', merely reflects his own
flamboyance, and the royal cipher can be tolerated, even in its
profusion; but the horror that Anne Boleyn was so soon to know
on Tower Green lends tragic point to the letters H and A en-
twined in a lover's knot.

So one sees this extraordinary foundation rather as a small
exotic plant that, long before it has taken root, unexpectedly
produces a blossom transcending all others in size and mag-
nificance—a foundation, moreover, that seemed unlikely to take
root at all in a University bitterly resentful of its privileges. Not
until 1724 did it flower again. Then, with the chapel completing
the northern side of the projected court that one now enters from
King's Parade through a pinnacled gatehouse, Gibbs undertook
his last work in Cambridge—the Fellows' Building. This forms
the western range in Portland stone, symmetrical about a central
arch, and inevitably there are critics; but whether the archway
enchants with its 'surpassing beauty' or merely rouses 'an unhappy sense of congestion', there can be no doubt that this
splendid building, often known by its builder's name, is not in the
least overpowered by its neighbour.

Then, yet again, the years slipped by with the college in a state
of suspended animation—an Etonian enclave stifled by the restrictions of its own statutes—and 1822 had come before the task of
completing an opulent court fell to Wilkins. A commodious hall
in a southern range, and the great stone screen to the east, all in

'Collegiate Gothic'—these were his contribution, and once more the townsmen had lost, this time their shops and houses along the High Street. But the street has now been widened, and when the broad verge of grass, such as only Cambridge grows, reached from the old Plott and Nuts Lane between St Catharine's and King's to the Senate House opposite Great St Mary's, the town had acquired a thoroughfare with a distinction all its own, and the college had at last taken its proud and rightful place on the parade that bears its name.

It has been said with some truth that K.P., as the parade is popularly called, owes much of its charm to this grass verge in front of the screen: it provides a foreground, and Cambridge colleges are renowned for their lawns. American visitors have been known to kneel and stroke them, reverently and in wonder. But only dons may tread them. Such a lawn greets the visitor arriving at King's. Centrally placed is the fountain—added in 1879—that forms a pedestal for the statue of Henry the Sixth, and it faces the many-pinnacled gatehouse. Behind it lies the broad sweep of the Gibbs' Building; to the right the new hall and worthy accommodation; to the left the chapel, hiding the site of the old and makeshift court which the college did not abandon, and sell to the University, until 1828. Now there is only its splendid gateway.

Inevitably, in the course of its long history, the chapel has been used for purposes unforeseen by its founder, and Queen Elizabeth's visit in 1564 was probably one; for then, in the ante-chapel, there was erected a stage 'containing the breadth of the church from one side to the other' in order that the side-chapels might be used as dressing rooms. Elaborate, too, were the arrangements made for the audience. 'Ladies and gentlewomen' were packed in the rood-loft, and below them were 'tables greatly enlarged and railed for the choice officers of the Court'. Only a few spectators were allowed on the stage, apart from the Queen. For her, 'from the quire door unto the stage was made, as t'were, a bridge, railed on both sides'. And when the imaginary curtain was due to rise, the Lord Chamberlain and Mr Secretary brought in a multitude of the guard, carrying torches 'for the lights of the play'. After that, until midnight, the Queen's Grace watched the *Aulularia* of Plautus.

So ended the Sunday. On the Monday, from 9 o'clock until midnight, the Queen saw *Dido,* and on the Tuesday, *Ezechias,* which was at least acted in English. But on Wednesday, when faced with *Ajax Flagellifer* in Latin, Her Majesty declined, 'being over-watched with former plays'. Her reluctance to attend until she had ascertained what awaited her on that later occasion in 1592, is therefore just as comprehensible as her refusal to come when she had, especially as the wear and tear of an official visit would be formidable without any plays at all.

At Elizabeth's visit in 1564, the Mayor undoubtedly had the first word, for he mounted his horse and, exercising his prerogative, met the royal party at Newnham, but the reception proper began at the west door of King's Chapel where the Chancellor waited with the Orator who proclaimed Her Majesty's virtues in such detail that his speech went on for half an hour. This, Her Majesty appears to have endured with more patience than her horse 'curvetting under her', for at the end she did manage a word of thanks and a tribute to the Orator's excellent memory. Then, inside a chapel hung with splendid tapestry and strewn with rushes underfoot, the Chancellor made his personal obeisance, and after the *Te Deum* and Evensong the ceremony concluded with the formal presentation of six boxes of comfits and—with fine solicitude for the protection of the royal fingers—four pairs of Cambridge double gloves. That done, the Chancellor rode away on his 'little black nagg'.

Sunday, being a day of rest, limited Her Majesty's entertainment to *Aulularia,* but on the Monday she not only had to watch a second play: she had also to attend a high-level disputation in the University Church where another great stage had been erected, and Dr Caius himself, with two professors, argued the important implications of *Simplex cibus praeferendus multiplici,* and *Coenandum liberalius quam prandendum;* or, as it might be put, 'Is a plain meal preferable to one of many courses?' and 'Should dinner be more generous than breakfast?'

Only once did the Queen have to ask the disputants to raise their voices. Then she did so in Latin, and as further evidence of her erudition, when Christ's welcomed her with an oration in Greek during her tour of the colleges, she at once replied in Greek. At 'Benet College', where she was late in arriving, she would hear no oration although she stayed long enough to receive some boxes of comfits and a pair of gloves. Undoubtedly her visit was a great success, reflected in her statutes given to the University six years later, but it is unlikely that every young man welcomed what must have appeared to some as interference with their pleasures. No longer were freshmen to be 'salted'—given an initiatory emetic, that is—and Peterhouse students were specifically forbidden to visit travelling theatres lest 'the reputation of the scholars be cheapened to the danger of soul and body and to the scandal of the whole House as often comes from such exhibitions'.*

Uffenbach, visiting King's, appears to have been far less astonished at finding the college library in a side-chapel than at not finding a manuscript in it, but he did unbend sufficiently to admire the stonework generally, and the organ particularly, enchanted, it seems, by the lingering note that wanders on 'as loth to die'. No one, however, appears to have been responsive to the chapel's 'breath-taking beauty', only the absence of heating, when the Fellows of the college assembled in its vast emptiness to elect their Provost on a freezing January day in 1743. It was not a straightforward election because there were three candidates with supporters—numbering twenty-two, sixteen and ten—of such stubborn loyalty that nobody would give way; and as no one was allowed to leave the chapel until a decision had been taken, 'nor

* Of the tremendous activity behind the scenes on the occasion of a royal visit, Cooper gives some idea when he tells how the Vice-Chancellor and Heads of Houses came to Catharine Hall and presented a pair of gloves to the Earl of Sussex who was staying there. His three hundred servants were quartered in the town, of necessity, and the townsmen also waited on His Lordship with 'a marchepane and a sugar lofe which cost them £1. By taking eight marchepanes and sugar lofes, for eight noblemen', they received a discount and paid £7 19s. 6d.—a lot of money to spend on marzipan and sugar in 1564.

none permitted to enter', there they remained—for thirty-one hours.

The sister foundation happily provides evidence of the suffering and fortitude of these devoted dons. 'A friend of mine, a curious man', the letter says, 'tells me he took a survey of his brothers at the hour of two in the morning, and that never was a curious and more diverting spectacle. Some, wrapt in blankets, erect in their stalls like mummies; others asleep on cushions like so many Gothic tombs; here a red cap over a wig; there a face lost in the cape of a rug. One blowing a chaffing-dish with a surpliced sleeve; another warming a little negus or sipping 'Coke upon Littleton', i.e. tent and brandy. Thus did they combat the cold of that frosty night, which has not killed many of them to my surprise.' Yet passion seems to have survived even this cooling interlude, for proceedings began during the forenoon of a Monday, and the winter's sun must have set on the Tuesday before the candidate with twenty-two votes enlisted sufficient support to give him a clear-cut majority. The Tory candidate failed.

Strange happenings indeed, yet the chapel must have known many like them in the changing life and unexpected hazards which the years have brought, even though—

> They dreamt not of a perishable home
> Who thus could build.

The few German bombs that fell on Cambridge during Hitler's war left the college scene no more than slightly scratched, but precautions had been taken: the chapel's priceless glass had been removed beyond the reach of bombs till peace returned. Some twenty more years had to pass before any damage was done, then by the foot of an undergraduate 'night-climber'—small but damage nevertheless.*

* The practice of night-climbing is old and, short of posting sentries, nothing, it seems, is going to stop it, for no one takes full advantage of a University education who does not, at some time during his three years of residence, climb into his college after midnight. But college railings, walls and drainpipes are nursery stuff compared with such Alpine structures as the Chetwynd Crack and the Fitzwilliam Chimney—and the pinnacles of King's College Chapel— where the climb is undertaken for bravado and the ultimate disaster is obvious.

The Fitzwilliam Museum

Today—surprisingly, some people think—the chapel is also the home of Rubens' *Adoration of the Magi,* the value of which alone sets a daunting problem in security, and as it stands in isolated majesty and state, discreetly radiant beneath the great east window, it lends its own distinction even to the chapel.

It has been said that the inevitable effect of such limiting statutes as those the founder gave to King's was to produce a college for the 'intellectually destitute', and that may be so, but Kingsmen of distinction were to be found in the national scene long before the statutes of 1861 opened the college to non-Etonians. Sir Francis Walsingham, one of the commissioners who tried Mary, Queen of Scots; Sir Robert Walpole, England's first 'prime' minister; his son, Horace, author and politician, famous for his 'curiosity shop' on Strawberry Hill as well as a dearly loved cat; Lord Stratford de Redcliffe, the diplomat, and Lord Camden, the jurist—all were products of the 'restricted era'. In Charles Simeon, too, the college produced a remarkable priest whose discovery that prayer was to him 'as marrow and fatness' led to what must surely be one of the most astonishing forms of 'revivalist' meeting in the University's history—a freshman 'instructing' his bedmaker and her friends on Sunday evenings. That he was a born preacher, time was soon to show in the vast range of his following. Yet his views, at first, aroused sufficient hostility for the parishioners to lock him out of Holy Trinity Church until a smith could open the door, and his services had all the tumult of the hustings. In later years his lot came near to adoration, and when he died, in 1836, some eight hundred members of the University attended his funeral service in the chapel. His rooms in the Fellows' Building were known as 'The Saint's Rest'.

At the turn of the last century, one finds Oscar Browning hailed as the 'undergraduates don'. Of him, F. E. Smith—later to be Lord Birkenhead—wrote: 'Take him away from Cambridge, and you will reduce that venerable institution to a picturesque but decrepit ruin.' And, such was the concern for

6

Clare College Court

him when age began to reveal itself with increasing weight, one of his adoring pupils expressed an appeal in verse:

> O.B., oh be obedient
> To Nature's stern decrees;
> For though you be but one O.B.,
> You may be too obese.

There was also, at the time, 'a young Apollo, golden-haired'—

> dreaming on the verge of strife,
> Magnificently unprepared
> For the long littleness of life.

—Rupert Brooke. But he was not destined to savour life's littleness for long: he died of acute blood-poisoning during the Gallipoli campaign in 1915.

'This place is rather funny to watch, and a little wearying,' he said of King's. 'At certain moments I perceive a pleasant kind of peace in the grey and ancient walls and green lawns among which I live; a quietude that doesn't compensate for the things I have loved and left, but at times softening their outlines a little.' He also found the people about him 'often clever' but 'always wearying', and if one should be moved to take his opinion of the townsmen seriously—

> For Cambridge people rarely smile,
> Being urban, squat, and packed with guile.

—it is well to remember that the habit may have resulted from the deprivations of those six hundred years when they had next to nothing to smile at, and a generous helping of guile was necessary for survival in the shadow of a medieval university. But there were those tiny houses that looked like 'huts for pigmies'.

VI

THE WIND OF CHANGE

WHEN the first stones of the great chapel were laid, the office of Chancellor had already been in existence for two hundred years, and if its nebulous period of birth and pre-natal existence as a student guild are taken into account, another hundred years can be added—three centuries of no significant academic progress. The University still clung to its *trivium* and *quadrivium,* with a further eight years of study for a doctorate in one of the hardy evergreens, Theology, Law and Medicine; its spoken word was still Latin; as late as the 1620s Milton described the curriculum as 'an assinine feast of sow-thistles and brambles'; and by modern reckoning the bulk of the 'scholars' were still schoolboys, to be treated as schoolboys, for the Master in Grammar had no monopoly of the 'rodde'. Punishment was then considered a necessary adjunct of education, and one—no doubt devoted—mother pleaded that her son's tutor should send her 'faithfully words ho Clemit Paston hathe do his dever i'lerning, and if he hathe nought do well nor wyll amende, prey him that he wyll trewly belash him tyll he will amend'. Major offences were expiated in the college hall where a 'menial' did the whipping.

The hand of the medieval Church also lay heavily on the University at this period, restricting that independence of thought which is the very life-blood of such an institution, and another century had to pass before it took its place among the great universities of Europe. For the moment the wind of change was a gentle breeze, conveying no hint of the hurricane which was to be the Reformation. Lollardy, so far, had made no impression on Cambridge, whereas Oxford was highly suspect—at one time Wycliffe was Master of Balliol—and it is reasonable to suppose that the cleaner ecclesiastical air at Cambridge influenced Henry the Sixth in his decision to build his chapel there, despite the 'sad mortality' that resulted from breathing the other sort.

Nevertheless, a slight friction—literally at ground level—was developing between the Church and the University, with its growing family of colleges, over the simple question of space. The great Augustinian Priory stood self-sufficient and aloof at Barnwell, with a church transcending in magnificence any building in Cambridge until the chapel at King's was completed. But the religious orders, as a whole, had been quick to recognize the advantage of an adjacent university. They had established themselves accordingly, and there simply was not room for two cuckoos in the Cambridge nest. Privileged by the University to 'keep terms' and study in their own commodious quarters, they had further obtained—from the Pope—not only the right of proceeding to their degrees in Theology without first qualifying in the normal course, but also release from the obligation of preaching to the University in Great St Mary's. To that extent were they affiliated to, and privileged within, the University. Going a stage further, in 1426, the Benedictines had founded their own college, and but for the dissolution, others might have followed. As it was, this offshoot from Crowland Abbey became Magdalene, just as St John's College emerged from the Augustinian Hospital of St John and, earlier, Jesus College from the Nunnery of St Rhadegund.

Although the religious houses were surrendered to the King—except that of the Carmelites which was 'gladly, freely and willingly' though inadvertently handed over to Queens', a surrender at once declared void—the benefit to the University, through the colleges, was considerable. In due course Sir Walter Mildmay founded Emmanuel on the site of the Dominicans, and that of the Franciscans passed to Sidney Sussex. For some time before the dissolution, and afterwards until demolition began, the University held its annual commencement or graduation ceremonies in the great church which was a feature of the Franciscan Friary. On these occasions it was converted into a 'theatre' with a large stage on which the candidates disputed. The site, too, was a good one, apart from the blemish of the King's Ditch, but as long ago as 1325 the brethren had largely offset the danger from that with an aqueduct bringing them drinking water from a spring near what is now the Observatory on the way to Madingley; and it still brings water to Cambridge, if only to the fountain in Trinity Great Court.

The Carmelites, who had first established themselves in Newnham, found water-trouble of a different kind, for the winter floods so frequently cut them off from their studies that they had to move—into Milne Street. This explains their premature settlement with Queens'. Happily it carried no significant penalty, for the college was allowed to buy the order's building for £20, and that, in effect, was a useful benefaction. But the Carmelites, being mendicant, had no settled income and were hardly opulent. In contrast, Barnwell Priory's annual income amounted to as much as £256, and among the colleges was exceeded only by those of King's, St John's, Christ's and Queens'.

Some idea of the accommodation that the richer orders enjoyed —and the townsmen ruefully contemplated—is found in the Augustinian Friary building of twenty-seven rooms, exclusive of outhouses, the 'great parlour' of which was seventy yards long; and the site was in proportion. Apart from its use as a 'Physic Garden' and finally accommodation for 'The Cavendish', at one time it also made room for six almshouses and the Perse Grammar School, from which the lane draws its present name, Free School. Stephen Perse, M.D., a Fellow of Gonville and Caius, left the money for both in 1615. He had in mind a school for a hundred boys from Cambridge and the immediate neighbourhood, and so it started; but it was to know temporary closure, use of its buildings to house the Fitzwilliam collection, and a law suit, before it acquired its present distinction and, in recent years, settled in its own vast grounds not far from the 'new' Addenbrooke's.

But the dissolution of the monasteries—in effect, their seizure by the Crown to the great benefit of an undeserving court—was only a beginning. Although it had cleared one cuckoo out of the Cambridge nest, repercussions were alarming, for the early University was itself not far removed from a monastic foundation while those in authority were celibates for the most part in Holy Orders, the 'scholars' in clerical habit, their studies mainly theological, and their ultimate allegiance owing to the Pope. The subsequent act for the dissolution of the colleges, passed in 1545, was therefore a clear and predictable indication of their peril. Expectant beneficiaries were gathered now for a second helping. Like 'wolves agape' for further spoils, the Vice-Chancellor said. Nevertheless, after Queen Katharine Parr, whom he petitioned, had 'attempted the King's majesty for the stablishment of their livelihood and possessions' so movingly that the King himself acknowledged an urge to advance learning and 'erect new occasion thereof' rather than 'confound the ancient and godly institutions of Cambridge', the outcome was hardly in doubt. As commissioners reporting under the act, the Vice-Chancellor—then Matthew Parker—assisted by the President of Queens' and a future Master of Trinity, further discouraged the wolves by revealing that, without exception, colleges were unable to make both ends meet, and the King's decision to found a college himself assured the University's survival.

King's College Chapel was still an airy vision when Andrew Doket, the Rector of St Botolph's and Principal of the neighbouring hostel of St Bernard, received the royal permission to build a small college between the High Street and what would ultimately survive as the end of Milne Street. It was to have a Master and four Fellows, and be named the College of St Bernard. But his ideas ran ahead of his purse, modest though they were, and two years later, in 1448, after observing that Cambridge had 'no collage founded by eny Quene of Englond hidertoward', Queen Margaret took over and founded the Queen's College of St Margaret and St Bernard on the larger site between Milne Street and the river, 'beside the most noble and glorious college royal of Our Lady and St Nicholas founded by the King's highness'. More importantly, she engaged Reginald Ely, the master-mason, busily engaged though he was next door. Fuller, however, sees her generous intervention as something less than altruistic. 'As Miltiades' trophy in Athens would not suffer Themistocles to sleep', he says, 'so this Queen, beholding her husband's bounty in building King's College, was restless in herself with holy emulation until she had produced something of the like nature, a strife wherein wives, without breach of duty, may contend with their husbands, which should succeed in pious performance.' And of Elizabeth Woodville, co-foundress in 1465, he adds: 'A good-natured lady whose estate being sequestered for the delinquency of her husband, makes her more merciful to the miseries of others.' But, whatever the inspiration, her act has been noted as the first symbol of reconciliation between the Houses of York and Lancaster.

The earliest statutes gave the new foundation a President— itself a departure from the customary Master, and in keeping with the choice of a Provost for King's—with twelve Fellows, all of whom were to be in Holy Orders and immune, by oath, from the heretical temptations of Wycliffe and Pecock; and to the great advantage of the college, Doket himself was the first President, for it was during his reign of some forty years that Queens' took its Tudor shape, so greatly admired today. To enter by the turreted gateway that fronts on the old Milne Street is not only to step into a Tudor court, clunch-built but faced with deep-red brick long since richly mellowed: it is to know the feel of stepping back in time. Only ten years after its completion, Doket began a second court to meet the demand for accommodation. Cloistered in part, with small brick arches, it carries the college buildings down to the river, and the President's Gallery, itself a perfect gem of Tudor half-timbered architecture, closes the northern side of what is probably the most intimate and picturesque court in Cambridge. Without ostentation—that is unavoidably reserved for the ancient decoration perpetuated in the hall—these two courts speak quietly for the age to which they belong, and if any comment on Uffenbach's almost inevitable condemnation is needed, it is to be found in his dismissal of them as old and mean.

He did, however, admit that the library contained some worthwhile books.

Andrew Doket had indeed done well for what was really his own foundation. Under his guidance Queens' had quickly taken a notable place in the University, and John Fisher's tenure as President was destined to put the college at the very centre of the critical thought that was then beginning to mark the University, for there is little doubt that on his suggestion Erasmus, the greatest scholar of the Renaissance, elected to spend three years at Queens'. As Fuller comments: 'Queens' College accounteth it no small credit thereunto that Erasmus (who no doubt might have pickt and chose what House he pleased) preferred this for his place of study for some years in Cambridge. Either invited thither with the fame of the learning and love of his friend Bishop Fisher, then Master thereof, or allured with the situation of the College so near the river (as Rotterdam, his native place to the Sea) with pleasant walks thereabouts.' Fisher had, in fact, been elected Chancellor of the University for life, and Bishop of Rochester, in 1504, and after a three-year stay Erasmus left Cambridge in 1513 to spend the next few years divided between Basel, Louvain, and visits to England.

Although Queens' gave their eminent guest 'the fairest chambers in the ancient building', and his study overlooked 'the best prospect about the colledge, viz., upon the river, into the cornefields and country adjoyning', he appears to have been a difficult man to please, reformers being, one can but suppose, critical by nature. He never ceased complaining about the cost of living and —while grudgingly admitting that 'nothing can be extracted from the naked'—the laxity of undergraduates in paying their lecture fees. Yet, in today's equivalent values, his yearly income has been estimated at several thousand pounds. He did not like the college beer, finding it 'raw, smal and windy', and as the wine available was just as bad in its way, he sought the help of a friend: 'If you can send me a barrel of Greek wine, the best which can be had, Erasmus will bless you; only take care it is not sweet. Have no uneasiness about your loan; it will be paid before the date of the bill. Meanwhile I am being killed with thirst. Imagine the rest. Farewell.'

But even this solution was far from satisfactory, for when the wine reached him, there was not enough of it. He had 'supposed' that his friend would have sent him 'a somewhat larger flagon which would have lasted some months', and lamenting that he had only the scent of the small one to console him, specifically ordered the larger. The carriers, however, discovering what they were carrying, promptly drank half of it on the way and filled up the cask with water—a dilution which Erasmus blamed for his subsequent attack of gravel. Only the Cambridge girls appeared to be above reproach, being 'divinely pretty, soft, pleasant, gentle, and charming as the Muses', and most of all he liked their feminine courtesy. 'When you go on a visit,' he said, 'the girls all kiss you. They kiss you when you arrive. They kiss you when you go away, and they kiss you again when you return.'

So Desiderius Erasmus, a Dutchman, descended on Cambridge, and when not grumbling, worked diligently on the New Testament, held the Lady Margaret Professorship of Divinity, introduced the teaching of Greek into the University—probably the printing-press into Cambridge as well—and, with John Fisher, gave impetus to the critical thought then stirring, for in these two, Queens' could claim scholars and reformers, both preferring adjustment from within rather than Luther's open schism.

The wind of change was freshening.

Nor was the voice of Cambridge silent. It was at last being heard in Oxford, although the idea that scholars from different universities should freely interchange to broaden their views dates back to Merton. But the Cambridge voice was not always appreciated. Of the scholars whom Wolsey arranged to go there, the Warden of New College lamented: 'Would God that his Grace had not motioned to call any Cambridge men to his most godly College! We were clear without blot till they came.' As Cambridge was then moving towards the Protestant faith and becoming its stronghold, this outcry is significant.

It is also interesting, though perhaps not significant, that the centre of the movement in Cambridge was close to Queens'.

With the clearance of the King's College site, the part of Milne Street where Queens' occupied most of the western side would have been a cul-de-sac but for a narrow lane at the very end leading down to the river, and, some twenty yards short of it on the other side of the street, another alley cutting through a cluster of inns and stables to the High Street. It was 'detestable and filthy', and it appears to have been known down the ages as Plute's, Plott and Nuts, and finally King's Lane. Among the surrounding stables were those of carrier Hobson, and of the several inns the nineteenth-century façade of the Black Bull still survives, strictly scheduled, as part of St Catharine's College. But the inn that lives in the Cambridge story is the old White Horse that narrowly fronted the High Street next to the Bull and reached back into the alley, for, by sheltering those who embraced the new noncomformity, it linked itself with the Reformation.

They were the scholars who called themselves 'Germans'—and even 'Heretics'—after the latest Germanic teaching, and 'Germany' was their name for the inn where they gathered in hopeful secrecy to avoid the Cardinal's spies. Here they studied the works of Martin Luther which Sygar Nicholson smuggled to them—books of a kind that were publicly burnt on Wolsey's orders in 1529, at a cost to the Proctors of two shillings. Thomas Farman, soon to be President of Queens', had contrived to evade the search for this dangerous literature, and to the inn, stealthily reached by the fetid alley, came men whose names are written in history. Robert Barnes, Prior of the local Augustinian house, attacked Wolsey himself from the pulpit of St Edward's Church where, four years later, Hugh Latimer preached his 'Sermons on the Card', and although he abjured and played the accuser's part against Lambert, his White Horse colleague, he went to the stake as a Protestant in 1541. Lambert, of Queens', was burnt at Smithfield in 1538, where Frith, of King's, had suffered five years earlier.

'Little Bilney', of Trinity Hall, was the first to die, burnt at Norwich in 1531. Himself converted by Erasmus, he in turn inspired the White Horse movement. 'The first framer of the University in the knowledge of Christ', John Foxe calls him in

The History of the Acts and Monuments of the Church, commonly 'The Book of Martyrs'. Through Bilney, Latimer confessed that he 'began to smell the Word of God, forsaking the school doctors and such fooleries', and suffered Bilney's fate, with Ridley at Oxford in 1555. In that same year, John Rogers, of Pembroke, was the first of the Marian martyrs. It was the good fortune of Miles Coverdale to avoid the fate of his Augustinian prior.

Oddly, in view of the prominence of the University in the Reformation, and the penalties its members paid, only one— John Hullier, a Kingsman—went to the stake in Cambridge, brought back to suffer on Jesus Green in 1556. To his enemies' derision he 'made no answer, but made him ready, uttering his prayer. Which done he went meekly himself to the stake, and with chains being bound and beset with reed and wood standing in a pitch barrel, and the fire being set to, not marking the wind, it blew the flame to his back. Then he feeling it began earnestly to call upon God. Nevertheless his friends perceiving the fire to be ill kindled caused the Serjeants to turn it and fire it to that place where the wind might blow it in his face. That done, there was a company of books which were cast into the fire, and by chance a communion book fell between his hands, who received it joyfully, opened it, and read so long till the force of the flame and smoak caused him that he could see no more, and then he fell again into prayer, holding his hands up to heaven and the book betwixt his arms next to his heart, thanking God for sending him it . . . and when the people thought he had been dead he suddenly uttered the words, Lord Jesus receive my spirit, dying very meekly.'

Although the circumstances of Hullier's martyrdom were not sufficiently abhorrent to deter spectators from taking 'what they could get of him' afterwards, the burning of the exhumed bodies of the two German reformers, Paul Fagius and Martin Bucer, one from St Michael's Church and the other from Great St Mary's, offered less opportunity when 'crated' and chained to stakes in the market place. Moreover, revulsion was such that, in 1560, not only were their degrees and 'titles of honour which they had

enjoyed' formally restored by grace of the Senate, but the
University itself assembled in Great St Mary's for a special
'oration' in their honour.

Two years before Bilney died at the stake, pestilence added still
further to the University's troubles by forcing the colleges to close
completely during the summer, and that, in turn, fortuitously
involved the University in a question of legality touching the
King's own marriage with Catherine of Aragon—a question of
some trickiness since, with Henry the Eighth, there was only one
acceptable answer. Back from a fruitless mission to the Pope in
Rome, the Provost of King's and the Master of Trinity Hall
chanced upon Cranmer, innocently tutoring at Waltham Abbey,
and from him received the suggestion that the King should consult
his own learned theologians. By doing so, he would at least avoid
the delays of the Papal Court. But the King's delight at referring
a problem involving divorce to an English jury—'Marry!' he
said, 'I perceive that man hath the right sow by the ear.'—was no
guarantee that the University, itself divided between papal
supremacy and reform, would give him the answer he wanted.

For William Buckmaster, D.D., of Peterhouse—the Vice-
Chancellor and 'referee' in a disputation that involved some two
hundred theologians with the question: 'Is a man allowed to
marry his brother's wife when his brother has died without issue?'
—the task of getting a clear-cut verdict was impossible, and the
King required a clear-cut No, followed by the divorce that would
make the surviving daughter illegitimate and avoid the danger of
civil war later. When the Vice-Chancellor asked the doctors as a
body, there was no agreement. Nor would the meeting consent
to a secret vote; and to his proposal, on the morrow, for a grace
appointing a committee of twenty-nine doctors and masters to
answer the question, a two-thirds majority being acceptable, the
opposition was at first so violent that the grace was defeated. Not
until the Provost of King's and the Master of Trinity Hall had
diplomatically 'caused some to leave the house which were against
it' was a third attempt successful, and the Vice-Chancellor able
to give the King, at Windsor, an answer that was only in part

satisfactory, although he did reward the Vice-Chancellor with twenty nobles before reaching the awkward clauses. It was poor consolation for one who had done his best and, on returning, was met with rioting and, at night, 'such a jetting in Cambridge as ye never heard of, with such booing and crying even against our College', all on his account. But the King, if 'scarce contented', was sufficiently sure of his strength to accept a breach with Rome. Wolsey had fallen. In 1530, only a year after the University's verdict, he pronounced the whole body of clergy guilty of treason under Richard the Second's law of praemunire, and pardoned them on payment of £118,840. Very soon he was dissolving the monasteries, founding Trinity College and, less happily, preparing the way for the Marian persecution.

In the midst of this religious upheaval at high level, the active protest of the townsmen against the enclosure of common land came as a further reminder of their own ill-fortune. Nor did the suppression of the religious houses ease the burden of the poor when rapacious bailiffs and others used the large tracts of land released. At Norwich, armed force was necessary to quell what amounted to insurrection. Prisoners were brought to Cambridge, and a reference in the local archives to expenses incurred 'for carrying out the Gallows and for a new Rope' reveals where some of them met their end. Cambridge, however, provided a far more unusual spectacle when the Vice-Chancellor and the Mayor joined in the task of pacifying their own rebels, and obtaining a general pardon for what amounted to little more than pulling up fences and, it seems, throwing them in the river.

Few Vice-Chancellors in these troubled years, however, found themselves in a position so delicate, and perilous, as Dr Edwin Sandys, the Master of St Catharine's, for he was in office when Edward the Sixth died, and not only had Lady Jane Grey been proclaimed Queen, but the Chancellor of the University, the Duke of Northumberland, had arrived in Cambridge 'with his army and a commission to apprehend the Lady Mary' who, hurrying south, was known to have reached Sawston. Nor were the Doctor's fears allayed during dinner by the ducal request that he should preach a sermon on the morrow, supporting the cause of Lady Jane in whose ultimate success he had no faith at all, and that night, in his perplexity, he sought for guidance in prayer. Having shut his eyes and opened his bible, he begged that the first words he saw might give him the text that would save him.

It was the Book of Joshua: *Responderuntque ad Josue, atque dixerunt: omnia, quae praecepisti nobis, faciemus, et quoqunque miseris, ibimus.* And they answered Joshua, saying: all that thou commandest us, we will do, and whither soever thou sendest us we will go. 'A fit text indeed for him, as in the event it proved,' Fuller says, for 'so wisely and warily he handled his words, that his enemies got not so full advantage against him as they expected'.

That was on the Sunday when Doctor Sandys apparently 'pulled many tears out of the biggest of them' with his sermon, and so moved the Duke and the nobility present that they appointed 'one Master Leaver to go to London with it and put it in print'. But a sermon delivered extempore takes time to reconstruct, and Wednesday had come when a weeping bedell came running to Sandys even as he gave the manuscript to a Leaver all booted and spurred. Only then did he learn of the Duke's abortive foray into Suffolk and his speedy return to Cambridge 'with more sad thoughts within him than valiant soldiers about him'. Worse still, the Duke hastened to proclaim Mary Queen in the market place, with the Vice-Chancellor and the Mayor officially in attendance, and 'among others, he threwe uppe his owne cappe, and so laughed that the tears ran down his cheeks for grief'. But to no avail. That night the Sergeant-at-Arms arrested him for high treason in the sanctuary of King's, having entered without hindrance a college which Fuller describes as 'fenced about with more privileges than any other foundation in the University'.

Swift, too, was Popish reaction. Hearing the Schools' bell tolling without any order from him, and finding, on his return to his lodge, that thieves had already taken the keys and books of his office, Dr Sandys went at once to the Regent House, and was addressing a highly perturbed congregation when 'in cometh one Master Mitch, with a rabble of some twenty Papists, some endeavouring to pluck him from the Chair, others, the Chair from him, all using railing words and violent actions'. But the Doctor's courage was never in doubt, and 'groping for his dagger, he would have despatched some of them as God's enemies, if Dr Bill and Dr Blith had not fallen upon him and prayed him for God's sake to hold his hands'. He did, and when the tumult was over, finished his oration, quietly handed over his office and 'repaired home to his own College', there to await the Queen's pleasure. That took him next day to the Tower of London with the Duke—a grim command upon which 'his stable was robbed of four notable good geldings' while he himself was 'set upon a lame horse that halted to the ground'. The yeomen of the guard, however, were content that a friend 'might lend him a nagg'.

Although he was allowed to live, imprisonment and self-appointed exile were his lot until Elizabeth's accession restarted his advance to high preferment. For a man notoriously impetuous in small matters, he had shown himself remarkably calm and steadfast in moments that were no less demanding for being normal to the period. 'I cannot', he said, 'blow hot or cold.' Only in his preaching, it seems, was there calculated excess, for his sermon to the Queen in which he first announced his intention of not being too long—'few words will be sufficient for the wise'— a distinguished bishop was later to describe as one 'of marked brevity: it only takes three-quarters of an hour to read it in a room'.

The hurricane died with the advent of Elizabeth, and her statutes of 1570, which endured for some three hundred years, put the University's house in order. But Papist and Protestant still had to achieve a tolerant acceptance of each other; there was still the Puritan clash to come, with civil war, apart from the townsmen's implacable hostility. But, for the moment, the University enjoyed the royal favour. The Vice-Chancellor and the Heads of Houses held the reins and controlled the University's finance, a burden hitherto borne and, one would think, gladly relinquished by the Proctors; and as if to set the seal of royal approval on their activities, three years after the new statutes were given, a grant of arms to the University followed—gules a cross ermine and four gold leopards with a book gules upon the cross.*

But the royal favour did little to help the University in its war with the townsmen, for they had cunningly acquired a powerful champion in the Lord Lieutenant of the County—an office created in Mary's reign—and Lord North, newly appointed High Steward of the Borough, also enjoyed the royal favour to the extent of entertaining the Queen with appropriate magnificence at Kirtling, his country seat near Newmarket. The townsmen evidently saw their chance in the first years of his appointment to the Lieutenancy, three years before his stewardship in 1572, when he not only complained to the Vice-Chancellor about the 'evyll and fowle wordes' which a student had used to the Mayor, but directed that 'the varlet' should spend three hours in the pillory with one ear nailed to it, and then seek the Mayor's forgiveness on bended knee. He did, however, relent sufficiently to spare the young man's ear.

The extent of the University's indignation at this interference with a traditional pastime is revealed in the attack made on Lord North's lodging by a mob of students armed with clubs and swords, their intention being—so he said in his complaint to the Privy Council—to kill him. He was undeterred, nevertheless, and he also appears to have won the battle of the wandering players, among them Lord Strange's company of which Shakespeare was once a member. Chesterton, too, under his protection, seems to have become a bigger nuisance than ever, although it is doubtful whether he would have condoned the local football team's stratagem of hiding staves in the church porch and then belabouring the scholars so heartily that 'divers of them were driven to runne through the river'. Nor would he have allowed Chesterton to assert its right to the pleasures of bear-baiting by thrusting a bedell 'upon the Beare in such sort that he could hardly keep himself from hurt'. Lord North was certainly fair-minded—inconveniently so, the University must have thought at the time

* Oxford's comment that learning at Cambridge is obviously a closed book, to which Cambridge crushingly retorts that Oxford's book is always open at the same page, is a pleasantry no doubt reversed when told by an Oxford man.

The Round Church, seen from St John's College

of the Spanish Armada, when the whole country was astir and he insisted that the scholars, excused the muster or not, should play their part in meeting the threatened invasion. Whatever the ethical questions involved, he undoubtedly earned the gifts, ranging from silver-gilt cups to frying pans, which the grateful townsmen showered upon him.

Yet all this tempestuous rioting was never more than a local feature, a conflict of incompatibles that would itself fade away. The wind of change had done its work in the wider field of history.

7

Wren's Chapel, Emmanuel College
The Gate of Virtue, Gonville and Caius

VII

THE FAMILY GROWS

A CURIOUS feature of the medieval University is that, in the most unpromising circumstances, nothing seemed to halt its growth. Dynasties might fall, monastic houses disappear, pestilence and persecution stalk the land while, locally, rioting was normal relaxation and the town itself one of the sorriest places on earth, but still the colleges grew. Over the period 1441 to 1596, ten came into being in fairly steady succession, starting with King's and ending with Sidney Sussex. Two of them, St John's and Trinity, are today the largest colleges—though Churchill is in pursuit—and with St Catharine's, they joined King's, Queens', Gonville and Caius, Clare and Trinity Hall, in filling the site between the old High Street and the river. Much common land had to be made available before 'New Town' could flow eastward and engulf Barnwell, and not until the beginning of the last century did Cambridge itself appreciably expand.

So, in the middle years while the University took shape, the town advanced but little beyond the Ditch and hardly at all across the river. Although a ribbon of small houses ran up Castle Hill, Chesterton, like Newnham, was still a separate village, and on the other side of the town, St Thomas's Leys—in due course to accommodate Downing College—was still open country. Only beyond the Trumpington gate was growth significant—a finger of dwellings that included two colleges and extended as far as Lensfield Road. Outside the Barnwell gate, God's House stood forlorn, opposite St Andrew's Church, and further on rose the

Dominican Friary, but there was little else. Along the Via Devana, Cambridge ended at the corner of what is now Parker's Piece.

St Catharine's, the college that followed Queens' in 1473, and now occupies the southern end of the site between Silver Street and King's, began with a small clunch-built court and, it might be said, the distinction of its founder. As Fuller comments: 'Herein he stands alone, without any to accompany him, being the first and the last, who was Master of one College, and at the same time Founder of another.' That was Robert Woodlark, or Wodelarke, Provost of King's, and for him the Wars of the Roses were disastrous. They put an end to all hope of lucrative prefer-ment, with the result that 'the Master and ten Fellows, students of philosophy and sacred theology', whom he had in mind, shrank to a Master and three, and inevitably the college suffered from 'lowness of endowment and littleness of receipt'.

'Far be it from me to resemble this Virgin Hall to a wanton woman', Fuller wrote, and having referred to a 'she favourite' of Edward the Fourth, of whom it was said that 'there was nothing in her body one would have changed except one would have wished her somewhat higher', made it clear that Catharine Hall's undoubted charm was likewise impaired by a slender purse; and with even less felicity the college has been called 'a sucker thrown up by the parent stem'. But at this suggestion St Catharine's can afford to smile, the sucker today being larger than the parent.

Nor did two of the most important benefactions which St Catharine's was later to receive fail to reveal disappointment among hopeful legatees, no less deeply felt for being quaintly expressed. When, in 1745, a wealthy Yorkshire lady left property giving a return that exceeded the entire college income from other sources, her relatives made their feelings perfectly clear on her monument in Adlingfleet Church, for this bluntly proclaims that Mrs Mary Ramsden 'bequeathed her whole Estate to Catharine Hall in Cambridge'—just that. Nor were the Fellows of Gonville and Caius less forthright after their Master had bequeathed his considerable property of the Bull Inn, for it is said that once a year they drank despondently to the unhappy memory of Dr Gosling who was such a goose as to give the Bull to Catharine. That was

ELIZABETHAN CAMBRIDGE (*Richard Lyne, 1574*)

in 1626, when the College had just entered a period of rebuilding and growth common to most of the earlier foundations. Also acquired, about this time, was the house of the famous Hobson, adjoining the Bull to the south with the legendary stables behind, and there is evidence that, as early as 1454 in the pre-natal days of the college, Woodlark purchased, and held for a time, a tenement called 'Fordham Place or the White Horse', the rendezvous of 'The Heretics'. History, grave and gay, therefore lurks in this once malodorous corner of Cambridge bordering Plott and Nuts Lane, but there is little to tell of it now that the lane is part of the college scene, and St Catharine's Chapel stands on the site of the stables. Hobson's memorial is the modern building that bears his name.

A wealthy carrier of parcels and passengers between Cambridge and London, appropriately to the Bull in Bishopsgate, Hobson is known in Cambridge for his conduit, and to the world at large for his 'choice', a that-or-nothing ultimatum which derived from his custom of making a would-be client seeking a horse—and notoriously 'the Scholars of Cambridge rid hard'—take the one by the stable door. Even Milton was strangely moved by Hobson's death on New Year's Day in 1631, at the age of eighty-six—sufficiently so to write of 'the University Carrier, who sickened at the time of the Vacancy, being forbid to go London by reason of the Plague':

> Here lies old Hobson: Death hath broke his girt,
> And here, alas! hath laid him in the dirt . . .
> And surely Death would never have prevailed,
> Had not his weekly course of carriage failed;
> But lately, finding him so long at home,
> And thinking now his journey's end had come,
> And that he had taken up his latest inn,
> In the kind office of a Chamberlin,
> Shewed him the room where he must lodge that night,
> Pulled off his boots, and took away the light:
> If any asked for him, it shall be said,
> 'Hobson hath supped, and's newly gone to bed.'

The 'visitation' during which Hobson died was not exceptional Nothing equalled the Black Death of 1348. But it was severe even by the standards of Cambridge where bubonic plague and typhus were common in the appalling squalor that prevailed. No doubt to the townsfolk they were plain acts of God, to be accepted and endured, and they were until, for no apparent reason, the great 'visitation' of 1666, following that of 1665, proved to be the last. In this final period, 1629 to 1666, the Audit Book of St Catharine's refers to seven outbreaks that called for ten payments ranging from one shilling to £32 2s. 11d., and there is the entry, dated 1629-30:

for allowance to yᵉ Butler for losses in beare in yᵉ tyme of infection —5 16 3½

—a sum, about £100 in modern currency, that could well indicate the closing of the college when tea and coffee had yet to slake the national thirst and beer was the staple beverage.

If the University did not disperse as a whole, infected colleges were put in quarantine with extra porters 'keeping the gate' if necessary. In a letter dated the 24th of April 1630, the Master of Christ's wrote: 'Our University is in a manner wholly dissolved; all meetings and Exercises ceasing. In many Colleges almost none are left. In ours, of twenty-seven mess we have not five. Our gates are strictly kept, none but Fellows to go forth, or any to be let in without the consent of the major part of our society, of which we have but seven at home at this instant; only a Sizar may go with his Tutors ticket upon an errand. Our Butcher, Baker and Chandler bring yᵉ provisions to the Colldg Gates, where the Steward and Cooke receive them. We have taken all our officers we need into the Colldge, and none must stir out. Yea, we have taken 3 Women into our Colledge and appointed them a Chamber to lye in together. Two are Bedmakers, one a Laundresse. We have turned out our Porter, and appointed our Barber both Porter and Barber, allowing him a Chamber next the Gates. Thus we live, as close prisoners, and, I hope, without danger.'

In a letter dated the 25th of May, following a grace for closing the Schools, the Master of Sidney Sussex gives a view of the

University from the outside. 'Our School-gates are shut up, and our Colleges left desolate and empty almost. There have died of this Infection, from the last of February till the 24th of April 24 Persons; and since then till May 15, 30 more and 7 more. The Magistrates are careful. But the Charge groweth great, both in maintaining the Infected and the Poor amongst us, which want both Means and Work.'

In 1556, seven years before Parliament made the poor rate compulsory, the common enemy had brought Town and University together for their own preservation. The result was a levy designed to cope with sickness as well as the poverty and even famine inevitable when the Town, like the University, came to a standstill; and Dr Henry Butts, the Master of Corpus Christi, who was Vice-Chancellor during the 1630 'visitation', reveals some-things of what was done. 'There are five thousand poor', he told the High Steward, 'and not above a hundred who can assist in relieving them.' Of the sick, he says: 'We have built near forty booths in a remote place upon our commons, whither we forth-with remove those who are infected—where we have placed a German physician, who visits them, day and night, and he ministers to them.' The commons referred to were Midsummer Green. 'Besides constables', he adds, 'we have certain ambulatory officers who walk the streets night and day, to keep our people from needless conversing, and to bring us notice of all disorders.' Horsemen, too, were hired to protect the fields in harvest time from 'the disorderly poor'.

At what cost to the Vice-Chancellor, one does not have to guess. 'Myself am alone,' he wrote, 'a destitute and forsaken man: not a Scholler with me in College, not a Scholler seen by me without. God, all-sufficient, I trust is with me; to whose most holy protection I humbly commend your Lordship.'

During the year there were 617 deaths from all causes, of which 347 were from the plague. Dr Butts hanged himself in his study.

The 'visitations' of 1665 and '66 differed only in their severity. Each time the University stagnated in a town that was stilled in isolation. Armed watchmen patrolled it. Some exits were 'cast up and boarded'. The Privy Council itself banned Sturbridge

Fair. Forty acres of Coldham Common were set aside for pest-houses—even as the common was used in the smallpox epidemic of 1903—and once a week the ailing occupants saw the Mayor and the High Constable appear 'at a distance, taking the windward side, to know their wants'. The deaths from all causes in 1665 were undoubtedly heavy enough at 413, but those a year later were 797, without the contribution from the parish of St Giles beyond the Great Bridge, and some twelve hundred deaths in a population of six thousand is a death roll sufficiently large to suggest, over the years, one reason why the town took so long to expand beyond the limits of river and Ditch.

Meanwhile St Catharine's emerged from its tiny chrysalis of decaying clunch, first with what was for the period a small but dominating range that bordered on Milne Street—a range, too, of significance far beyond the purpose of its unknown architect, for it set the pattern of development:

> O wise unknown, who used thy skill to raise
> These walls for us to copy and to praise,
> Thy name forgotten, moves us to recall
> That 'Man is nothing, but his work is all'. *

That impressive start was made in 1634, and the Bursar's accounts for 1634–35 show that the expenses incurred for bricks, lime, hair, sand, slate, tiles, lead, timber, nails, workmanship, and the smith, the mason and the glazier, amounted to no more than £260 5s. 10d. Ownership of the Black Bull Inn made this new building possible, and its deep-red brick and stone set the pattern of the major development some forty years later. Started by Robert Grumbold and finished by Essex, it led to the complete disappearance of Woodlark's court, and has produced homogeneity and, as one architectural authority puts it, 'the beautiful three-sided effect of the present court as it looks across Trumpington Street'. When Grumbold built the Baroque gateway opening on to Milne Street, it was the college front door. Today it is the back, opening on to Queens' Lane, and St Catharine's joins with Queens', St John's, Magdalene and others in supporting the charge

* The late Dr W. H. S. Jones, Litt.D., F.B.A.

that Cambridge itself is also, in small though charming part, a red-brick university.

Until 1921, when it was cut down, a grove of elms between the college railings and Trumpington Street added to that charm, and during the Napoleonic threat of invasion a note of belligerence as well, for *The History of the Cambridgeshire Regiment* records: 'Tradesmen and youthful aspirants for military fame marched and counter-marched in Sidney College Gardens (at the time an open pasture) as well as on Clare Hall Piece, in Peterhouse grounds and in Catharine Hall Grove where a juvenile band (with wooden guns and sabres) under the command of Captain Sharpe, designated the 'Cat-in-Hall Fencibles', mimicked the martial fame of a Marlborough and a Granby.'

As there is little point in wasting an Army captain on the training of street urchins, one can but assume that undergraduates made up the 'juvenile band' and 'youthful aspirants', their differences with the local tradesmen properly suppressed in the hour of peril. Nor are 'wooden guns' evidence of puerility. In the Kaiser's war of 1914 they were used by recruits drilling on Parker's Piece. Over two thousand were killed and some three thousand wounded of the fourteen thousand members of the University, past and present, who fought in that war. Today the C.U.O.T.C.—the Officers Training Corps—is the only one with a battle honour, a number of volunteers having served in the field with the Suffolk Regiment during the final Boer War.

Of the Puritan assault on the old Woodlark chapel, and the vain but courageous protest of Dr Ralph Brownrigge, the Master and Bishop of Exeter, there is Dowsing's own record:

At Katharine Hall, 1643, Decemb. 28.
We pulled down St George and the Dragon, and the Popish Katharine and Saint to which the Colledge was dedicated. Dr Brunbrick the Bp. manifested more reverence due to the place called Church than any other place, the Communion Plate not to be used for no other use in any Church, and he said it was an Error to break down John the Baptist there and these words 'Orate pro Anima qui fecit hanc Fenestram': 'Pray for the Soul of him that made this Windowe.'

But Uffenbach was not entirely disappointed. The new St Catharine's, in 1710, was 'a large and fine building', and in a library that contained some 350 books, he did find one manuscript.

The College of the Blessed Virgin Mary, St John the Evangelist and the Glorious Virgin St Rhadegund, commonly called Jesus College in the University of Cambridge, followed St Catharine's in 1496, and like St Catharine's, it has peculiar distinction in its birth, being the only college to make its home in a nunnery. Over three and a half centuries had slipped away since St Rhadegund's had risen outside the town, to prosper awhile, outlive its purpose, and settle in slow decay; and it was the prescience of John Alcock, Bishop of Ely, that led him to convert the neglected and tumble-down buildings into the college, commonly known as Jesus, before it could be swept away in the dissolution soon to follow. Today, it is the only college that keeps to the plan of its heritage, and its pride and glory is the nunnery church, mostly of early Gothic, part of which survives as the oldest college chapel in Cambridge. Nor was the college other than happily placed from the start, for St Rhadegund's in its early days had attracted the young King Malcolm the Fourth of Scotland, and he, as Earl of Huntingdon and a local landowner, had given some ten acres of 'Grenecroft'—part, that is, of what is now Midsummer Common and Jesus Green. The nuns had also been allowed to hold what was later known as Garlic Fair during the Feast of the Ascension, but this the college did not perpetuate although the Fair continued to be held in the college grounds for the next three hundred years.

Alcock died before he could give his college its statutes. They reflect, therefore, the views of his successor at Ely, Bishop Stanley, and suggest the early whispers of the changing wind. Both Master and Fellows—and there were eight—were given unusual freedom. One of the Fellows had to confine himself to the study of Civil and Canon Law, but the others could enlarge their studies beyond Theology if they so desired, and only one had to be in Holy Orders. Even the Master was exempt from that requirement. Also, teaching within the college was encouraged, and that was a striking departure from custom, for it anticipated a change in college purpose that became general after Elizabeth had reformed the University. Then, in addition, the Jesus statutes not only provided for the instruction in Arts of four 'youths', and in grammar of four 'boys' who were to sing in chapel: they established a school for them and boys from the town under a schoolmaster and usher who were on the foundation and, it seems, better paid than the Fellows.

Jesus College, in short, was different, as Uffenbach was quick to note. It resembled a monastery. But he liked everything about it, including the library although it was on the small side; and he could hardly fail to admire the famous walnut-tree—nearly a hundred feet in width, so it was said. Lawrence Sterne, the eighteenth-century novelist and one of many illustrious Jesus *alumni* to contemplate this remarkable tree, wrote:

> At Cambridge many years ago,
> In Jesus was a walnut-tree;
> The only thing it had to show,
> The only thing folk went to see.
>
> Being of such a size and mass,
> And growing in so wise a college,
> I wonder how it came to pass
> It was not called the 'Tree of Knowledge'.

This is hardly kind to the college chapel, or the founder's elegant gatehouse, but it does throw a small gleam of light on one who 'read a great deal, laughed more, and left Cambridge with the character of an odd man, who had no harm in him, and who had parts, if he could use them'.

Much of that could also be said of Samuel Taylor Coleridge, another distinguished *alumnus* who came up in 1792. Scholar as the word is used today; winner of the college prize for Latin Declamation, and the Browne Medal for a Greek ode on the Slave Trade; and one of the four selected candidates for the Owen Scholarship—he had everything except Sterne's inherent stability. In a word, Coleridge was 'wild'. Of his extravagance and confessed 'Bacchanalian sympathy'; of his sudden exchange of the local scene for the barracks at Reading as Silas Tomkins Comberbatch of the 15th Light Dragoons, followed by his penitent return to the college after his brother had bought him out—of all this it can be said the man is revealed as he was. There is, too, the gay defiance with which he challenged those of the Trinitarian faith in their traditional black raiment by preaching a sermon to them as the 'Reverend' S. T. Coleridge clad in a sky-blue coat and white waistcoat; and one cannot overlook his mad-cap scheme for a communist—though he called it 'pantisocratic'—settlement on the banks of the Susquehanna where 'the females of the party' were to 'cook and perform all domestic offices'. So it is hardly surprising that, in his moments of depression, 'the colleges looked like workhouses' in muddy alleys full of cats and dogs, mingling with priests and proctors. He never took his degree, but slipped away a second time to recall, in later years, the 'inauspicious hour' in which he left 'the friendly cloisters and happy grove of quiet, ever-honoured Jesus College, Cambridge'.

Nor was the conduct of Thomas Cranmer while at Cambridge all that one would expect of a future Archbishop who exchanged the See of Canterbury for the stake. He entered Jesus in 1503, at the age of fourteen, and had been elected a Fellow when 'it chanced him to marry a wife'. So much was alleged at his trial some forty years later—'that he, being yet free, and before he entered into Holy Orders, married one Joan, surnamed Black or Brown, dwelling at the sign of the Dolphin at Cambridge'. To this he answered 'that whether she were called Black or Brown he knew not, but that he married there one Joan, that he granted'. It seems a remarkably casual union for a man of his intellectual promise, especially as he must have known that the college statutes made no provision for married Fellows. The future Primate of All England therefore resigned his fellowship, taught Theology for a living at the Benedictine college soon to be Magdalene, and stayed at the inn with his wife until she died in childbirth a year later. Recognizing his 'towardliness in learning', Jesus then restored his fellowship.

Coleridge, in a magnanimous moment, described the Cam as 'a

handsome stream', its only blemish being 'a muddy complexion', and there was Wordsworth to recall 'his own beloved Cam', and regret that Coleridge had not been there with him to see—

> the light of evening fade
> From the smooth Cam's silent waters.

But it was not always so. Two hundred years earlier Bacon had deplored its weeds and found no pleasure in 'the naked fields' through which it slowly drained. For him, Cambridge still bore traces of Cantebrigge, inland port and trading post, whereas Coleridge knew only a country town that was foremost a seat of learning, a Cambridge not markedly bigger than the one that Bacon had known, but studded now with sixteen colleges, the youngest nearly a hundred years old, and a seventeenth soon to be added. In short, the cuckoo had won—and made the town known to the world.

Grumbold had built Clare bridge and the Backs were taking shape when Coleridge admired 'a handsome stream'. Commerce, too, was dying on the Cam as water-transport died elsewhere with the coming of passable roads and railways, and it mattered little that only eight years before Coleridge came into residence, the Town and University had jointly, and successfully, petitioned Parliament to pass a bill for 'erecting Sluices and other Engines' for keeping the river open to barges from Lynn. From the millpool that survives today without the mill, to the Great Bridge and Jesus lock beyond, the canoe and the punt have long since replaced the barge and the fenland wherry. The Cam is now an amenity. Downstream from the lock, it glides imperceptibly past the college boathouses backing on Chesterton—a 'town' no longer addicted to bear-baiting and annoying 'our University'—and apart from a small built-up area on the right bank which unhappily includes the gas-works, it moves quietly through the fenland scene to join the Ouse near Ely. Like Cambridge, it has changed its character. No longer tidal as far as Waterbeach—fen-drainage saw to that—and cured of its one-time habit of serious flooding, for many years now it has provided Town and Gown with a race-course.

Although racing goes on for most of the academic year in craft of various sizes and construction, the climax on the river is undoubtedly the May Week Races which, oddly, take place on four 'nights' in the first week of June. They decide the 'Head of the River'—a title Jesus oarsmen once regarded as their own with such feeling that, on being ousted after holding it for eleven consecutive years, they appeared on the towpath in mourning. That was in the 'eighties, and it does reveal that Jesus has long enjoyed its reputation as a 'rowing college'. The narrowness of the river restricts the racing to the 'bumping' type wherein each boat strives to touch the one ahead and change places with it in the race next day; and as there are some twenty colleges all putting on as many boats as possible—in 1965 St John's had fifteen—the races are rowed in divisions with the head of a lower division acting as sandwich boat in the division above. The 'Head of the River' is the leader of the 1st Division. A racing 'eight' derives its name from the eight oarsmen who, with the cox, make up its crew, and usually there are sixteen eights in a division. In 1966, when there were eight divisions and the Jesus first boat was third on the river, 128 crews took part in these 'May' races—well over a thousand undergraduates, that is. The University, however, was not always so numerous, and in its less populous days Sidney Sussex is said to have met the challenge with only ten. But they sufficed. As the poet sang:

> There were eight to row and one to steer,
> And one to run on the bank and cheer.

May Week at Cambridge is still a climax in University life, but it is no longer the colourful social occasion it used to be when punts were moored two deep, and even three, at Ditton Corner where the Pitt Club entertained on a riverside lawn; and after the races were dinners and dances, and the University's own hilarious dramatic club, 'The Footlights'. That still prospers. May Balls, too, linger on, though not a yearly affair with every college, and Cambridge itself, plagued now with motor cars, is just as crowded as ever. Much of the old sense of culmination also survives, with its attendant gaiety, but, in one way and another, everything is just a little different—outside the Senate House. Here, at least, the Latin formula of the admission ceremony maintains its antiquity unchanged.

All in all, Jesus did well by its occupation of St Rhadegund's, for in recent years with modern sport ever demanding more acres, Jesus alone had its cricket pitch on its doorstep until Churchill settled opulently on the Madingley Road; but it is still the only college that can see its boathouse on the river where it has so often triumphed. The splendid heraldic cock on its founder's arms is not altogether inappropriate for his college.

King's College Chapel and Gateway

VIII

'LADY MAGGIE'

THE University owes much to Lady Margaret Beaufort, Countess of Richmond and Derby, mother of Henry the Seventh and heiress of the Duke of Somerset as well as 'all King Henry the Sixth's godly intentions'. Of her it has been said: 'She was a gentlewoman, a scholar and a saint, and having been three times married, she took a vow of celibacy. What more could be expected of any woman?'

Although the voice of heresy was for the moment still, and neither the townsmen's hostility nor the incidence of the plague abnormal, the turn of the fifteenth century hardly encouraged those concerned with the University's prosperity. God's House, originally intended to support a 'Proctor' and twenty-four scholars in a post-graduate college, rose forlorn and penniless by the Barnwell gate without even a table in the dining hall, and with no more than thirteen books in its library. Meanwhile King's Chapel, to which it had given space, stood potentially magnificent but only half-built, all work having ceased for some twenty idle years, and the rebuilding of Great St Mary's was proving no less tardy. Around them, the religious houses might be in slow decline, with the brethren drifting away, but no threat of dissolution yet disturbed them. The Hospital of St John even ranked as a college. It was the calm prelude to reformation, and for the moment the University was outwardly stagnant, droning its interminable Latin and recognizing its inadequacy by employing an Italian scholar to write its official correspondence at twenty

Emmanuel College Garden
The single-span wooden bridge at Queens'

pence a letter. Several years had to pass before Erasmus came to give point to uneasy stirrings.

It was against this background that Lady Margaret founded Christ's College in 1506 and St John's in 1511.

That Lady Margaret was herself a woman of unusual learning can be accepted. As her friend and spiritual adviser, John Fisher, put it, 'right studious was she in books, which she had in great number both in English and in French', as well as being 'of singular wisdom far surpassing the common rate of women', but there is little doubt that in 1506 she allowed Fisher to guide her in the detail of her foundation. Officially, and in effect, she gave new and lasting life to God's House. Only Fisher could have urged her to this rescue operation, and his influence is further apparent in the new society which enlarged that of God's House to a Master, twelve Fellows and as many as forty-seven scholars. King's alone was larger. Furthermore, pensioners were to be admitted—young men who not only paid for their keep but received their instruction from an officially appointed college lecturer. The idea of teaching within the college was growing.

Since the foundation of Peterhouse in 1284, the colleges had been cramped by their statutes into what were very close to monastic houses, supplying students for the Schools opposite Great St Mary's. Now, by teaching themselves, they were not only encroaching on the University's prerogative: by gathering their pupils under their roofs, they were surely killing the hostels and the wild disorder inseparable from their undisciplined occupants. Within two years of its foundation, Christ's was fighting St Nicholas' Hostel, and soon afterwards the turbulent members of St Gerard's and St Hugh's, both in St Michael's Lane opposite Gonville Hall, broke into that college by burning the postern gate and poured away all the beer, while the butler, fearing for the college silver, dropped it down a well. These were 'northern' students, and it is significant of a tendency for the University to cater for 'southerners' that the statutes which Lady Margaret gave to her foundation, and copied from God's House, laid down that half the society, including the scholars, should come from the north of England. But, wherever the young men of Christ's,

or any other foundation, were born, the seemingly great im-
mutables of the University, the *trivium* and the *quadrivium,*
awaited them.

In following the conventional pattern of an early foundation—
a four-sided court to which others could be added—Lady
Margaret had the advantage of a small but substantial college
already on the site, for God's House was far better built than
endowed, and a good deal survived in what was, when completed, the most spacious court in Cambridge at the time. Moreover, Bingham's modest entrance from the highway, then called
Preachers' Street, had been enlarged to a turreted gatehouse,
complete with Tudor heraldry and the baffling yales of the
Beauforts upholding the college arms above the gate itself. Most
people are content to dismiss them as deformed antelopes, but the
late Sir Arthur Shipley, at one time Master of Christ's, has pointed
out in his *Cambridge Cameos* that the yale—or cale—can be traced
back some four thousand years to an eastern and apparently long-
abandoned custom in animal culture that trained the animal's
horns 'fore-and-aft', one extending over its nose and the other
pointing to its tail. It therefore seems that the yale is not entirely
the mythological animal suggested by its heraldic appearance as a
supporter.

In its subsequent expansion the college achieved what is held to
be one of the more distinguished pieces of Renaissance architecture in Cambridge—the Fellows' Building and 'a very noble
erection' with, one might add, all the fascination of conjecture
because nobody is sure who designed it. Inigo Jones is suggested.
Others ascribe it to the Grumbold family. Less happily, the
common enemy of the period, clunch-decay, was soon to involve
the college in the extensive refacing of the earlier buildings with
the more enduring 'freestone' that so often came from Ketton.

Not the least remarkable feature of Lady Margaret's foundation
was the interest that she displayed in its detail. 'Our wish', she said,
'is that the Fellows sleep two and two, but the Scholars four and
four, and that no one have alone a single chamber for his proper
use, unless perchance it be some doctor, to whom, on account of

the dignity of his degree, we grant the permission of a separate chamber'. Although such 'doubling-up' was not unusual then, her wish does suggest that her generosity did not run to pampering her young men, and evidently her insistence on 'primary chambers built for our own use' was to ensure that it did not. These, in the event, were the first-floor rooms of the Master's lodge, from which two small windows enabled her to look down into the hall. Through one she chanced to observe the college Dean thrashing a young man with such vigour that, in pained astonishment, she called out: 'Gently! Gently!'

That Lady Margaret was genuinely shocked may well be possible, for the sixteenth century did not spare the rod—certainly not the Vice-Chancellor in 1571 when he ruled that 'if any scholar should go into any river, pond, or other water in the county of Cambridge, by day or night, to swim or wash, he should, if under the degree of bachelor of arts, for the first offence be sharply and severely whipped in the common hall of the college in which he dwelt, in the presence of all the fellows, scholars, and others dwelling in the college, and on the next day should again be openly whipped in the public school where he was or ought to be an auditor, before all the auditors, by one of the proctors or some other assigned by the Vice-Chancellor'. For the second offence the young man was 'to be expelled from his college and University for ever'.

Although it is unlikely that Milton was one of the last students at either Oxford or Cambridge to suffer 'the public indignity of corporal punishment', as Dr Johnson asserted, there is no doubt that he was rusticated for a short time in 1626 during his second year. Nor is it likely that he planted the mulberry tree in the Fellows' Garden which is ascribed to him. Sixteen years before he came into residence—also at the age of sixteen—the college had purchased three hundred mulberry plants for eighteen shillings to further the cultivation of mulberries at the wish of James the First, and 'Milton's tree' is probably the surviving one of three hundred, growing 'in a certeyn parcell of Grounde lying in the bakeside of the said Collegge', first hired and then bought from Jesus. This, the 'grett orchard', now forms part of the

Fellows' Garden, and with its bathing pool surrounded by trees, is one of the most delightful in Cambridge. Milton's bust, among others, looks down from the pedestals that are spaced around the pool.

Nevertheless, there is one record that surely belongs to Milton. Where the truly great are concerned, there is little doubt that their mere residence in college gives to the rooms in which they kept— to use the old expression—an aura to which later occupants and visitors justly point with pride. But there can be few among them who have been sufficiently moved by the experience to get drunk; fewer still to record the experience in verse; and when the poet is Wordsworth, and the verse impeccable, Milton's fame must be unique.

> O temperate Bard!
> Be it confessed that, for the first time, sealed
> Within thy innocent lodge and oratory,
> One of a festive circle, I poured out
> Libations, to thy memory drank, till pride
> And gratitude grew dizzy in a brain
> Never excited by the fumes of wine
> Before that hour, or since.

Christ's College has never lacked for famous men among her *alumni*, yet one whose name must have been among the most familiar in the University for many years is today almost unknown—William Paley who came up in 1759, was senior wrangler four years later, and published his famous *Evidences of Christianity* in 1794. It might have been called 'A Mathematical Approach to Christianity', and there was none other than Charles Darwin, a Christ's man himself, to write that the logic of the *Evidences* gave him as much delight as Euclid. 'The careful study of these works, without attempting to learn any part by rote, was the only part of the academical course which, as I then felt, and as I still believe, was the least use to me in the education of my mind. I did not at that time trouble myself about Paley's premises, and taking these on trust I was charmed and convinced by the long line of argumentation.' At one time, with his *Moral Philosophy,* the *Evidences* were essential for the B.A. degree. Now they have slipped away with the coming of the Scientific Age and the broadening of theological conception.

For a man who could argue so convincingly on orthodox Christianity, Paley was remarkably broad-minded and even roguish. His suggestion that a suitable text for the sermon when the great Pitt arrived as Prime Minister with patronage to bestow—

> There is a lad here who hath five barley loaves and two small fishes; but what are they among so many?

—completely overshadows the poet Gray's unhappy ode on a similar occasion; and he did point out that as some of the Thirty-Nine Articles were contradictory, not even the learned men who framed them could expect everyone to believe them. So it is perhaps as well that he did not live a few centuries earlier.

The risk of letting mathematicians loose in the golden treasury of prose is now recognized, and it is reasonable to suppose that John William Colenso of Lady Margaret's other foundation, St John's, and a second wrangler in 1836, did as much as anybody to bring about this recognition. The list of Johnian mathematicians is both long and illustrious, among them John Couch Adams and Sir John Herschel, who carried on his father's work, both senior wranglers and astronomers. But the laurels for the most resounding discovery must go to the humble Colenso, for he, as Bishop of Natal, used his mathematical genius to unravel the doubts of a Zulu chief, and justified them instead. Afterwards, in *The Pentateuch and the Book of Joshua Critically Examined,* he pointed out that, among much else, the Mosaic narrative implied:

1. That the number of boys in every Hebrew family must have been on the average forty-two.
2. That the mother of Moses must have been at least 256 years old when he was born.
3. That 603,350 warriors assembled in a court that held on the most liberal estimate, only about five thousand.
4. That, on the occasion of the Second Passover, the priests sacrificed fifty thousand lambs at the rate of four hundred a minute.

Condemned by Convocation and deprived of his See by the Metropolitan Bishop of Cape Town, he yet won an appeal to the Privy Council, only to be excommunicated the following year, and today his textbooks for the young, on school algebra and arithmetic, are his faded memorials.

All colleges have their outstanding years, memorable for those whom chance brings together. Recently, at Christ's, it was the almost monopolistic number of rugger and soccer blues that gathered there. In the middle of the last century it was the presence of Seeley, Besant and Calverley—Sir John Seeley, the austere and free-thinking historian whose *Ecce Homo* 'excited an extraordinary commotion in the religious world' only three years after 'an avalanche of criticism' had overwhelmed Bishop Colenso; Sir Walter Besant, novelist and first Chairman of the Society of Authors; and Charles Stuart Calverley, the second classic and 'prince of parodists' who, while entertaining his voluntary candidates with oysters, beer and milk punch, set the famous examination on the *Pickwick Papers* in which Besant came top. Among the questions were:

1. What are the components of dog's nose, and a red-faced Nixon?
2. Who, besides Mr Pickwick, is recorded to have worn gaiters?
3. Mention any occasion in which it is specified that the Fat Boy was not asleep.

More significant, however, is the glimpse that two of these gifted men afford of the freedom of thought and the nonconformity now astir in a University soon to shed its old religious emphasis and embrace a wider scholarship. Besant himself had intended to take Holy Orders, and towards the end of his life he wrote, in thankfulness, that Seeley had left him without 'a single rag or scrap of ecclesiastical rubbish'.

He also wrote of the life that he and his gay companions led, not much over a hundred years ago when the profligacy of the eighteenth century was happily past and the Town and University were on the point of shaking hands. Day then began with a 'good honest breakfast with cold pie and beer', and dinner in hall, as now, was the principal meal. But it was eaten earlier, about four o'clock in the afternoon. That done, he says, 'men divided into little sets and went in turn to each other's rooms and drank port and sherry till six. I dare say it was not good for the boys to be drinking fiery port, but it generally amounted to a bottle between four and five, and if it was wrong, it was pleasant.'

'It seems wonderful after all these years', he adds, 'to relate that, at midnight, when the whist was knocked off, we always sat down to a great supper with copious beer, and after supper to milk punch, and talked till four. And yet some of us survived.' He died in 1901 at the age of 65.

But that is a way of life which has vanished from a University where evening supervisions are all-important, and hall is round 7 o'clock. Let, then, Calverley himself recite its epitaph.

> I go. Untaught and feeble is my pen:
>   But on one statement I may safely venture:
> That few of our most highly gifted men
>   Have more appreciation of the trencher.
> I go. One pound of English beef, and then
>   What Mr Swiveller called a 'modest quencher';
> That home-returning, I may 'soothly say',
>   'Fate cannot touch me: I have dined today.'

When Lady Margaret founded Christ's, the King's Ditch lay obliquely across the end of Petty Cury—a name of uncertain origin*—and it skirted the college along what is now Hobson's Street. But this menace, augmented by 'visitations', which the college had to accept for another hundred years, Lady Margaret herself alleviated by making her manor house at Malton in Yorkshire a refuge for the scholars of Christ's College—'to resort thidder and there to tarye in tyme of siknes at Cambrige'. Hardly less sinister, on the opposite side of the college, was Hangman's Lane—happily no more.

For her second foundation, Lady Margaret intended to convert

---

* In the City's official Year Book it is said to derive from 'Petite Curye' or 'Little Cookery', the street in the reign of Edward the Third being remarkable for its large number of cookshops.

the Augustinian Hospital of St John into a college in much the same way as she had taken God's House and refounded it as Christ's, but she died in 1509, and two years passed in obstruction that reached litigation before Fisher, who acted as her executor, was able to carry out her wishes with a much reduced endowment. There were even objections to dissolving the Hospital of St John, almost empty though it was. Nevertheless, in 1511, the year that Erasmus introduced Greek to the University, the College of St John the Evangelist came into being with a Master and thirty-one Fellows, and, like its sister foundation, it had a strong link with the north.

Again there were buildings available for incorporation, some of the oldest in Cambridge that called to mind Balsham's unruly clerks before the birth of Peterhouse. One range provided the Master's lodge and—after some drastic and unfortunate modification—the college chapel. But the very antiquity of the Hospital ensured that the early court could never be homogeneous. Built of clunch, with a pleasant facing of red brick, the rest of the court is further enhanced by a period gatehouse which repeats the heraldic decoration at Christ's—Plantagenet roses, Beaufort portcullises, the foundress's own marguerites and yale supporters —and is considered by many to be the finest of its kind anywhere. There is, however, nothing discordant about the second court which became necessary by the end of the century. It has been described as well-nigh faultless, late Tudor at its best, and today it survives largely as Ralph Symons built it. Brick had to come from Stow in Norfolk or 'some other place where very good bricke is to be had'. Stone to face the best Barrington clunch had to be 'Cliff free ston' from King's Cliffe in Northamptonshire; and today, from its niche in the splendid gate-tower, Burman's statue of the Countess of Shrewsbury looks down on the court that her generosity provided. It cost £3,400.

The flurry of building undertaken by the University as a whole during this period—in large part a direct consequence of the comparatively short life of unprotected clunch—led Fuller to comment: 'The University began to be much beautified in buildings, every college either shedding its skin with the snake, or renewing its bill with the eagle, having their courts or leastwise their fronts and gatehouses repaired and adorned. But the greatest alterations were in their chapels, most of them being graced with an accession of organs.' St John's, having yet to be concerned with decay, found its problem to be one of space, for it achieved an eminence in the University so quickly both in lustre and numbers —William Cecil (the great Lord Burghley) and Thomas Wentworth (Earl of Strafford) were among them—that a third court was soon essential.

Built around 1670, Carolian, and just as charming in its way as the second, this new court took the college to the river itself. Two bridges now give access to the other bank, though scarcely enhancing the river scene, for the older one, splendidly built in the style of Wren around 1700, blends ill with the other that connects with the controversial buildings of the 1830s. It may have been 'ingeniously contrived' to resemble the Bridge of Sighs and embody 'some of the delicate serenity of its counterpart in Venice', but there are dissidents to deplore a 'Cockney Gothic affair', and note that a certain decency of proportion alone makes it slightly 'less detestable than the main structure to which it belongs'.

At this period it seems that the college suffered from what one critic calls 'an unfortunate frenzy of megalomania' which culminated in the 1860s. Then it swept away the last relics of thirteenth-century Cambridge surviving in the Augustinian Hospital, including the old, if much altered chapel, with Fisher's chantry attached. In its place stands Sir Gilbert Scott's elaborate Gothic chapel, of which another critic morosely observes that the new tower at least helps to fill the Cambridge skyline; and in unhappy comment on the overall effect, there is a third who declares that for anybody entering the court 'the eye is at once offended'. Yet, to ordinary mortals, the overall impression is that of a stately college, obvious though it is that architectural style has changed with the passing years, and one can only regret that the most charming survival of all, the Combination Room, is of necessity a private treasure, for it is a typical Tudor gallery, and to see it by candlelight is to carry away a picture of unforgettable beauty.

Nor must one forget the Backs which are an integral part of the Johnian scene. Once, the Hospital of St John stood on a built-up island in the swamp, as a good deal of Cambridge did. Now the college shares in a sylvan glory, and its Wilderness is a woodland glade that is surely peerless. During a festival in honour of the Duke of Northumberland's installation as Chancellor in 1842, the college entertained 1,400 guests in its grounds.

Among Johnian *alumni* of unusual distinction are William Wilberforce, who came up in 1776, and Thomas Clarkson who followed him four years later—Wilberforce a robust roistering Yorkshireman who notoriously kept a large pie in his rooms to sustain his hungry companions; Clarkson a scholar who converted himself to the cause of freedom by winning a prize essay on the ethics of the slave-trade. The University sought its abolition with petitions to Parliament; the Master of Magdalene even dispensed with the Bidding Prayer when preaching in Great St Mary's, and prayed instead for the brethren in the West Indies; and later Wilberforce himself, as member for Hull, with the backing of Clarkson and the Quakers, embarked on his victorious campaign of liberation that lasted nineteen years.

But no name in Johnian history springs so readily to mind as William Wordsworth, for he, alone among the Cambridge poets, has not only described his undergraduate life in retrospect, some ten years after going down: he has done so in blank verse. Whether all that he has to say matches the dignity of such high expression is doubtful, certainly when he calls himself a 'man of business and expense' going—

> From shop to shop about my own affairs,
> To Tutor or to Tailor, as befell,
> From street to street with loose and careless mind.

Yet from *The Prelude* there does emerge a glimpse of the University in the eighteenth century as seen by one of England's greatest poets.

The change from his village in the Cumbrian hills to the flat Cambridge scene was in every sense abrupt, and he was conscious, on his own confession, of—

> a strangeness in the mind,
> A feeling that I was not for that hour,
> Nor for that place.

But he was in no way troubled. The weeks went roundly on, with invitations, suppers, wine and fruit, and—

> As if the change
> Had waited on some Fairy's wand, at once
> Behold me rich in monies, and attired
> In splendid garb, with hose of silk, and hair
> Powdered like rimy trees, when frost is keen.

Although in later years he saw his earlier companions as 'chattering popinjays' and the period itself as one in which 'imagination slept', he appears to have enjoyed both their society and the freedom afforded. But there was a stirring of revolt. More as a sense of duty than desire, he attended lectures that, in the main, he considered 'timid' when not tyrannical, and he had little patience with—

> The dangerous craft of culling term and phrase
> From languages that want the living voice
> To carry meaning to the natural heart.

Wordsworth was undoubtedly fortunate in his years of residence, for they might have been sadly disturbed. The period was that of revolution in France and acute apprehension at home, and the doctrine of equality is catching. Cambridge, however, had its own problems arising from a period that was also—and notoriously—corrupt. Not until 1792, the year after Wordswoth went down, did the Mayor form a local association for preserving Liberty and Property against Republicans and Levellers, and a renewal of rioting seriously disturb the local peace, this time led by two chimney-sweeps against the Dissenters. To that extent, the embryo poet of seventeen was free to develop in any way he chose within the limits of college discipline. His most irksome restraint —and one that he doubtless shared with others—was 'compulsory chapel'.

> Was ever known
> The witless shepherd, who persists to drive
> A flock that thirsts not to a pool disliked?

It was an early protest, for Cambridge men had to endure this compulsion for another century, and more, until—with a notable exception—colleges expanded far beyond the capacity of their chapels.

Nor did he think highly of the dons—

> men unscoured, grotesque
> In character, tricked out like aged trees.

But in thinking that, he was merely exercising the undergraduate's prerogative, a parlour game analogous to that of denigrating architecture, and one may leave his epitaph in his own safe hands:

> For myself
> I grieve not; happy is the gowned youth
> Who only misses what I missed, who falls
> No lower than I fell.

So, 'furnished with ability and dwelling peaceably', Lady Margaret Beaufort wrote her name modestly in the pages of Cambridge history, and it survives today, not in the titles of the splendid foundations which are her memorials, but in the University's first endowed professorship of Divinity, and in the Lady Margaret Boat Club of St John's.*

* In 1966, 'Lady Margaret' had eleven boats in the May Races, and finished second on the river. St Catharine's had ten boats competing.

IX

BEYOND THE DITCH

WHEN the University took shape in the thirteenth century with the coming of the clerks, the local population appears to have been about two thousand. Four hundred years later it was only five thousand, and its living space for the most part was still enclosed within the bounds once set by river and Ditch—a confinement that in large measure Cambridge drew upon itself as an inland port at the head of a fenland river. Wider and appreciably more shallow than it is now, the river then flowed sluggishly through a belt of marsh until it spread in vast areas of reedy water above which rose the several isles. In name, Ely still remains one.

Fen drainage goes back to monastic times when the monks reclaimed patches of ground so fertile that 'they could be mown three times a year'. The Romans, too, set bounds to the flood with their Car Dyke, and built a sea-wall from Wisbech to Lynn. For a while the great religious houses did their well-intentioned best by digging ill-placed leams—that connecting the Great Ouse at Littleport with the Little Ouse from Brandon merely drained one part by flooding another—and with the dissolution of the old abbeys, the fens reverted to a web of neglected waterways that took three centuries and four successive companies of 'Adventurers' to unravel, with Cromwell overcoming opposition to the fourth. Drainage was not the wish of the fenmen.

Nor were the fenmen alone in seeking to preserve their heritage. Cambridge itself was just as deeply concerned with any adjustment that might affect its link with the sea, and as no approach to such a problem could be neglected, the resulting argument was undoubtedly forthright and not unamusing. The fenmen and their supporters claimed that as God had said to the waters 'hitherto shall these come and no further', it was clearly 'a trespass upon the Divine prerogative for man to presume to give other bounds to the water than what God had appointed'; but, said those in favour of draining, that argument applied only to salt water. Then there was the Cambridge alderman who affirmed that the fens were 'like a crust of bread swimming in a dish of water', and that draining them was clearly impossible. He was reminded that 'such as have sounded the depth of the ground find it to be Terra Firma', from which it followed that 'his brains seemed rather to swim than the floating earth'; and the further claim that the fens afforded 'great plenty and variety of fish and fowl', met the quelling retort: 'Who will not prefer a tame sheep before a wild duck? A good fat ox before a well-grown eel?' Even so, the fenmen's opposition did not fade until the mid-nineteenth century, and today it is noted with alarm that the famous 'black soil', the legacy of the fens, is rapidly disappearing.

But the draining of the fens lay centuries ahead when the University established itself in a trading centre where only two corridors offered ground that was tolerably dry and east of the river—the slight ridge along the old High Street and a similar one that widened as it ran towards the 'uplands' of Newmarket Heath. On this lay the Barnwell Field of 'East Anglian' Cambridge. (The Cambridge Field, lying beyond the river to the west of the town, was 'Mercian'.) Here, then, in embryo, were the two great highways that, as the A 10 and A 45, today connect the city with London and with Norwich, and no one is going to challenge the A 10's importance. Nevertheless, in earlier times the A 45 was the old Barnwell highway that skirted the Sturbridge fairground as it headed for Newmarket, and it could hardly fail to hold the local interest. Especially was this so after James the First had taken to hunting on the famous heath, and Charles the Second had not only introduced horse-racing, but established a yearly race-meeting, the first of its kind in the country.

'It was not uncommon for the whole Court and Cabinet to

go down there,' Macaulay wrote. 'In places of public resort peers flirted with maids of honour, and officers of the Life Guards, all plumes and gold lace, jostled with professors in trencher caps and black gowns. For on such occasions the neighbouring University of Cambridge always sent her highest functionaries with loyal addresses, and selected her ablest theologians to preach before the Sovereign and his splendid retinue. . . . With Lords and Ladies from St James's and Soho, and with doctors from Trinity College and King's College, were mingled the provincial aristocracy, fox-hunting squires and their rosy-cheeked daughters, who had come in queer-looking family coaches drawn by cart horses.'

Although in the reign of King John, and for long afterwards, Cambridge itself was girt by river and Ditch, and in the number of its inhabitants was little more than a modern village, the extent of its common land—the Cambridge and Barnwell Fields—indicates that in acreage it compared with a sizeable modern town. Its bounds, indeed, were sufficiently wide for the Mayor and alderman to fish within the limits of the borough from Newn-ham to Fen Ditton, a right they formally exercised until the Restoration, and in those early days the importance of fish was such that rents were often paid in the currency of eels. But these distant bounds encircling a core of religious houses, tenements and hovels, and later, colleges, do reveal that the medieval borough was essentially rural with, one would have thought, sufficient arable land and pasture for its needs. Yet as late as 1577 it was said that 'Cambridge hath not such store of medow ground as may suffice for the ordinarie expenses of the towne and uni-versitie wherefor the inhabitants are inforced to provide their haie from other villages about.' It is possible, however, that behind this suggestion of inadequacy, there lay the undoubted attraction of sheep-farming now that East Anglia had developed a flourishing woollen industry. Nor is it without significance that the largest section of Sturbridge Fair, at this time and for many years to come, was the Duddery or Cloth Fair.

Like so much else at Cambridge, a strong religious emphasis marked the birth of Sturbridge Fair in 1211. In that year King

Queens' College: The President's Gallery

John granted to the Hospital of St Mary Magdalene—with its leper chapel—the right to hold a fair in its close on the vigil and feast of the Holy Cross, the 13th and 14th of September, that is; and the suggestion is made that he was doing no more than reviving a much older fair. Lysons, the historian, plumbs antiquity for Irish merchants selling their cloth in the reign of King Athelstan. Fuller, too, recalls the traditional belief that Westmorland cloth dealers, caught in a rainstorm while making for Norwich, afterwards spread out their goods to dry and found so ready a market that they went no further. But there is no doubt that after the dissolution of the religious houses, Henry the Eighth sold the rights and profits of the Fair to the Town for one thousand marks, a transaction in due course confirmed by Elizabeth.

The effect of this acquisition on Town and Gown relations had a Gilbertian touch. It mattered not that the Town owned the Fair. The University saw a University responsibility, and as the Town refused to forgo its moment of glory, both parties were driven to express their importance independently. The University's *Crye of Sturbridge Fayer* began:

> Wee charge & straightlie comaund in yᵉ name of the Kinge of England or Soveraigne Lord, and in yᵉ name of the Lord Chauncellr of yᵉ Universitie of Cambridge, yᵉ all manner of Schollers, Schollers Servants, and all other persons in this Fayer, and the precincts of yᵉ same, keepe the Kings peace, & make no fraye, cry, owtass, shrekinge, or any other noyse, by yᵉ which Insurations Conventicles, or gatherings of peopl may be made in this Fayer, to yᵉ trouble vexinge and disquietinge of yᵉ Kings leage people, or lettinge of the officers of yᵉ Universitie to exercise there offices, under the payne of Imprisonment & Further punishment as the said offence shall require.

Here one sees both the shadow of the Chancellor's Court and the University's assumption of precedence, from which stemmed a quarrel that seemed without end, and the existence of two courts at the Fair did nothing to make for harmony. Within ten years of the Town's acquisition of the Fair's 'rights and profits', two knightly gentlemen were acting as umpires in the search for a code of procedure, acceptable to both parties, in matters which

9

The Backs: Spring
Autumn

strikingly reveal the extent of the University's interests outside the academic. The first clause reads:

> That no common Pultar or taker take up or grosse any victualls in Cambridge markett, or within V miles of the towne by virtue of commission. Excepte it be fisshe for yᵉ Kings Majesties household or others, or other such victualls sold as merchandise in Stirberch or mydsomer fayres.

Time and the Award Act of 1856 were to solve this problem of precedence, and during the heyday of the Fair, in the eighteenth century, its proclamation continued to involve both University and civic ceremonial. Accompanied by their noble guests, the Vice-Chancellor and University officers drove in state to the Fair, the Senior Proctor having first provided cakes and wine at the Senate House. This sustained them until they were free to dine in the University's 'tiled booth' where custom had long restricted the Vice-Chancellor's table to a large dish of herrings, a neck of roast pork, a plum pudding, a boiled leg of pork, a pease pudding, a goose, a large apple pie, and, forming the centrepiece of the collation, a round of beef. Add to this a generous refreshment—'ale and bottled porter in great profusion' at the Vice Chancellor's table—and it is not difficult to believe that even 'tipsy Masters of Arts, many fellows of colleges and clergymen were to be seen with linked arms jostling the passers-by'.

On their side, the townsmen appear to have ignored the University, for an eighteenth-century historian of the County not only declares that the Mayor and Corporation first 'set out' the Fair on St Bartholomew's Day, having ridden to the site 'in grand procession, with music playing before them and most of the boys of the town on horseback after them, who, as soon as the ceremony is read over, ride races about the place', but also states that 'on the 7th of September they ride again in the same manner to proclaim it, which being done, the Fair begins and continues three weeks'. Among the civic dignitaries who rode in state was the Bellman who patrolled the streets at night, and to lend further colour there were eight red-coated stalwarts to escort the Mayor and act as attendants at his court.

The site of the Fair—a cornfield that was itself no more than half-a-mile square—was only two miles from the Market Hill in Cambridge, and it lay between the highway and the river, ominously opposite Chesterton. The Stour brook and its bridge gave the Fair its name, and the site had one transcending virtue: it was accessible. Practically all merchandise came by water, through Lynn and up the river; manufacturers arrived from all over England; according to Defoe, wherries were brought from London on wagons 'to plye upon the little river Cam and to tow people up and down from the Town and from the Fair'; and the volume of trade was enormous. It is said that, in the Duddery alone, a week's sale would amount to £100,000. But whatever the turnover within the Fair, Cambridge itself did well enough, drawing its profits from the fines and tolls which it levied, and the rents it charged on the site. Even the sun of opportunity shone brightly on the townsmen through the lodgings they provided on the spot. Defoe writes: 'Not Cambridge only but all the Towns round are full: nay, the very Barns and Stables are turned Inns and made as fit as they can be to Lodge the meaner Sort of People.' Yet the very success of the Fair was telling against it. There was little point in collecting vast quantities of merchandise in one spot when the difficulties and expense of transport could be largely avoided, and long before the coming of the railways and the industrial revolution, the Fair had evolved into a 'shop window' for wholesale buyers.

It might be said that, during the time of the Fair, Cambridge life moved to this converted cornfield. Everybody went. Browsing along the booksellers' row in his first year, Isaac Newton chanced upon the astrological treatise that led him to study Euclid in order to understand it. At the Fair, too, he bought the three prisms with which he studied the spectrum. They cost £3. 'The Fair', wrote Carter, about 1750, 'is like a well-governed city, and less disorder and confusion to be seen there than in any other place where is so great a concourse of people.' But there were incidents. On one occasion, while crossing the river by ferry, a notorious Chesterton bruiser caused an affray so damaging to a number of scholars that the bedell declined the privilege of arresting him, and a strong-armed B.A. of Trinity and a singing-man of King's had to be enlisted. The question of University privilege also arose, inevitably, and in 1701 when the Mayor licensed a theatrical performance at the Fair, as many as sixty-two Masters of Arts assisted the Proctors in preventing this overt breach—an objective achieved with great simplicity by pulling down the booth and sending the leading actor to prison. Normally the Proctors concerned themselves with complaints involving weights and measures, the scholars' behaviour, and the 'seeking out of lewd women'.

Nevertheless, the eighteenth century was soon to see, if not the dawn of reason in Town and Gown relations, at least a small deviation from strict conformity with age-old custom; for in 1772 the Vice-Chancellor did license a genuine playhouse at which a Norwich company performed with distinction during the three weeks of the Fair. It was built on the highway which is now the Newmarket Road; everybody of note attended, from the Lord Lieutenant downwards, with the lively Richard Farmer, D.D., Master of Emmanuel, an almost permanent member of 'Critics Row' in the pit. Dr Farmer also takes his place as a Shakespearian authority and one of the more worthy members of the colourful eighteenth century at Cambridge. Once, when called upon as Vice-Chancellor to affix the University's seal to a loyal address and denied the key by a disgruntled scrutator, he, like Simeon, promptly sent for a blacksmith. The theatre, it seemed, had suddenly become respectable, and after a fatal outbreak of fire had destroyed the old playhouse in 1802, it was not only rebuilt as the Barnwell Theatre, but licensed for plays throughout the vacations. To that extent had tolerance grown, and although in the great abrogation of 1856 the University retained the privilege of licensing theatrical performances, sharing it with the Mayor, it was clearly an outworn intrusion and renounced in 1894.

As for the Fair itself, that died with the age which gave it life. Born to fulfil the needs of a period, it dwindled until, in 1927, even the Mayor gave up its formal proclamation, and by order of the Secretary of State it was abolished in 1934.

The horse-fair attached had already died with the passing of the horse.

Much of the common land bordering the river at the time of the Sturbridge Fair has long disappeared, built over in the nineteenth-century expansion, but enough remains near Jesus College to suggest its earlier state, and the part known as Midsummer Common takes its name from the fair that is held on its grassy acres at midsummer—in practice, the 22nd of June and the next three days, exclusive of any intruding Sunday. Again there is uncertainty of origin, and like much else, it seems to have grown from age-old custom that once a year, at midsummer, brought children to the wells from which Barnwell is said to take its name, the Children's Wells. Here they danced and played, the boys in particular showing their skill in wrestling, and it is not unlikely that to this cheerful gathering came the vendors, seeking opportunity. But, whatever the detail, a fair was undoubtedly born. King John gave the rights to the Barnwell canons. For long years the townsmen claimed that the tolls were theirs, and as the dispute was settled to the Town's advantage in 1506, Cambridge still has a fair of its own, hardly comparable with Sturbridge but one that may well be of greater age, and one that still retains its early purpose in the 'droll' that survives today even when the motorized circus comes to town.

Mystery also surrounds the steps by which the Rogation Fair that King John granted to the Burgesses of Cambridge in 1200 —and was held there apparently up to 1278—found its way to the village of Reach about seven miles distant from Cambridge, on the edge of the old-time fen. There, with no less certainty, it was held in 1388, and has been ever since. That the Mayor and Corporation continue to open it in state at least suggests a friendly connexion.

The slowness with which Cambridge itself expanded, even when it had broken the bonds of river and Ditch, is seen from the census of 1801 which shows that there were still only ten thousand inhabitants, apart from the University, and but for that qualified blessing, the town would have been as moribund as Sturbridge Fair. The dawn of the Industrial Revolution shed no gleam of hope on Cambridge. Yet the nineteenth century saw it change out of recognition in status as well as size.

Although the great peace that entered into Town and Gown relations in 1856 transcends all else in local affairs, the coming of the railway must not be overlooked if only because it enabled the University to trumpet its wrath with a finality matching the occasion. As early as 1825 there had been a proposal to build a railway through Cambridge, connecting London with the north, and for a time, during the national exuberance at the thought of covering the land with a spider's web of railway lines, schemes were four-a-penny. Not until 1842 was the critical one approved. Then Parliament agreed that Cambridge should connect not only with Newport in Essex, on the way to London, but also with Brandon in Norfolk and Peterborough in the west, and the isolation of the horse-age was at an end.

It was apocalyptic.

Henceforth the ungodly would be able to come and go at will, even on Sundays, and not only was the University itself appalled: the Vice-Chancellor was so indignant that, on hearing the railway directors' decision to carry foreigners and other unseemly persons who, 'having no regard for Sunday themselves, would inflict their presence in the University on that day of rest', he roundly stated that 'the contemplated arrangements were as distasteful to the University authorities as they must be to Almighty God and all right-minded Christians'.

But the University, although unable to stop the trains, could still ensure that the railway station itself lay dauntingly isolated in the fields and pastures by the Via Devana, remote and accessible only to the athletic. That was in 1845. Today, in the light of modern expansion coupled with the traffic chaos in the rush hours, one can be thankful that there is not a busy railway station near the city centre to stop the traffic completely.

Nor was the University content with the insulation of mere distance. Represented in Parliament, it had the regrettable act so framed that the Eastern Counties Railway Company was not only denied the privilege of conveying anyone *in statu pupillari*, even if he had paid his fare, but also liable to a fine of £5 if it did not report the delinquent who wanted to travel; and the University's officers were granted free access to all parts of the station at the times of departure and arrival of the trains. As railway stations then had the charm of novelty, this restriction on the undergraduate was undoubtedly hard, especially as the Company had contrived a station resembling an open arcade, of sufficient merit for some of it to survive today, and, in 1867, for its praises to be sung in frank advertisement of Cambridge: 'The progress of the train has ceased, the rebounding of the carriages coming to a state of rest is over, the voices of porters and the opening of doors has commenced, and here we are on the pavement of Cambridge station. What a surprise! I had no idea of such a length of building, all covered over and comfortable; it cannot be much less than four hundred feet. This is really one of the best stations I have seen for many a day. But how is it the stream of passengers is dividing? Oh, I see, one half are taking themselves off to that handsome refreshment room, and the other half are passing through the building to trudge on foot into the town, or to indulge themselves with a cheap ride to the same place.'

There is an ominous ring about 'trudging on foot into the town', and the reference to a cheap ride can hardly fail to rouse nostalgic memories among elderly Cambridge men, whether Town or Gown, who recall the old horse-trams that yielded to the bus in the early years of this century. They were hardly designed for anyone in a hurry, but they were in keeping with the hansom cab, attuned to the academic calm that Cambridge knew before being flooded with bicycles and choked with petrol fumes. The station, too, has altered, apart from its unusual façade. Once there were two main platforms, flanking the normal 'up' and 'down' lines. Now there is only one. But it does give Cambridge another oddity—what is said to be the longest platform in the country— for the 'up' and 'down' platforms are now end to end, and cover some three hundred yards.

Apart from this curiosity, the traveller will see nothing abnormal as the train draws clear of the station, certainly not in the featureless development of modern Cambridge through which it glides when northward bound, for that development engulfs historic Barnwell and floods along the old Newmarket road. 'The greatest fair in Europe' has left no trace for the fleeting glance. Nor, further afield, do the flat acres of sugar beet suggest that Ely was once an isle.

X

'MAUDLIN'

CAMBRIDGE town having expanded beyond the Ditch and over
the Barnwell Field in the general direction of Newmarket, it seems
only proper, as well as inevitable, that the University should
expand beyond the river and over the Cambridge Field in a
direction roughly opposite; and the stranger who follows the
route of Wordsworth's coach today, noting Girton's Waterhouse gate-tower and a suggestion of the Arabian Nights in the
new Fitzwilliam College, may be pardoned for wondering if he is
indeed approaching an old University town. Nor will the ancient
buildings of Magdalene at the foot of the hill by the Great Bridge
immediately reassure him, for they have been likened to a
gracious old country house overtaken by an expanding suburb;
and in so far as the hostel for student monks from neighbouring
Benedictine monasteries was a 'country house' in 1428, Magdalene
College in the University of Cambridge, founded in honour of
St Mary Magdalene in 1542, certainly has its roots in one. Financed
by Crowland Abbey at its inception, and enjoying the patronage
of the Duke of Buckingham, the hostel so nearly resembled a
normal college in its development that long before the customary
court was completed, and the monasteries dissolved, the University knew it as Buckingham College. Chapel, chambers,
domestic quarters, hall—the third Duke built that about 1519—
all were there, with red brick pleasantly facing the suspect clunch,
and the dissolution meant no more than a change of ownership
when Thomas, Lord Audley, the newly enriched occupant of

Walden Abbey, decided to found a college. The student monks walked out in 1539, and after a seemly interval of three years, the lay scholars walked in—with one servant combining the duties of gyp, bedmaker, porter and cook. Forty years later, according to Dr Caius, there were still only three attendants.

Lord Audley died in 1544, and the University shed few tears over a judge who had joined in sending Fisher to the block. 'The stone is not harder, nor the marble blacker than the heart of him who lies beneath,' wrote Fuller of Audley's tomb at Walden, and to such an extent did the college of his foundation suffer at birth, like St Catharine's, from lowness of endowment and littleness of receipt, that the eight Fellows who, with the Master, made up the original society, speedily fell to four. But for his untimely death, it is possible that the founder would have increased his endowment, as he could easily have done, being a beneficiary of the dissolution. Such assistance, too, would doubtless have been more appreciated than his stipulation that the mastership of Magdalene should be the gift of the holder of the Barony of Braybrooke as the founder's representative. Normally the Master of a college is elected by its Fellows. Trinity and Churchill, where the mastership is a Crown appointment, and Selwyn, where it rests with a council not wholly drawn from the college, are exceptions.

So, in those far-off days when the town still lay penned by river and Ditch, the University spread across the river, and down the centuries Magdalene College has not only assumed the appearance of a gracious old country house: it has reclaimed an ancient splendour by restoring the old Buckingham court. Less happily, the city fathers would say, the traffic problem being theirs, it has also spread across one of the city's most important roads where it narrows by the bridge. For here, at the foot of Castle Hill, old Cambridge still survives in the timber-framed Tudor houses backing on Benson's Court, and with a wing by Lutyens in the early thirties of this century, and other assorted additions, the court itself takes an honoured place in Cambridge if only for the reason that it is like no other. It has been described, with some felicity, as a pleasant architectural cocktail for the connoisseur.

But Magdalene's peculiar treasure is the personal library and diary of its distinguished *alumnus* Samuel Pepys, housed in a building of considerable charm though uncertain origin. There is reason for thinking that its parent stood on the site in the early part of the seventeenth century, and that today one sees the old building suitably fashioned for its present role. The inscription over the central arch of the arcade—*Bibliotheca Pepysiana 1724*— dates the legacy. It was Uffenbach's misfortune to have suffered his usual disappointment only fourteen years earlier when he found several hundred books, some of them quite good but stowed away in the roof of an old and inevitably mean building, and, he says, mostly covered with mould.

Pepys himself came into residence in 1651, calling himself a 'cheerful roundhead' in a college that was unavoidably Puritan. His tutor's reproof, however—

Pepys and Hind were solemnly admonished by myself and Mr Hill for having been scandalously overserved with drink, the night before. This was done in the presence of the fellows then resident, in Mr Hill's chamber.

—suggests that he was even then anticipating the Restoration, and his not infrequent visits to his old college in later years reveal no trace of repentance. 'At the Three Tuns we drank pretty hard to the King.' Or they continued 'till it began to grow darkish'. Or, with friends, he went 'to the Rose Tavern where we sat and drank till sermon time was done, and then Mr Perchell came to us, and we sat drinking the King's and his whole family's health till it began to grow dark', after which he found his father and a friend waiting at his lodging and returned to the Rose where he 'gave them a quart or two of wine, not telling them we had been there before'.

Undoubtedly Pepys fills his own little niche in the hall of fame, but more than one of his kind in a college could hardly fail to be embarrassing. It is therefore just as well that a college derives its reputation from its family of young men and not from a single member, however illustrious. If, then, a taint of 'overserving' should be thought to linger, it is sufficient to record that during one evangelical period towards the end of the eighteenth century,

Magdalene men were not only given to prayer-meetings but reproached for 'choking up the river with tea leaves'.

It was during this outbreak of piety in the name of Low Church methodism that a devout young mathematician found himself only a senior optime in his Tripos, and explained his failure to be a wrangler as a form of religious persecution. 'A Maudlin man', he wrote to a friend, 'stands little chance in the Senate House. The world is not fond of seeing a religious man honoured.' The University lightly knew these earnest young men as 'The Saints'.

Samuel Morland, on whom had fallen the task of admonishing an overserved Pepys, was also a Magdalene man, with barely ten years seniority, and although he never achieved the fame of his erring pupil, he did, as 'mechanician' to Charles the Second, add a pump to his several inventions—among them a speaking trumpet —and become a baronet. It was therefore a sad coincidence that none other than the Reverend Charles Kingsley, who entered Magdalene some two hundred years later, should be requested in his Mechanics paper to describe this important Magdalene product: for many though his virtues were as a brilliant novelist, at one time Professor of Modern History at Cambridge, and as an exponent of what is sometimes called Muscular Christianity, he knew nothing about the inside of a pump. He could do no more than draw the outside of one—on a village green with the church in the background, the beadle in the fore and women with buckets gathering round, and, on the pump itself, a notice: 'This pump locked during Divine Service.'

Charles Stewart Parnell came up to Magdalene in 1865. Like Cromwell of Sidney Sussex, to whom he bears some resemblance as an opponent of established order, he did not take a degree. But whereas Cromwell went down after his father's death, Parnell was sent down for reasons that allow a choice between vulgar brawling in which he was sued for damages and relieved of twenty guineas, and his love for a lady with blue eyes and golden hair who cast herself into the Cam. Of his subsequent career as an Irish political ruler in pursuit of Home Rule, with a flair for obstruction particularly where Gladstone happened to be, it is sufficient to say that he contributed much to a sad chapter in Anglo-Irish relations which is happily closed.

There is, too, A. C. Benson, Master during the Kaiser's War, who contemplated life 'From a College Window' and released his 'smooth, melancholy essays in a course as unceasing and un-ruffled as that of the Cam itself'.

It was a proud yet discouraging period in Cambridge history that saw the foundation of Magdalene, a child, one might say, of the Reformation. Only thirteen years after its birth, Ridley and Latimer were to die at the stake, and Cromwell—from a college yet unborn—had come and gone before external pressures ceased to plague the University. But to Pepys, the 'gay cavalier', returning to drink through sermon time at the Rose, the town itself must have seemed no different from the one he had known as a 'cheerful roundhead'.

Nor could there have been anything, apart from the growing splendour of the colleges, to distinguish Cambridge from other small country towns of the period. Its narrow streets were filthy, unpaved, and still unlighted as the word is understood today. First to be paved was Petty Cury, in 1788, and the University's decree forbidding undergraduates to carry 'lighted torches or links' because of the 'great terror and apprehension' which they caused, provides all the comment necessary on the plight of ordinary pedestrians after dark. Householders who could afford to do so were required to create a small gleam in the darkness, usually a rushlight, and for nearly a hundred years from 1575 a watchman went his rounds crying 'Lanthorn or whole candle-light, hang out your lights', but only for three hours from 6 p.m. between the 1st of November and the 2nd of February, except on 'such nights as the moon shall shine'. Not until 1788 was a gleam sought from lamps permanently fixed to buildings, and another thirty-five years had to pass before gas, derived from oil, burnt in a Cambridge street-lamp—soon to be followed by 'inflammable air or gas obtained from coal'.

Pepys chose well when refreshing himself at the Rose. It was central, large and roomy, being foremost among the several

Cambridge inns that started as student hostels, and from it, three times a week, a stage coach left for London—the fare, ten shillings. Rose Crescent marks its site today, curling round St Michael's Church to the old High Street from a market square that Pepys would not have recognized. He knew only a narrow strip, little more than a street connecting Shoemakers' Lane (now Market Street) with Petty Cury. Then the market place was L-shaped, for Petty Cury opened into a broader strip in front of the old tol-booth and connected with Peas Hill. A huddle of tenements and cottages packed most of the area which is now the cobbled market. They backed, too, on Great St Mary's Church, separated from it so narrowly by a passage known as Pump Lane that part of the congregation knew the distraction of looking straight in to a bedroom. Nearly two centuries had to pass before, in 1849, fire destroyed eight houses and provided the opportunity, wisely taken, to create the market square of modern Cambridge.

Fire-fighting on this scale was not easy on Market Hill in 1849. Hobson's conduit was hopelessly inadequate, and the river at Garret Hostel Bridge, the main source of supply, was three hundred yards away. But from the river water had to be carried, and what this involved in labour when the roof of nearby St Michael's Church caught fire that same year, is vividly told by the future Canon of York who found the 'vulgar rabble' so alarming. One can understand, though hardly credit, his state-ment that 'all Cambridge was thrown into consternation by the cry that Prof. Scholefield's church was on fire', but, he goes on: 'As soon as I heard of it, I hurried to the spot and found a great crowd already assembled and the firemen and engines hard at work. The congregation, just collecting for morning service when the fire was discovered, were instantly employed in supplying the engines with water. Crowds of gownsmen from all the colleges came flocking together to render aid to their favourite minister. Soon two long double rows were formed from the conduit and the river, gownsmen and townsmen working cordially together, the Vice-Chancellor, Proctor, Masters of colleges, fellows and undergraduates all placed on a level in the hour of danger. I soon fell into one of the lines and passed buckets of water along most vigorously for an hour. Two of our fellows were working in the same line. . . . The fire was arrested before it did much damage to the organ, but they had begun to pull it down, and the Professor was seen rushing through the crowd with some of the organ pipes under his arm.'

'Gownsmen and townsmen working cordially together' becomes a significant phrase on the eve of the University's great abrogation of privilege, only seven years later.

When Pepys sought distraction in Cambridge, nothing was friendly in Town and Gown relations, particularly inside the guildhall, for that should have been the Mayor's stronghold yet, even there, the Vice-Chancellor came first at public functions. It was this slight that moved the Mayor—in 1705—to behave in a manner made clear in his 'humble submission', admitting his guilt in having 'denied unto Sir John Ellys, the Vice-Chancellor, the precedence on the joynt seat at the upper end of the guildhall, which refusal was the occasion of a great deal of contempt and indignity offered to the said Vice-Chancellor and his attendants'. Two aldermen, having supported the Mayor, also found it expedient to apologize for conduct 'whereby divers unworthy affronts and indignities were occasioned the said Vice-Chancellor'. Nor were these confessions freely made. The University had first to discommon so widely that about half the local tradesmen lost their University business.*

Had Pepys, with Benet Street in mind, strolled along the narrow strip of market opposite the Rose and crossed the end of Petty Cury, he would have entered Butchers' Row. By turning right at Slaughterhouse Lane, he would have continued down Short Butchers' Row behind the tolbooth, itself a combination of tax-office and townhall with a prison adjacent. In Benet Street, which continued Short Butchers' Row, he would have passed the site of the old Augustinian Friary, and the end of Free School Lane, before reaching the oldest building in Cambridge, St Benet's Church with its Saxon tower. Almost opposite, in the sixteenth

---

* The University still retains, though seldom uses, this jurisdiction which prohibits members of the University from doing business with a particular person or firm.

century, lived John Mere, a King's don whose commemoration service, preached in St Benet's, gives a start to the third, or Easter, term in the University year. The others are the Michaelmas and Lent Terms.

The directions in John Mere's will were precise. The preacher was to begin: 'John Mere, Esquire Bedell, long since of this University, gave a tenement situate in this parish; in consideration whereof the sermon is here today. He left a small remembrance to the officers of the University provided they were present at the Commemoration; and was also not unmindful of the poor in the Tolbooth and Spittal-house.' But the distribution, made after the service as the beneficiaries leave the church, worked out at three shillings and fourpence for the preacher, sixpence for the Vice-Chancellor, and a groat each for the other officers. The poor had three shillings. Nevertheless, as one officer was heard to remark a few years ago, it is rather nice, being paid to go to church, if only fourpence.

St Benet's to Magdalene is barely a ten-minute stroll, and the narrow High Street that Pepys knew had yet to be transformed. Then it was—and so it remained until early in the nineteenth century—'the narrowest of the narrow streets of Cambridge, wherein the foot passenger walked as it were beneath the first floors of the houses, and their walls formed the street border'. Senate House Hill did not then exist: there was no Senate House, only tenements bunching opposite Great St Mary's, hiding the Old Schools and stretching as a fringe along the frontage of King's. And so it would remain for a while. The entire site had to be cleared before Gibbs could begin his magnificent Corinthian Senate House in 1722, and even thirty years later, when Stephen Wright added his splendid façade to the library front of the Old Schools and completed the University centre, another seventy had to pass before the High Street changed to King's Parade with its verdant fringe. Probably apocryphal, yet no less revealing, is the story of the lady who wondered how such wonderful grass could be made to grow, and was told: 'Nothing to it, mam. You just cut it, roll it, weed it, and water it for a hundred years or so.'

Pepys, in his maturity, saw little more than the town of his

St John's Gatehouse

student days, when barges still poled their way to the mill, and the river still carried some waterborne trade. Six taverns then stood in the short length of Quayside, and as further distraction for Magdalene men, there were scolds to be ducked in the river. Nor, in that era of solid construction, could the scold have been rare when a ducking stool was worn out in twenty-one years.

Today the Via Devana is known hereabouts as the A 604, and it crosses the river by Magdalene Bridge.

Winter on the Cam:
'The Wedding Cake', St John's
Trinity College Bridge

XI

'NOBLE AND MAGNIFICENT'

FOUR years after Buckingham College had become Magdalene, one of the smaller colleges today, Michaelhouse and King's Hall had coalesced, as it were, to form the largest—the College of the Holy and Undivided Trinity, and one of such splendour that even the *University Calendar* is moved to abandon its usual non-descriptive neutrality and refer to this 'noble and magnificent college'.

As King's had done, Trinity enjoyed the benefit of the royal inspiration but, unlike King's, it also profited by an endowment in keeping with the royal idea, and that, with Henry the Eighth, was nothing less than to found a college equalling in magnificence, if not exceeding, any other in Europe. He was not competing with his holy predecessor in building a monumental chapel. He clearly had in mind a court that was to symbolize a college in its entirety —what is now the Great Court of Trinity. Furthermore, his disposal of the spacious Franciscan Friary which the University used for its commencement ceremonies, gave at least a glimpse of his determination. Apart from any 'wolves agape for further spoils' of the dissolution, the University wanted it; so did the Town, as a hospital for the indigent poor; but Trinity had it, and later sold it to the executors of the Lady Frances Sidney, widow of the Earl of Sussex, when they set out to found her college.

In taking over Michaelhouse and King's Hall, and using their buildings in part, Henry the Eighth was doing no more than taking advantage of two colleges that had outlived their usefulness. He had still to clear a site, and that meant the violation of Milne Street, the northern end of which started in what was to be the Great Court. Trinity, in fact, was destined to complete the conversion of the area between the High Street and the river into a University island, a task demanding time as well as careful thought, and happily, by using the large refectory of Michael-house and the sizeable chapel of King's Hall for a start, the college had that time. Although, in 1564, the new chapel took an honoured place as the largest and best of its kind, that of King's being in every way exceptional, at the turn of the century Trinity was still an irregular jumble bearing little resemblance to the noble magnificence finally achieved. For that posterity must thank, in particular, Dr Thomas Nevile, Master during twenty-two years from 1593, for to his imaginative plan the Great Court largely took shape, and to him also, by his personal gift, the college owes the splendour of its second court which bears his name.

Nevile's bold removal of the Edward the Third gateway from what had been King's Childer Lane to the west end of the new chapel, and the clearance of parts that still intruded from King's Hall, made possible a court not only approximating to a rectangle, but also one of a size that is deservedly called Great. It is some 90,000 square feet in extent—over two acres. The gateway, too, has changed its purpose, being now the home of Wordsworth's 'loquacious' clock that strikes the hour twice 'with male and female voice'—first in A flat and then in E flat—and innocently challenges the more athletic undergraduates to race round the court, 383 yards, in the 43 seconds between the first and last strokes of the double chimes at midnight.

The chapel fabric is both Marian and Elizabethan, having been started in one reign and finished in the other, and into its walls and buttresses went much good stone from the Franciscan Friary; but the woodwork of the stalls—the gift of the tempestuous Bentley—is early eighteenth century. For most people, the outstanding feature is the statuary of Trinity's great men grouped in the ante-chapel. That of Sir Isaac Newton, by Roubillac, in the place of honour, has been called the noblest of English statues and among the finest works of art in Cambridge. With him are Bacon, Macaulay, Tennyson, and two Masters of more than usual lustre, Barrow and Whewell, but not Byron. His statue, by Thorwaldsen, proudly gazes down the full length of Wren's magnificent library, Westminster Abbey having rejected it on grounds of Byron's personal reputation. Commemorated also are Trinity men who fell in the two world wars. The names of six hundred who died in the first are inscribed in the chapel, and, in the ante-chapel, the names of four hundred who died in the second—figures that starkly reveal the greater carnage in the first.

Apart from its length and the impression of narrowness that results, even Uffenbach could find no fault in a chapel otherwise very handsome and well-lighted. But the great Elizabethan hall, built by Symons about 1605 and held by many to be one of the finest examples of its kind—for that he could find no word of praise. It was ugly and, on the occasion of his presence, smelling so strongly of bread and meat that he would not have been able to eat a bite. Fortune, however, was less unkind when he called on Dr Richard Bentley at the Master's lodge which, with the hall, largely formed the western range. Nevile had been responsible for building it; a hundred years later Bentley had panelled much of it; and Uffenbach, meeting this tall spare man, 'red in the face', was moved to record not only that he had created for himself 'an excellent house, so that he is as well lodged as the Queen at St James's, or better', but also that 'for an Englishman he speaks good and tolerably intelligent Latin'. The window panes also caught his attention, 'being of extraordinary size, and the windows themselves very large and high'.

Some two hundred years passed before the holder of the English native record at putting the weight, who was also twice England's representative at the Olympic Games, tentatively thrust his hand between the curtain over one of these mullioned windows with the intention of letting in a little fresh air at a dance, and inadvertently 'put' the entire window into the court.*

Meanwhile, under Nevile's direction, the Queen's Gateway with its statue of Elizabeth had been inserted, as it were, in the

* *Cambridge Doctor,* by Rex Salisbury Woods, M.D., F.R.C.S.

southern range so as to match the Edward the Third Gateway or Clock Tower in both style and positioning. That was in 1597, and a few years later, in the centre of the vast court, there appeared the delightful canopied fountain which sets the seal of completion on his work. Who designed it is a mystery. Symons could have done. But from the point of view of the visitor entering by the Great Gate from the old High Street, as most visitors do, it suffices that the fountain is there, in a setting mainly of Tudor Gothic that is majestic.

So one finds the Great Court today—a superb conception in stone that has come down the years not entirely as a monument to a king's vanity. In its south-east corner are the turret rooms where Byron lived with his bear and threw unorthodox parties. At one were gathered 'jockies, gamblers, boxers, authors, parsons and poets'—an interesting cross-section of his friends, but, as he said, 'the place is the devil'. Next to the Great Gate, on the first floor of E staircase, are the rooms in which Newton wrote his *Principia Mathematica*. In the set below, before it was embodied in the porter's lodge, Thackeray once dwelt. Macaulay, too, kept on this famous staircase. But Newton is supreme. Planted in the little garden between the college and the street, overlooked from Newton's window, even the historic apple which, in falling, suggested to him 'the notion of gravitation', has an authentic relative. Shabby, dishevelled, his long untidy hair prematurely white, Newton was everything that the popular idea demands of an absent-minded professor, and there was really no need for him to stress his abstraction by leaving his books and papers on the table in his room and forgetting to blow out the candle when he set off to chapel. Some of the papers destroyed had taken 'twenty years in the making'. As for the occupants of the Master's lodge, it will suffice for Sir Francis Doyle, an Oxford man of the last century with a roguish eye on Whewell, to express an opinion of curiously modern significance:

If you through the regions of space should have travelled,
And of nebular films the remotest unravelled,
You'll find as you tread on the bounds of Infinity,
That God's greatest work is the Master of Trinity.

Nevile's own court, sometimes known as the Cloisters, lies on the other side of the hall—between the western range and the river, that is—and since 1682 a discreetly admirable rostrum of three semicircular alcoves backing against the hall, has done much to harmonize its Tudor Gothic with the classical or Italianate style of the cloisters and Wren's exquisite library which provides the fourth side of the court, parallel with the river. A close friend of Isaac Barrow, Master of Trinity for five years from 1672, Wren gave his services without charge; Robert Grumbold, responsible for the building, received four guineas a month for his labour; but, for each of the statues representing Divinity, Law, Physic and Mathematics which adorn the eastern parapet of the roof, Gabriel Cibber was paid £20; and, in 1775, William Peckitt of York earned one hundred guineas for giving effect to Cipriani's idea of a painted window that would show a lady 'in a somewhat scanty robe of yellow', thought to personify Fame or Cambridge University, introducing Isaac Newton (who died in 1727) to George the Third (who was born in 1738) while Francis Bacon (who died in 1626) noted the proceedings.

Wren also designed the furnishings in the Library itself, with particular attention to the splendid avenue of what he called 'celles', each with its table, desk and stools. Grinling Gibbons did the carving. It is down this avenue that Byron casts an appraising eye on Roubillac's busts of Newton, Barrow, Bacon and Bentley, and among others, Tennyson and J. J. Thomson whose name is so often associated with Rutherford. Not without reason does Trinity claim the library to be its finest building. It has been described as 'certainly one of the very greatest works of the great master of English architecture', and Uffenbach himself was not only moved to acknowledge a library handsome in itself, but to pay a second visit to continue his study of its books and manuscripts. Among the college treasures today are the manuscripts of Thackeray's *Esmond*, Tennyson's *In Memoriam*, and some of Milton's poems, including *Lycidas*, the first edition of which was printed at the Pitt Press.

Unexpectedly lurking south of the Great Court and the tourist track, where the old Milne Street comes to an end, is the Bishop's

Hostel, part of which is thought to be the work of Wren, but there is nothing uncertain in the opinion of one critic about New Court south of Nevile's, built in the reign of George the Fourth, and about Whewell's, across the street opposite the Great Gate and completed in 1868, for, he sourly comments, 'these are fortunately so situated that the sightseer can easily avoid looking at them'. In Angel Court, however, pleasantly tucked away between the Great Court and the shops in Trinity Street, and completed in 1959, there is at least a suggestion of Michaelhouse in the name of the hostel it bears.

As Henry the Eighth died in 1547, the year after the foundation of his challenging college, others had to give effect to his intention that the society should consist of a Master and sixty Fellows, apart from scholars, and the revised statutes under which the college ultimately settled down were Elizabethan, granted in 1560. These allowed for the Master and sixty Fellows, and added sixty-nine scholars, sixteen sizars, six chaplains, six lay-clerks and ten boy-choristers. There were also to be nine lecturers among the college officials, and—most importantly in that it cleared the path to intellectual eminence—the customary restrictions on the choice of Fellows, such as one only from each county and equality between 'northerners' and 'southerners' were abandoned so that Trinity was free to pick the best on the market. Pensioners, moreover, were admitted on the same conditions that governed scholars, and apart from the tremendous emphasis that was still placed on the study of 'dead languages', the Trinity curriculum was just about as broad as sixteenth-century knowledge and ideas between them permitted.

Odd though such a training appears today, it nevertheless produced men of the calibre of Newton and Bacon, and a rich variety of others, notorious as well as notable. Among them were Charles Montagu, Earl of Halifax, who was largely responsible for creating the Bank of England in 1694; John Ray and Francis Willoughby, the seventeenth-century naturalists; George Jeffreys of the 'Bloody Assize', who became Lord Chancellor soon after sitting in judgment on Titus Oates; and Robert Devereux, Earl of Essex, who appears to have come up to Cambridge at the early age of thirteen to collect his degree, and twenty-one years later, the Chancellorship, in the meantime having had his ears boxed by Queen Elizabeth as, it would seem, a preliminary to his later execution in the Tower for high treason. Nor has this lustre dimmed with the passing of the old concepts of a university education. Trinity has achieved all that its royal founder intended, and for that fulfilment there is at least the explanation lightly offered by Sir Francis Doyle. The Masters of Trinity undoubtedly make an interesting list.

In John Whitgift, Master for ten years from 1567 and afterwards Archbishop of Canterbury, Trinity was doubly fortunate in having a disciplinarian at a critical time, and a theologian able to cope with the rising Puritan as well as the surviving Catholic, for religious dissension did not die overnight with the crowning of Elizabeth. There were still Fellows who broke stained-glass windows 'wherein did appear superstition' and refused to wear surplices in chapel. There was the teaching, too, of Thomas Cartwright, a Trinity man who, as Puritan leader, united his unofficial title with that of Lady Margaret Professor of Divinity. Whitgift persuaded him 'to travel and depart from the college to Geneva'. At the other extreme, he assisted at the bonfire of 'Popish trumpery' so dear to the heart of Dr Caius. Nor did he hesitate to have the erring scholar whipped in hall, and the bachelor put in the stocks.

Although Trinity has never lacked Masters of distinction, if assertiveness is added to that virtue, then Isaac Barrow and Bentley must surely rank by themselves. It is, however, Trinity's misfortune that Bentley, who reigned forty-two years from 1700, must also qualify as the most contentious, whereas Barrow, who lasted only five years from 1672, merely loved a rough house for itself. As a schoolboy he proved so rowdy that his father was moved to exclaim that 'if it should please God to take away any of his children, he could best spare Isaac'; and when Algerine pirates attacked the ship in which he was travelling on his grand tour, which took him to Constantinople, he fought one of her guns with such accuracy and enthusiasm that the pirates hastily withdrew. In the academic field he was eminent as a classical and a mathematical scholar. At one time—until he gave up the Chair to his pupil, Newton—he was Lucasian Professor. But his fame as a theologian, firmly though its rests on his vigorous expression and lucidity, as well as his *Treatise on the Pope's Supremacy* published after his death, is not quite unsullied. It should not be necessary to demonstrate that Charity faileth never with a sermon lasting three-and-a-half hours. Nor can he rightly blame the congregation of Westminster Abbey where he once held forth with such eloquence that they persuaded the organist to play 'till they had blowed him down'.

He died at the age of forty-seven, and was buried in the Abbey.

But for Richard Bentley, the Johnian from Yorkshire, there was no such tribute. By turning his long reign into a series of quarrels, punctuated by litigation, he did no more than achieve a notoriety in strange contrast with his scholarship. No one challenged that. The year before his appointment to the mastership, his *Dissertation upon the Epistles of Phalaris,* which he denounced as forgeries, had given him a European reputation, and during the most astonishing feud in college history that followed, he yet contrived, in 1717, to become Regius Professor of Divinity.

Beyond all doubt there was much in eighteenth-century Cambridge, its most unsatisfactory era, to justify the energetic reforms of an able man, but the sharp practice and blatant contempt with which he set about his task of reviving Trinity's slack society were intolerable, and 'war' broke out immediately over the Master's lodge. That it needed attention was never in doubt, and readily sanctioned. Bentley's idea of repair, however, included among other improvements the construction of a magnificent panelled staircase, and the college was faced with a bill so far exceeding expectation that the Bursar could hardly do other than demur. Bentley threatened to send him away 'to feed his turkeys'. Nor did the Junior Bursar fare any better when he had the temerity to protest against meeting the cost of a newly-built hen-house. Bentley stopped his commons—the daily rations supplied from the college buttery.

Also engaging Bentley's early attention was the chapel, for

that was in a state of some decay, and he proposed to make it worthy of the splendid new organ, the building of which he had arranged when he first became Master. With a show of generosity in his own gift of £200 towards the cost of restoration, he persuaded most of the Fellows to give up their dividends for a whole academic year, but even so the total subscribed was only one-third of the amount expended, and this deficit on top of the expense incurred at the lodge put the college into real financial trouble. It was so serious that Bentley tried to abolish even the simple pleasures of the college feast in order to save money; and to deny the Fellows a meeting place to discuss their grievances, he further sought to deprive them of their combination room by turning it into chambers. There is, indeed, more than a touch of sadistic humour in his opening moves against the dons, for, by exercising his statutory powers to the full, he was able to compel everyone to perform academic tasks and disputations daily in the college hall, fine them if they forgot to attend chapel, and force the dilatory among them to take their degrees in Divinity—all this apart from the amiable threat of turning the college into a prison by gating them. The wonder is that the Fellows stood this treatment for nine years.

The explosion came when the rapacious Bentley proposed to increase his share of the college income beyond the statutory limit of his dividend. Not even his own supporters could tolerate that, and the meeting closed with Bentley's stormy departure from the combination room and his promise that 'peace in Trinity College' was now at an end. But this time he had gone too far, and in May 1710, on the advice of a legal expert, a number of Fellows appealed to the college Visitor, the person, that is, authorized to adjudicate in college affairs. But even here an awkwardness intruded, for Bishop Moore of Ely had been largely responsible for Bentley's appointment to the mastership, and to him Bentley promptly wrote. The petition of the dons he dismissed as 'the last struggle of vice and idleness against virtue, learning and good discipline', and—what must have been a relief to the Bishop—astutely claimed that the Queen was the College Visitor, and requested her intervention.

Three years passed before it was ruled that the Bishop was in order to proceed, and another year before, in May 1714, the trial began in London, at Ely House, with an ex-Chancellor and Sir Isaac Newton as assessors—a trial that should have seen the end of Bentley's mastership. When the Bishop condemned his conduct in open court, Bentley fainted. But the Bishop caught a chill and died, leaving his written judgment among his papers, and the death of Queen Anne next day quickly led to the fall of the Government and a country thrown into turmoil. The trial therefore lapsed, and Bentley continued to reign in Trinity.

Although his escape from deprivation and ignominy could not have been narrower, Bentley was quite unrepentant, and as the new Bishop refused to revive the old proceedings, and the Fellows' appeal to the Privy Council brought no result, his position in the college was unassailable. Disheartened and divided among them-selves, the Fellows could do nothing except agree. Nor did Bentley spare them, for having—with apparent generosity—persuaded the lawyer who had prompted the first petition to resign his fellowship in consideration of £528 to cover his costs in the trial, and then claimed £500 for his own expenses, he had no difficulty in making the Fellows see that the college should not only provide both sums but also refurnish the lodge.

It was during this period of bribery and violence in Parlia-mentary elections that, in 1715, Bentley took advantage of one in Cambridge to propose that two vacancies among the twenty-four retainers that Trinity assisted in their old age should be filled by a publican and a notorious mob-leader significantly recommended by 'a gentleman in the county', and when the Fellows hesitated, announced that he himself would elect the bruiser on the single vote of a feeble-minded don 'who was his never-failing supporter'. His rapacity, however, was nearly—and again, should have been—his undoing when George the First, during his visit to Cambridge in 1717, presented thirty-two honorary degrees in Divinity, and Bentley, using his position as Regius Professor, first collected four guineas from each of the recipients. But among them was an ex-Trinity don who, being aware that this extortion was illegal, paid without demur and then sued Bentley in the Vice-Chancellor's court.

Months slipped by, and when at last the Vice-Chancellor sent a bedell to arrest Bentley, there was high comedy, for Bentley, in effect, arrested the bedell by locking him in the lodge.

Whether or not Bentley did this to provide the glorious red herring it proved to be, there is little doubt that if the Vice-Chancellor had met cunning with cunning and not with indignation, Bentley would have fared badly. As it was, the Vice-Chancellor led the Senate in passing a grace that deprived Bentley of all his degrees, an illegality which Bentley pounced on with delighted ferocity. He was now the aggrieved party, in a position to rout his would-be persecutors, and rout them he did. One he sent to prison. At the same time, apparently, he pocketed his 128 guineas, for the ex-Fellow of Trinity, who merely wanted his small contribution returned, had to apologize.

The 'war' had lasted seven years when, in 1724, the Court of King's Bench bluntly ordered the University to restore Bentley's degrees, but there could be no peace at Trinity while Bentley occupied his magnificent lodge. He was insufferable, and after three years of uneasy truce, the Fellows again sought to deprive him. Moreover, they persisted down the years until, in 1733, they not only brought him to trial at Ely House: they heard the sentence of their own release. Bentley, the court said, was to lose his mastership, and with any other man that would surely have been the end. But not with Bentley. The Vice-Master alone had authority to perform the act of deprivation, and Trinity's statutes said nothing about what was to be done when Dr Richard Walker —he of the 'Physic Garden' and Vice-Master at the time— bluntly refused to deprive his personal friend. In vain the Fellows besought the King's Bench to issue the necessary writ compelling him to do so, desperately persisting throughout five troubled years. Clearly death alone would remove this astonishing man from the lodge he had made his own thirty-eight years earlier. Yet his contribution to learning and the smooth-running of the University, cannot be overlooked, indirect though it was. He did encourage Newton to publish a second edition of the *Principia,* and even built an observatory over Trinity's Great Gate for the first Professor of Astronomy. But his most enduring work is found in the University Press, for to that he gave its present organization as a University department governed by a University syndicate.

He was eighty when he died in 1742.

Today, in the chapel for which he did so much, however unorthodox his methods, his name can be read over the Master's stall, but on his tomb there is no mention of the proud title he once bore with such curious distinction.

Restoring Trinity's eminence after forty-two years of Bentley's mastership was not a task to be accomplished even in a comparable period. Numbers were down; the dons, it was said, drank too much; scholarship, like the University itself, was at its lowest ebb; and the relief at escaping from a seemingly invulnerable despot could hardly fail to express itself in lassitude. Not without reason, therefore, had the century itself slipped by before the college saw the work begun by Robert Smith, the Plumian Professor of Astronomy who had succeeded Bentley, blossom in a world of expanding scholarship and religious emancipation. Whether the Prime Minister of 1798, prescribing for a convalescent college, chose an adequate disciplinarian when he appointed William Lort Mansel, Bishop of Bristol, must be open to doubt when Byron kept a bear and undergraduates sought forgiveness for their sins by chanting under the Master's window: 'We beseech thee to hear us, good Lort!' Nor did Christopher Wordsworth, the poet's brother, appear to grasp the new freedom of thought when he ruled against voluntary chapel-attendance with the challenge that the college had the choice of compulsory religion or no religion, and a tutor murmured that the distinction was too subtle for him to grasp.

It was during Wordsworth's mastership, after being ordered to attend chapel twice on Sunday and once on every other day of the week, that the young men of Trinity formed their 'Society for the Prevention of Cruelty to Undergraduates'. Operating secretly, they struck by keeping a register and publishing weekly

—to the delight of the University at large—the embarrassing omissions in chapel attendances of the Fellows themselves. They did, however, give a prize for the most regular attendance—a bible, afterwards cherished by the first Bishop of Melbourne.

Then there was William Whewell, 'Willie Whistle' to the undergraduates. He flung an offending young man out of Trinity by the scruff of his neck after a midnight rag, yet was so conscious of his dignity when an undergraduate offered him shelter and a cigarette during a thunderstorm, that he loftily reminded his benefactor of the college rule which allowed undergraduates to communicate with the Master only through their tutors. He was thrown from his horse and died in 1866, two years before the completion of the court that bears his name. W. H. Thompson, too, his successor as Master, deserves immortality within the University if only for his epigram: 'We are none of us infallible, not even the youngest of us.'

The display of versatility that Trinity produced in this period of resurgence is unrivalled. One can start with three Prime Ministers—Campbell-Bannerman, Baldwin and Balfour—and note with an almost casual eye such products as Byron, Macaulay, Praed, Thackeray, Tennyson, Sedgwick (the geologist), Airy (the astronomer), Jebb (the Greek scholar), Frazer (of *The Golden Bough*), Fitzgerald (to whom the world owes an English version of the *Rubaiyat of Omar Khayyam* that is reputedly finer than the original), Maurice (the inspiration of what was so unhappily known as 'Christian Socialism', who also studied at Trinity Hall without graduating at either college), and Westcott (the Bishop of Durham whose memorial is the clergy training house named after him in Jesus Lane).

Tennyson came up in 1828. Of the Chancellor's Medals for Classics in the ten preceding years, Trinity men had won fifteen, St John's five, and the other colleges none; and in 1829 Tennyson himself won the Chancellor's English Medal for a poem on the subject of *Timbuctoo*. One gathers that he entered the competition merely to please his father, who was no doubt well satisfied, but Charles Wordsworth wrote from Christ Church, Oxford, to his brother, the Master of Trinity, saying that 'if such an exercise had been sent up at Oxford, the author would have had a better chance of being rusticated, with a view to his passing a few months in a lunatic asylum, than of obtaining a prize'; and going one better, Thackeray parodied the style with impudent gaiety and a sad confusion of geography, but nevertheless a touch of remarkable foresight:

> The day shall come when Albion's self shall feel
> Stern Afric's wrath and writhe 'neath Afric's steel.
> I see her tribes the hill of glory mount,
> And sell their sugars on their own account,
> While round her throne the prostrate nations come,
> Sue for her rice and barter for her rum.

It was, incidentally, Thackeray's first appearance in print.

Thackeray, who was born in Calcutta, also came up in 1829, and those were days when the old barriers were falling and strange thoughts free to stir, not least as intellect found itself in conflict with traditional belief. But it was little more than a leaning towards the new nonconformity, a gentlemanly rebellion that did not obstruct the way to high preferment in the orthodox church. F. D. Maurice, who came up in 1823, and John Sterling, a year later, were the founders, Tennyson an honorary member, and they took for their name a title bestowed in jest but proudly adopted—the Society of the Apostles. Not everyone took them seriously. One critic was unashamedly amused at Maurice's conception of 'a moderately hot Hell to which nobody would go'. It is therefore pleasant to record that Maurice went on to graduate at Oxford, take normal Holy Orders, and finish at Cambridge in the Chair of Moral Philosophy. Never a strong man, Sterling died at the early age of 38, and Tennyson succeeded Wordsworth as Poet Laureate in 1850, the year of *In Memoriam*.

Although this 'elegiac treasury stored with the grief and meditation of many years' is Tennyson's tribute following a pilgrimage to the rooms of his friend, Arthur Hallam, who kept in New Court and died in 1833, there can be few men who have made no more than a sentimental journey to their own old rooms and have not known the poignancy of the first half-dozen simple words:

Another name was on the door:
  I lingered; all within was noise
  Of songs, and clapping hands, and boys
That crash'd the glass and beat the floor;

Where once we held debate, a band
  Of youthful friends, on mind and art,
  And labour, and the changing mart,
And all the framework of the land.

Tennyson named his elder son Hallam.

So this royal college of Henry the Eighth rose from the tangle of buildings that had themselves been colleges, keeping the best of them, and shaping itself to the further glory of Cambridge. For most visitors, Trinity Great Court and King's Chapel are the University. Today, Trinity wears the royal flag of Edward the Third, and the Queen's judges on circuit stay at the Master's lodge, a privilege—but only a privilege—they have enjoyed since the reign of James the First, 'that pierles and most noble Prince and morninge starr' who stayed there himself in 1614. The royal connexion is, in fact, a living reality, and when Queen Victoria, with Prince Albert, came in 1843, 'a little incident, trifling though it may appear to some, but full of the right feeling, seemed to give Her Majesty more gratification than all that she had yet witnessed since her arrival in the precincts of the University'.

On this occasion the royal party entered Cambridge by the southern approach, and at the entrance to Trumpington Street passed beneath a floral arch, with an escort of Whittlesea Yeomanry and the Mayor walking beside the carriage. At Trinity, Whewell made formal submission with mace and key, first as Vice-Chancellor, then as Master, and soon the Queen was enthroned on the hall dias, receiving those lengthy addresses of welcome and loyalty which, if still inevitable, were now delivered in English. Not until that evening, after visiting King's, did the Queen express her wish to see Trinity Chapel, and the undergraduates hastily formed a torchlight procession. Then, 'on leaving

Trinity Great Court

the Chapel, it was perceived that there was a short deficit in the carpeting that led to the lodge, and quick as thought, a hundred gowns were off and strewed three deep beneath her Royal path'.

Trinity is still the largest college, but one cannot overlook the new Churchill, expanding rapidly, for its buildings off the Madingley Road are said to be designed for the accommodation of over six hundred.*

* In 1966, the average number of undergraduates in twenty-three colleges was about 350, to which a further ninety can be added for research students and postgraduates, and these figures are independent of the dons who form the permanent staff. The largest of the colleges in purely undergraduate population were Trinity with 664, St John's 548, Queens' 406, St Catharine's 403, Fitz-william 401; and the smallest were Corpus Christi with 199, Peterhouse 218, Sidney Sussex 245, and Magdalene 253. Although a recent foundation, Chur-chill already had 359 undergraduates apart from 140 'advanced' students.

In the Michaelmas Term 1966 the 'freshman' entry into the University was:

	Men	Women	Total
Undergraduates	2,403	292	2,695
Postgraduates	714	138	852
	3,117	430	3,547

The total of all full-time students was then:

	Men	Women	Total
Undergraduates	7,301	865	8,166
Postgraduates	1,788	259	2,047
	9,089	1,124	10,213

11

St John's College from the river
Summer on the river by Trinity Bridge

XII

SOUTH-EASTERN APPROACH

THERE is, in the chalk hills of the Gogs to the south-east of
Cambridge, a seemingly unending but pleasant country lane.
To anyone at its starting point near the golf club, it turns not
aside but follows the same direction to the horizon, and it survives
as part of the Roman road that antiquarians—though not the
Romans—decided to call the Via Devana. In the opposite direction, where the ground falls away to the flat expanse of Cambridge, it has long been lost in the ravages of expansion, but its
site is never far from the city's south-eastern approach, a road
that roughly cuts Cambridge in halves and, it seems, in pieces;
for innocently though it starts as the Babraham Road, it soon
changes to Hills Road and continues as Regent Street, St Andrew's
(once Preachers') Street, Sidney (once Conduit) Street, and,
helpfully, Bridge Street, before it crosses the river to become
Magdalene Street and Castle Street. Only then does it resume its
swallow-flight as the Huntingdon Road. In these names, however,
one can discern the impact of history.

On the whole, Cambridge is fortunate in its main approaches.
No one who arrives from Newmarket and meets an airfield, a
factory or two, the Borough Cemetery and that most unlovely
of modern inventions, the building estate, is going to linger, even
to ponder the vanished glories of Barnwell, but there are ways
into the city that are not at once engulfed in expansion, the
southern approach being one, and among others the Via Devana's
descendant enters and leaves with dignity. There is no compulsion

to study Addenbrooke's transplanted hospital, although one's glance may linger in pained astonishment. Not for another mile, at the railway bridge, does commerce intrude with siding and shunting, a flour mill and a cattle market, and there is still a mile and a half to Magdalene Bridge. Distance, no less than the deplorable railway, doubtless discouraged a drift of learning towards the Gogs, and the only attempt was a failure. Cavendish College, founded in 1876 for the sons of the less well-to-do died of its own isolation after a mere fifteen years, and today its buildings survive as part of the red-brick citadel of Homerton College for the training of women teachers.

Recently a timber yard and Tait Mackenzie's War Memorial marked the junction of Hills Road and the one that slants in from the station, but now the hatless soldier, striding prodigiously back from the Kaiser's war, stands on a flower-bedecked island and is seen against a spruce and modern office block, flat-roofed with acres of glass—not, perhaps, the ideal background for a memorial held to be among the finest in the country, yet a marked improvement on the yard.

Hills Road becomes Regent Street where Lensfield Road cuts across and, heading for the old Barnwell highway, gives a fleeting glimpse of Parker's 24-acre 'Piece' which it skirts. Dominating this nodal point in the local traffic problem, rather as the chapel dominates King's Parade, is the Roman Catholic Church of Our Lady and the English Martyrs. Its lofty spire is a feature of the Cambridge skyline. The generosity of a French lady, who earlier had 'won fame and fortune as the most renowned ballet dancer of the London stage', enabled this splendid monument to be built towards the end of the last century; and today, from its position at the south-west corner, it looks in compassion across Lensfield Road at the tiny dwellings which welcomed the one-horse tram, then diagonally at a modern petrol station, and finally across Hills Road itself at one of the more remarkable excesses of modern architecture—the 'random' window. Even a building that resembles a flat-sided coffin, being long and low and boxlike, must have windows, but why they should be of the same height and vary only in width so that the smallest is no more than a slit, and placed 'at random' in rows, is not so clear. Nevertheless, whatever the staff of the Local Examinations Syndicate thinks about them from the inside, to the contemplative traveller at the bus-stop outside, they do avoid monotony. And there is a fringe of the greenest grass to give the University touch.

Parker's Piece, which backs on the shops lining Regent Street throughout most of its length, is one of the joys of Cambridge, a well-kept public playing-field, summer and winter, almost in the heart of the expanded town. When Trinity exchanged it for a site near the river, Edward Parker held the 'piece' as tenant, and as Parker's Piece its name has survived—evidence, too, of a college cook's importance even in 1612. But motorists now cast their covetous eyes, seeing no more than a wonderful parking place.

Regent Street becomes St Andrew's where a gorgeous supermarket, with offices above, joins a substantial block that once sufficed for the Fire Brigade and the Police Force. But the population of Cambridge has doubled since, at the turn of the century, the Borough paid £16,000 for a building in stone of almost collegiate dignity, and now the firemen have moved to adequate quarters and the policemen are due to follow. Preening itself with new buildings, St Andrew's Street gives the impression of welcoming clients to mercantile Cambridge, and no one can say that it does not succeed. But one does step back in time, and quickly too, almost on leaving its Regency prolongation, for on the right is the first college that the visitor sees when coming from the station. This—Emmanuel—is the college that followed the Preaching Friars from whom the street took its earlier name. Today, opposite the college main gate, is Downing Street along the far end of which ran the infamous Ditch before it cut across the old Hog Market to skirt Christ's College and head for the river by Hobson's Street.

That Thomas Hobson, the carrier, contributed much to local welfare is gratefully acknowledged in this perpetuation of his name, but whether the little canal that brings the water from Nine Wells is rightly known as Hobson's Brook, and not attributed to Dr Perne who suggested the basic idea, and Dr Montagu who helped to promote its fulfilment, is open to question. Contractors—unhappily known as 'undertakers'—dug the canal, and it is possible that Hobson was concerned with them, but his great contribution was in the town itself, of which he was at one time Mayor. In 1628, fourteen years after the blessing of fresh water had reached the very centre of the town through the conduit of Market Hill, he provided ground and property for a 'house of correction' which Cambridge knew as the Spinning House until it made way for the police station in 1901.

Whatever Hobson had in mind about the purpose of his 'house of correction'—and his intentions, in part at least, were kindly— the emphasis in its normal working fell heavily on correction, and that, in the seventeenth century, did not pamper the criminal. The town prison, adjoining the tolbooth, was then part of a house acquired in 1224, with a hole in the ground floor still in use as a cell for criminals 552 years later. Nor could the Spinning House have been much better, in construction or management, when it is on record that, a hundred years after Hobson's death, the Town Crier whipped delinquent women there, and that on one occasion the Vice-Chancellor himself intervened to release the survivors among seventeen women, crowded into a room only nineteen feet square with neither warmth nor sanitation. The others had died of fever. There were, apparently, one room for men, two for women, and a 'dark room' for the refractory. Yet Hobson spoke of his 'house' as one for 'setting poor people to work' as well as for dealing with 'stubborn rogues' and the lazy.

Not until the nineteenth century did Cambridge outgrow its 'houses of correction'. Already the old prison adjoining the tolbooth had been replaced, in 1790, by a new one behind the Spinning House, and yet another followed, quickly too, over-looking Parker's Piece 'in the outskirts of the town', and costing £25,000. It was an enormous sum in 1827, and called for a special rate. Even so, it lasted only fifty years. Prisoners were then committed to the county jail on Castle Hill, and now that has gone. Today the 'local' prison is at Bedford. As for the Spinning House, the Vice-Chancellor's repository for 'common women', that continued until one of them proved to be not so common as the

Proctors thought, and in 1894, when calm had returned and the University had freely surrendered to the Borough its rights in this house of suspect correction, there ended a curious chapter on human behaviour that hardly worked out as Hobson intended.

The visitor passing along St Andrew's Street today, and acquainting himself with Cambridge, sees Emmanuel not only as a normal college, but also one that is fringed with a garden—clearly an oasis in the traffic now plaguing the city. Yet its foundation in 1584, during the reign of a Protestant Queen, was both abnormal and perilous, for Sir Walter Mildmay was known as a whole-hearted Puritan, and Puritans Queen Elizabeth did not encourage. Her approach was ominous. 'I hear, Sir Walter, that you have erected a Puritan foundation.' Sir Walter, however, was Chancellor of the Exchequer as well as Treasurer of the House-hold, and skilled accordingly. 'No, madam', he answered. 'Far be it from me to countenance anything contrary to your estab-lished laws, but I have set an acorn which, when it becomes an oak, God alone knows what will be the fruit thereof.' And the acorn continued to germinate.

Courageously, in the circumstances, Sir Walter made his pur-pose quite clear. His college was to be 'a seed plot of learned men for the supply of the Church' in a country that was itself leaning towards his faith. Emmanuel, in short, was to infiltrate. Life-fellowships were ruled out. 'We would not', he wrote, 'have any fellow suppose that we have given him in this college a perpetual abode.' Instead, Emmanuel dons would become Doctors of Divinity and reform the Church of England with a continual flow of Puritan inspiration. It was a curious reversion to the old-time religious emphasis, yet in its early years, when the tide of Refor-mation was still running, it brought Emmanuel astonishing success, and the Commonwealth was its heyday. In 1644 this 'pure house' had eighty-one admissions against a mere nine at St John's, and in the same year—that preceding the battle of Naseby—when nine Heads of Houses refused to renounce episcopacy at the call of Cromwell's commissioners, Emmanuel men replaced seven. Earlier, the college had contributed twenty-one of the Pilgrim Fathers and thirty-five of the hundred Cambridge men who formed the bulk of the graduate settlers in New England. Among them—briefly, but with great consequence—was John Harvard.

The popularity of Emmanuel in its early days is the more remarkable when seen against the founder's disciplinary code, for that was undoubtedly severe although a report to Archbishop Laud—itself significant of the times—suggests a casual approach to serious matters which is not easy to reconcile. 'Before prayers begin', the report said, 'the boys come in and sit down and talk about what they list. They receive the Holy Sacrament sitting on forms about the Communion Tables, and do pull the Loaf one from the other, after the minister hath begun. And so the Cup, one drinking, as it were to another, like good fellows, without any particular application of the said words, more than once for all.' Against this, one finds Sir Walter enforcing his belief that 'the idle gossip of youths was a waste of time' and 'a bad habit for young minds', not only with a ban on playing and feasting and even talking, but also with inspection of the young men's chambers at least twice a week by the Fellows, and at night, for the purpose of 'carefully examining what they were doing'. Offenders were to be whipped. Furthermore, there were to be 'frequent hearing of sermons', chapel attendances, nightly prayers by the tutor at 8 p.m., and special Sunday lectures on the Christian faith by the Dean, after which he catechized the whole college. If, then, the young men's behaviour was accurately reported to the Archbishop, there must have been some curious interpretations of the founder's wishes.

For some time after the dissolution a townsman held the Dominican site on lease, and Mildmay was in the happy position of being able to take over property so readily adjusted to his ideas of a Puritan power-house, that he appears to have found additional pleasure in turning the Dominican refectory into a chapel, defiantly running north and south, and the Dominican church into a refectory. It was left to Sir Christopher Wren, nearly a hundred years later, to build the present chapel on Anglican lines. That was after the Restoration, during the mastership of William

Sancroft, High Churchman and later Archbishop of Canterbury, whose immediate purpose was to rid the college 'of that former singularity which rendered it so unhappily remarkable'. Clearly with his uncle's chapel at Peterhouse in mind, Wren placed Emmanuel's centrally, with cloisters each side supporting the Master's Gallery, and by so doing gave an eastern range to the attractive court which one enters from St Andrew's Street today. The Ionic pillars and simple pediment that add distinction to the frontage of the western range, seen from the street, are later additions that Essex made in the 1770s. Uffenbach, making his inspection sixty years earlier, graciously allowed that, apart from the library where the books lay in confusion, the college itself was tolerable, as indeed it should have been, for Emmanuel hides much in the old Dominican site, not least an attractive garden. But its position today, with main-road motor traffic on one side and a bus-station on the other is not the happiest.

There can be little doubt that in Emmanuel's list of eminent *alumni,* transcending all others in popular assessment, is John Harvard, the one man about whom probably least is known. The college has no record of him except his name in a book of receipts and his autograph on a small religious volume, and his adopted country has little more. It is reported that in Charleston he 'preached and prayed with tears and evidence of strong affection', and that he died at the early age of thirty-one after no more than a year in America. Yet his name is borne by one of the great universities of the world, for the founding of which his legacy amounted to £779 17s. 2d. and some three hundred books.

John Harvard was a product of Emmanuel in its Puritan ascendancy, a generation in time before Sancroft set out to remove its 'former singularity'. William Law's arrival as an unabashed Puritan, after a like interval, therefore reveals a splendid tolerance in the college, especially as he rose to a fellowship in 1711. His book, *A Serious Call to a Devout and Holy Life,* published in 1729, led to his association with John Wesley who was later to give life to Wesleyan Methodism, and he was also 'the much honoured and spiritual director' of the entire Gibbon family, but his own Puritan intolerance remained. Of the theatre, he thundered: 'Actors and spectators must all be damned. The playhouse is the porch of Hell, the place of the Devil's abode, where he holds his filthy court of evil spirits: a play is the Devil's triumph, a sacrifice performed to his glory, as much as in the heathen temples of Bacchus or Venus.'

Law died, at the age of seventy-five, four years after Richard Farmer, himself an Emmanuel man, had graduated—an interval long enough to spare the Master of Emmanuel, as leader of the Shakespeare Gang, the indignity of being denounced as the Devil's disciple.

As for the 'Whig Johnson', Samuel Parr, who came up in 1765, his memory is enshrined in his retort to the lady who pleaded that the privilege of women is to talk nonsense. 'No, Madame', he said, 'it is not their privilege but their infirmity. Ducks would walk if they could, but nature suffers them only to waddle.'

Beyond Emmanuel, St Andrew's Street soon adjusts its name, but not until it has swept along the front of Christ's and shown the visitor a college that contrives at least an air of academic calm amid the tumult of today, and there is nothing to tell that, on changing its name to Sidney Street, the road itself enters the Cambridge once girt by river and Ditch. Nor does Petty Cury, branching to the left, call to mind a lane of 'little cookeries'. Yet antiquity still survives in Sidney Street, first by the bus-stop in the heart of the modern city, where Market Street cuts down from 'The Hill'; for here stands the Church of the Holy Trinity, its ancestry lost in time, and, less remotely, Simeon's scene of triumph with his Evangelical Movement. Further along, too, nearer the bridge, there is also the last of the older colleges, Sidney Sussex, founded in 1596 and completing the ten in that unhurried progression which started with King's in 1441. Two hundred years had to pass before the next arrived—Downing in 1800. Fortunately, in view of the traffic in this narrow one-way street, Sidney stands back from the road, sheltered by a wall that hardly adds to external beauty but does make for internal peace.

It seems that Frances Sidney, the great Sir Philip's aunt and widow of the Earl of Sussex, consoled herself with the idea of erecting 'some goodly and godly monument for the maintenance of good learning' in the distress of her declining years, and the idea was her own. She died in 1589, and her will states that she 'had yearly gathered out of her revenues so much as conveniently she could'—£5,000 and certain residues. It was little enough for the purpose, but seven months after her death effect was given to her wishes, and as Fuller, himself a migrant to the new foundation, happily explains: 'We usually observe infants born in the seventh month, though poor and pitiful creatures, are vital, and, with great care and good attendance, in time prove proper persons. To such a *partus septimestris* may Sidney College well be resembled, so low, lean, and little at birth thereof. Alas! what is five thousand pounds to buy the site, build and endow a College therewith? Yet such was the worthy care of her honourable executors that this Benjamin College—the least and last in time, and born *after* (as he *at*) the death of its mother—thrived in a short time to a competent strength and stature.'

The chosen site was that of the old Franciscan Friary, purchased from Trinity, but of the Friary buildings only one remained, and that was in use as a malthouse. For a time, however, it sufficed as a chapel, and 'The College of the Lady Frances Sidney Sussex' owed its first three-sided court to the architect Symons. He faced the basic clunch with dark red brick. A second, and similar, court followed some thirty years later; Essex built a 'proper' chapel, destined to be enlarged in the early 1900s and take its place among the finest of its kind in the University; and except that large-scale renovation during the last century led one critic to deplore that 'a charming Elizabethan college has been ruthlessly turned into a thoroughly bad stucco dwelling gothicized in the Wyatt manner', its architectural development down the years has been far closer to normal than its early history, and Ketton stone has done something to repair the ravages of Sir Jeffery Wyattville, as Wyatt afterwards became.

So this 'godly monument' took shape, and whatever Lady Frances had in mind for its religious allegiance, there is no doubt that in its early days it mirrored Puritan Emmanuel, even to a chapel running north and south. All its young men had to be ordinands; the same prying and catechizing ordered their lives; and the Master himself, on election, had to proclaim his abhorrence of Popery.

It was during the years of its Puritan infancy that the college accepted Oliver Cromwell as a fellow-commoner.

Of Cromwell the undergraduate enough is known to suggest his sad indifference to the charm of scholarship in a Puritan foundation, as well as little affection for it. But he was never more than a freshman, for he came up at seventeen and went down on his father's death a year later, thereby just missing his future associate and rival, Edward Montagu, Earl of Manchester, who also came up as a fellow-commoner. In this brief sojourn he appears to have been more concerned with 'his exercises in the fields than in the Schools, being one of the chief match-makers, and players of football, cudgels or any other boisterous sport or games'; and as it is on record in All Saints' Church at his birthplace, Huntingdon, that he did public penance for scandalous living at the age of twenty, one cannot ignore his subsequent confession that he had not only 'lived in and loved darkness and hated light', but also had been 'a chief, a chief among sinners'.

In the dark years of civil war and Puritan ascendancy that were to follow, the University paid dearly for its allegiance to the King, and with good warning. With Cromwell himself in Parliament and member for the town, the future was bleak enough without the threat of civil war and the county's petition for Puritan dogma to be enforced in every college. Yet, as late as 1642, on a Saturday in March, the Prince of Wales who was to be Charles the Second received the University's full ceremonial welcome at the tender age of eleven. At King's, where he said his prayers, he was 'so little ashamed that, in the midst of that multitude, he hid not his devotion in his hat', and after lunching at Trinity, he sat through a comedy, in English, with all the 'signs of great acceptance which he could, and more than the University dared expect'. Nor did the University fail with its orations and hospitality when, on the Monday, the King himself, with Prince and retinue, dropped in for a 'travelling banquet' on his way from Newmarket to York; and even the Master of Puritan Emmanuel, preaching in Great St Mary's later in the week, was able to assert that 'never were the riches of the Kingdom so great, its peace so constant, the state of it for all things so prosperous'.

To complete the University's inevitable humiliation in a Cromwellian stronghold was the position of Cambridge itself at a river crossing. The drainage of the fens had started, but the town was still the all-important link. Only its function was reversed. The Normans built their castle to deny the crossing to invaders from East Anglia. Now earthworks took its place to guard the town from an English king who threatened to come by the Huntingdon road. For Cambridge had changed its status, being now the 'fortress' base of the Eastern Counties Association gathered for its defence, encamped meanwhile on Triplow Heath. Even when the threat had passed at Edgehill, a garrison a thousand strong stayed to torment the colleges. But long before the King had raised his standard at Nottingham, 'war' had broken out in Cambridge where the townsmen, having been given muskets, improved their practice on the college windows; and when the colleges sought to defend themselves by obtaining arms from London, the Mayor contrived to capture ten of the fifteen cases. Trinity managed to retain the other five.

While at York, the King twice requested colleges to help him, in June with money on loan at eight per cent, and in July with plate which, if not returned in the meantime, would be paid for 'when it shall please God to end these troubles'. Some colleges sent what they had, apart from communion plate and that of sentimental value; the loan came to nearly £6,000, and to it Sidney, Emmanuel and Magdalene contributed, Puritan though they were; but not all the plate reached the King. Although its escort succeeded in avoiding Cromwell's ambush on the Huntingdon road, he did manage to 'stay' some in Cambridge, that of King's as it waited collection in the college court, and his reaction was swift and ruthless. Soon afterwards his troops surrounded the chapels of St John's, Jesus and Queens' during service, and arrested the Heads of these Houses who had led the response to the royal request. They were sent to London and imprisoned in the Tower.

That Cromwell, in turn, should request a contribution to his own cause could not have been unexpected, but even so his response to the inevitable refusal must have exceeded the University's worst fears when it saw what happened to the Master of Sidney Sussex. Rounded up with other members of the University assembled in the Convocation House, the elderly Samuel Ward suffered with them as 'prisoners in the Public Schools on an exceedingly cold night till near one in the morning, without any accommodation for food, firing or lodging; and to complete the outrage, it was done on Good Friday, whence it may be supposed that they went with empty stomachs, and all this for no other reason than because they could not in conscience comply to contribute anything to that detestable war against His Majesty'.

On that Good Friday in 1643, when the Book of Common Prayer was formally destroyed, Cromwell himself had presided in Great St Mary's, and in the fate of the Master of his own college one sees the Puritan scourge that Cromwell so clearly encouraged. It meant nothing that the House of Lords should give the University its protection, specifically condemning interference with the normal life of the colleges and their worship according to the rules of the Church of England, and that Lord Essex should order his men to avoid damaging the colleges in which they were quartered. Not the slightest notice was taken, and the plight of the University during the next few years is best described as occupation by a vindictive thieving rabble. Already St John's old court had become a prison—'for the King's loyal subjects'—and although the Master of Sidney was soon released, he was by then a dying man. At the election of his successor, after his death in September, Cromwell's soldiers not only 'violently plucked' the likely candidate from his communion, but cast him into jail in order to clear the way for 'a creature of their own'.

The early destruction of Garret Hostel Bridge and five others belonging to colleges, all of them wood, may pass as defensive precaution. Only Grumbold's recently completed stone bridge at Clare escaped. Against this reprieve, however, the college had the rueful experience of seeing the stone and material collected for its own reconstruction, used in the castle's defences.

But far worse affliction was in store. A contemporary Royalist account complains bitterly that 'four score ragged soldiers, who had been lowzing before Crowland nigh on a fortnight, were turned loose into Pembroke Hall, being one of the least Halls in the University, to kennel there, and charged by their officers to shift for themselves, who, without more ado, broke open the Fellows' and Scholars' chambers, and took their beds from under them'. Nor was this behaviour exceptional, for the garrison itself contained many townsmen, 'poor tapsters' and the like, who saw only an opportunity. Rooms were wrecked, woodwork and furniture heedlessly burnt; stolen property sold in the market place. Meanwhile, at King's, troops drilled in the chapel; for sixteen months St John's provided a prison; and when Dowsing appeared, seeking his 'monuments of superstition', nothing, it must have seemed, was either safe or sacred.

In the June of that year, 1643, desperation could have driven the University to address itself humbly to the House of Lords, pointing out for their 'honourable Consideration the sad dejected state of the said University, how our schools daily grow desolate, mourning the absence of their Professors and their wonted Auditories; how, in our Colleges, our numbers grow thin, and our revenues short; and what subsistence we have abroad, is for the most part involved in the common Miseries; how, frighted by the Neighbour Noise of War, our Students either quit their Gowns, or abandon their Studies; how our degrees lie disesteemed, and all hopes of our Public Commencements are blasted in the Bud; besides sundry other Inconveniences which we forbear to mention. We cannot but conceive your Honourable Piety (out of a noble Zeal for Learning) will cordially pity our Condition, and, as the present calamities give way, afford some Succour and Encouragement.'

Yet, in the Earl of Manchester who enforced the will of Parliament, the University found, if not exactly a friend in the hour of need, at least an honourable enemy who carried out his duties with restraint and even solicitude. To the House of Lords he wrote, in the December of the same year: 'I doubt not your Lordships in your wisdom will think it better to endeavour the reforming of the University, rather than to hazard the dissolving of it'—a clear indication of what their Lordships had in mind. In his letter he also stressed the sorry plight of the Fellows and scholars in those colleges which 'did convey their Plate to the King', and found themselves now with all college land and profits sequestered, and with 'no other livelihood or subsistence'.

Refusal to subscribe on oath to the Convenant and, five years later, the Engagement, meant expulsion, and of the sixteen Heads of Houses during the period, twelve were ejected, two died, and only one retained his mastership apart from 'the creature of their own' whom Cromwell's men had installed at Sidney. Nor did the Fellows escape. Queens' lost its entire society, Peterhouse and Jesus all but one, and Trinity nigh on fifty. In the University as a whole more than half were ejected, and two of the smaller foundations, Trinity Hall and St Catharine's, alone escaped the purge. But the Earl did persuade Parliament to allow the colleges to retain for their own use, under his supervision, all revenues other than those hitherto paid to 'delinquents'—a concession that gave the college some voice in their own affairs, if only a small one.

In the town itself at this period, the Mayor and Corporation faced an unexpected hazard of the revolution in the problem of finding ministers for ten of their fourteen parishes, but they were Parliamentarians almost to a man, with the authority of their prescience in electing Cromwell himself. Thanks to him, the very existence of their age-old enemy was already precarious, and within a few years the Barebones Parliament was to argue that if Oxford and Cambridge were to exist at all—which was not recommended—two colleges in each 'should wholly and solely apply themselves to the study of attaining and enjoying the spirit of our Lord Jesus', where 'few books or outward human helps' were needed, and then only in English. Cromwell's dismissal of this visionary Parliament before it had time to vote was therefore opportune if not providential, however disappointing for the Mayor. Perhaps Cromwell had a kindly thought for Cambridge. One does not know—other than that he did enter his second and elder surviving son as a pensioner at St Catharine's in 1641. Like father, whose Christian name he bore, this 'civil young man' did not stay long. A cornet in the same troop of horse as Cromwell himself, he fought at Edgehill, and died of smallpox in 1644.

Meanwhile no battle raged in sight or sound of Cambridge; Huntingdon marked the limit of Royal endeavour; and into the squalid medieval town, further crowded by its unruly garrison, the wreckage of civil war alone intruded, and that was ill-received. When a number of prisoners were brought 'famished and naked in triumph by Cambridge to London', if the Royalist account is correct, 'some of our scholars were knockt down in the Streets, only for offering them a cup of small beer to sustain Nature, and the drink thrown in the kennel, rather than the famished and parched throats of the wicked, as they esteem'd them, should usurp a drop of the creature'.

It might be said that Naseby, in 1645, ended the military threat to Cambridge, and Dunbar, in 1650, clinched the University's submission to the Puritan yoke, for the Engagement binding those who subscribed to be 'true and faithful to the Commonwealth of England, as the same is now established, without a King or House of Lords', meant another Committee of Regulation sitting in Cambridge with its inquisition and inevitable expulsions. Covenant or Engagement—each spelt the suppression of the enquiring mind. Even the Presbyterian Earl of Manchester, who became Chancellor in 1649, had to go, and the University might be said to have followed in all but name. In what seems to have been a last despairing flicker, only a year before the King's execution, 'some disgraceful expressions in the Schools against the Parliament and army' had led to a fight in which 'the Parliamentiers prevailed' although the scholars of Trinity 'did gallantly' and some were killed.

Now the voice of the Quaker was heard in the land: nor was it the voice of freedom. Rather did it condemn the little that was left, for whereas the Puritan sought to enlarge the Reformation by ridding the Church of ceremony and 'superstition', George Fox and his Society of Friends added the Universities and learning to Puritan oversight. One preached naked in the streets of Cambridge until the Mayor 'did nobly' by putting his cloak around him, and Fox himself, in 1655, had to be rescued—again by the

Mayor—from 'apprentices in the trade of preaching', his name for the scholars who nearly pulled him from his horse and jostled him in the streets. As he described the incident: 'I passt to Cambridge y^t eveninge, and when I came into ye tounde ye schollars was uppe hearing of mee: and was exceedinge rude. . . . They was exceedinge rude in ye Inn and in ye Courtes and in ye Streetes.' It therefore appears that the later days of the Commonwealth were not entirely devoid of incident, and that the University's young men probably found more diversion than their elders.

For the Commonwealth rulers of the town, the Restoration of 1660 meant a swift reversal of fortune. It availed nothing for the Mayor to proclaim Charles the Second the lawful King of England in the Market Place 'amid acclamation of Joy from all sorts', especially as the County had declared for Parliament and a King, and a settlement with the Church, whereas Cambridge had shown its feelings by choosing the two opposition candidates whom the County had rejected. Nor was it helpful to light four bonfires—seemingly in hopeful expiation—after one had sufficed for Cromwell's 'crowning mercy of Worcester'. The Borough's turn had come to face a Commission of Enquiry, and it fared no better than the University had done with the Covenant and Engagement. Wholesale ejection from office followed, including the Mayor of this later day when his Commonwealth sins were remembered against him.

So Oliver Cromwell, leader of ungodly footballers and a fellow-commoner at Sidney, swept to heights of glory and execration that together make embarrassment. Apart from his suppression of the Barebones Parliament at a critical moment, and his acquiescence in the Earl of Manchester's policy of moderation that enabled the colleges to live, he did little to warrant their thanks. He came up and went down, a loutish young man from Huntingdon, but impressive, and no doubt to ensure his later patronage, with its promise of favours to come, the Borough gave him the Freedom of Cambridge. That he 'caused a good quantity of wine to be brought into the Town House, with some confectionery stuff, which was liberally filled out, and as liberally

12

The Woolfson Library, Churchill College
The History Faculty, Arts Precinct

taken off, to the warming of most of their noddles', suggests the
adolescent Cromwell in its crudity. Yet, as a soldier and statesman, he stands apart, with the faithful Milton content to be no
more than his Latin secretary.

Today the famous portrait which, at Cromwell's direction,
remarks 'all those roughnesses, pimples, warts, and everything
as you see me', hangs in the college hall. His death-mask is
respectfully curtained.

In the thunderous surging of modern traffic, Sidney Sussex still
maintains a slight monastic air behind its sheltering walls, but
there is nothing in the street to suggest the Cambridge of its birth.
Nor has Jesus Lane much more, apart from Jesus College. It still
branches to the right and connects with the old Barnwell highway
as it did when St Rhadegund's was young. It still contrives to
suggest that the motor car is an intruder, and not without reason:
those who plan relief roads in the struggle with local traffic have
promised that, one day, Jesus Lane will cease to be a 'trunk road'.

Only when Sidney Street changes its name to Bridge Street,
where the old High Street slants away to the left, does antiquity
return unchallenged. Here, opposite the corner of St John's, is the
Round Church of the Holy Sepulchre, not quite resembling its
prototype in Jerusalem but, one gathers, reconstructed in 1841
according to the Camden Society's ideas on what the design of the
first builders should have been. Ahead lies Magdalene bridge,
marking the one-time ford of a fenland river without which there
would have been no Cambridge, and today this many-named road
which is the axis of a world-known city, still holds to the path of
the Romans and sweeps on with no less authority.

If one turns to the left at the cross-roads just above Magdalene
bridge, one can follow the old route to Oxford—through Bedford, Buckingham and Bicester—and today it has a new importance, for the stretch to Madingley Hill marks the line of University
expansion. Not long ago its milestones recorded the distances
from Oxford and Cambridge, focal points in the world of learning
between which the traffic mainly flowed. Indeed, so many

graduates availed themselves of the privilege of being admitted by the sister University to the degrees that they held in their own, without further examination, that the road itself was privately known as the '*Ad Eundem*'.

Buildings in Cambridge are many and so varied in style that the white domes of the University's Observatory just off the Madingley Road cause no astonishment. Built in 1822 and replacing Bentley's eyrie on top of Trinity's gate-tower, much was expected of it, and but for the prior claims of the tea-break, however critical the moment, Cambridge might have had the honour of discovering Neptune. As it was, the sky clouded over during the sacred interval, and before the moment was again propitious, the Frenchman, Leverrier, had established his claim to the discovery with the help of Berlin University.

One imagines that the venerable Adam Sedgwick, Professor of Geology, was interpreting a general feeling when word of the defeat came during dinner at Trinity, and in the shocked silence he banged his clenched fist on the table and muttered: 'Confound their lymphatic souls!' But his language was notoriously vivid. The future Canon of York whose letters on Cambridge life are so revealing, referred to the Professor's geological lectures as 'a rich mine of strong, rugged and picturesque English even were one uninterested in the mysterious truths which he develops'.

XIII

THE LEARNING OF THE CLERKS

To Richard Wilton, the future Canon of York, posterity is indebted for much light on a University education in the middle of the last century, and that, in turn, affords a no less interesting comparison between the almost static syllabus of the earlier years and the vast expansion which has followed the recent change to a scientific emphasis. Xenophon, Virgil, Greek Testament, Paley and Old Testament History are strangely sounding names now that Greek and Latin and Paley's *Evidences*—'the rock', according to Wilton, 'on which many a gallant ship strikes and is wrecked'— are gone with the Little-Go itself. But he 'floored them all'. What is revealing of the times, however, is that he, an ordinand, then treated himself to a few guineas worth of lectures from the Professor of Botany who took his pupils on 'herbonizing excursions in the neighbourhood', and also paid heed to the college chaplain who 'justly observed that, in a few years, it will be monstrous for an educated man to be ignorant of music and architecture'. Taken out of its context, this definition certainly leads one to smile, but in Wilton's day undergraduates still wrote such exhortations as 'Down with the Pope!' and 'Ye sons of Granta, stand by the Church!' on pavement and wall. Emboldened by milk punch and kopas, they still sallied forth 'to meet any stray townsmen or cad' whom they could conveniently knock down, and they could even improve their vocabularies by listening to Professor Sedgwick; for the University had still to shake off the fetters of religious intolerance; Town and Gown had still to make peace. In 1850,

Science, as the word is understood today, was still no more than
beating at the door; it had still to burst it open and induce a
suffering but kindly English scholar to assist its devotees with a
most useful book on how to write English.

That a religious emphasis should lie heavily on the University
in its early years was inevitable: it owed its official existence as a
studium generale to a papal bull. That this emphasis should change
in its impact over the years was no less so, for doctrine itself was
mutable. Papal Supremacy; Reformation; Marian reversion;
Protestantism with the Puritan edging in; Laud's High Church
reaction against the Calvinist; the Puritans rampant, and finally
the Restoration—it is a formidable list, and beside its implications
such local centres of thought as the Platonists who strove to
reconcile religion with metaphysical philosophy, the 'Saints' with
their evangelical revival, and the 'Apostles' with their Low
Church, were no more than passing distraction. Anglican
allegiance had been enforced in 1662, following the Restoration,
and not until 1871, after a number of graduates had petitioned the
House of Commons thirty-seven years earlier and the House of
Lords had thrown out the bill in the meantime, were the controversial religious tests abolished and nonconformity allowed.
Until then, a Dissenter could neither proceed to his M.A. degree
nor hold a college fellowship.

It is also inevitable that one should suspect the purpose behind
this religious emphasis in the early days when the 'scholars' themselves were grouped in small communities and made to wear
clerical habit; and it is not difficult to see a rebellion against it
when the pensioner arrived and paid for his education. But it is
remarkable that as late as 1637, a hundred years after the dissolution of the monasteries, a report to Archbishop Laud on the
University's shortcomings should read: 'The clericall habit
appointed for students here is generally neglected unless it be at
King's Colledge only, wherein they reteine the ancient manner
both for color and fashion'. But King's then stood as a college
apart, drawing its members from Eton, whereas the others had,
in effect, absorbed the hostels with their less inhibited occupants.
'Undergraduates', the report went on, 'wear the new fashioned

gowns of any color and fashion . . . blew or green or red or mixt, without any uniformity but in hanging sleeves. And their other garments are light and gay, some with bootes and spurs, others with stockings of divers colours reversed one upon the other, and round rustic caps they weare (if they weare any caps at all) that they may be sooner dispised. . . . In all places, among graduates and priests also, as well as the younger students, we have found Roses upon the shoe, long frizzled hair upon the head, broad Spred Bands upon the shoulders and large Merchant Ruffs about the neck, with fayre feminine cuffs at the wrists, nay, and although ruffled shirts . . . be expressly forbidden by the statutes of the University, yet we use them without controule, some of our Drs, heads and all, to the laudable example of others.'

In conjunction with what is known about the curriculum of the period, this report leads one to think that the University had given freer rein to personal adornment than to scholarship, and in truth its early progress had not been rapid. Even the old *trivium* and *quadrivium* endured until the reign of Edward the Sixth, unchanged apart from the substitution of mathematics for Latin grammar in the *trivium* during his father's reign, and mathematics as the word was understood in the early part of the sixteenth century bore little resemblance to what it is now. Then it was numbered with the 'black arts'. At the time of the Reformation those skilled in its mysteries were eyed cautiously as 'nigromancers' with, it seems, good reason, for Pythagoras and Ptolemy were its gods, the one with his mystical properties of numbers, and the other with an approach to astronomy that embraced what would pass today for astrology and 'natural magic'. Pliny's cosmography helped. Elizabeth's statutes do not mention mathematics, and John Wallis, of Emmanuel, who migrated to Oxford and its Chair of Geometry in 1649, did so because, at Cambridge, 'mathematics was scarce looked upon as academical studies'. Cambridge founded its first Chair of Mathematics, the Lucasian, in 1663, with Isaac Barrow its first holder and Sir Isaac Newton its second, in 1669. His *Principia,* published in 1687, set the seal of his own fame on Cambridge mathematics.

In view of this early suspicion, it is satisfactory—and not

unamusing—to find none other than Wordsworth extolling the
virtues of Euclid and thereby suggesting that even his compulsory
studies for the Little-Go were not completely barren. As he put
it:

> Yet may we not entirely overlook
> The pleasure gathered from the rudiments
> Of geometric science.

Nevertheless, some may demur that neither the mystical properties of the three angles of a triangle, nor the square on the hypoten-
use of a right-angled one, could reward anyone with—

> A pleasure quiet and profound, a sense
> Of permanent and universal sway
> And paramount belief.

Although the Renaissance at large was no more than a revival
of ancient classical influences, and to that extent hardly 'new
learning', in this country it was confined almost entirely to
literature and scholarship—to the great renown, in passing, of
such men as Ascham and Cheke, Fellows of St John's who
followed where Erasmus had led with his introduction of Greek
and the germ of criticism. Latin translations of Aristotle were
no longer necessary, and Thomas Cromwell, the Chancellor who
followed the martyred Fisher, abolished lectures on Canon Law,
but apart from that, and the college teaching of Latin and Greek
which he made compulsory, the old studies remained. Theology
and philosophy were still paramount.

Trinity's private tuition was remarkable.

That authority should give the young student, the freshman of
today, two years in which to provide himself with copies of
Aristotle, Plato, Demosthenes, Cicero, a Greek Testament and a
Bible in Latin, is a pointer to both his travail and the scarcity of
text-books, yet failure under either heading—to obtain the books
or take his degree at the proper time—meant his expulsion. His
first year is clearly preparatory, for when he is not studying the
elements of Euclid and acquainting himself with the rules and
modes of reasoning, he is translating Demosthenes into Latin and
Cicero's orations into Greek—an exercise he varies in his second

year by translating Plato into Latin and Cicero's philosophy into Greek. In this year he also studies logic according to Aristotle. From now on, indeed, Aristotle appears to live at his elbow with ethics, politics, and rhetoric in his third year, physical science— in spite of its taint of 'nigromancy'— in his fourth, and as a general guide to his M.A. degree thereafter. That achieved, he is expected to learn Hebrew. Meanwhile, to further his proficiency, he is not allowed to speak English except at permitted times, although at others he can at least choose between Latin, Greek and Hebrew. Each aberration costs him a farthing—double for a Fellow. Also, three times a week there are declamations in hall, English now joining Latin and Greek, and if the young man does not find himself performing in a Latin or Greek play lasting several hours—there is one in each tongue every year—six-line verses, one in Latin and the other in Greek, still remain to be written, being unavoidable decoration on feast-days.

Yet the attention to detail in these statutes reveals nothing abnormal in the scope of a University education in Elizabeth's reign. Some three centuries had to pass before that significantly altered, and the tremendous advance of scientific knowledge turned young men into specialists. Until then this curriculum continued as it had been down the ages—philosophical, classical and religious. Its detail the Master of Magdalene revealed in his *Advice to a Young Student*, published in 1706, a hundred and sixty years after Trinity's foundation, and his advice starts by following the Trinity pattern exactly with the elements of Euclid. The young man then moves on to the *Opticks* of Newton, the *Astronomy* of Whiston, a Fellow of Clare whom the University expelled for Unitarian nonconformity, and Locke's *Essay Concerning Human Understanding*; his classical reading—recommended for the afternoon because, of the three branches of study, it is the least demanding on 'coolness'—ranges from Terence and Xenophon to Cicero and Sophocles, and his copious religious reading includes Pearson's *Exposition of the Creed*—an inevitable selection, one would think—and *De Veritate Religionis Christianae* by the Dutch jurist, Grotius. It was at least a liberal education in its day, and whatever significant difference there is between the studies pursued at the turn of the seventeenth century and those at Trinity in the sixteenth, must have followed the Restoration when Plato was preferred to Aristotle, the prop of medieval scholasticism.

In those far-off days when Latin was the spoken language and the written examination unknown, the candidate proceeded to his B.A. degree by disputation at the end of his third year. That is to say, after completing his *trivium,* he performed the necessary 'acts' and 'opponencies' by arguing questions of scholastic philosophy, twice in support as Respondent and twice as Opponent, and this oral approach continued until the vast and diverse expansion of knowledge led to the introduction of written examinations in 1772 and printed examination papers fifty years later. Even so, aspirants for the LL.B. had to remain vocal until 1851, and the medical student submitting his 'Thesis' is still said to 'Keep an Act'.

Today the undergraduate seeking an Honours degree takes the Tripos covering his particular branch of study, and to explain this odd name for the University's normal examinations, legend goes back to the sixteenth century, before the Reformation, when an 'ould bachilour' known as 'Mr Tripos', presumably because he sat on a three-legged stool called a tripos, argued with the 'eldest son' or senior candidate from each college. The Honours degree was then unknown, and although an *Ordo Senioritatis* appeared in 1498, it was not until the advance of learning itself outran the disputation that the list became an order of merit with those deserving Honours referred to as wranglers in the first class, senior optimes in the second, and junior optimes third—names that still survive in the Mathematical Tripos. Those deemed worthy of the B.A. degree, but not the distinction of Honours, were known as οἱ πολλοί or pollmen, another name that still survives for those who take a pass degree. But, until 1824, there was still only one Tripos examination, in Mathematics, and that the candidate had to pass for his B.A. degree, as well as show himself reasonably well-acquainted with Natural Religion, Moral Philosophy, and Locke on *Human Understanding*.

It appears that the solemnity—and dignity—of a ceremony that had once followed High Mass in Great St Mary's vanished with the Reformation, when Protestant fervour had to show its contempt for what had suddenly become Popish superstition, but why it was necessary for 'Mr Tripos' to degenerate into a buffoon, and the ceremony into a farce, is not so clear. It is on record that, in 1657, two Oxford men, made up as hobby-horses, presented themselves for degrees on the grounds that 'they had smith's work at their digits' ends', Smith being a writer of school-books, and they were accepted because 'such equitation gave them an equitable claim'. Meanwhile the 'ould bachilour' became a sort of jester delivering the prologue, and that—the Tripos speech—in due course changed to Latin verse. It was a curious prelude to serious business, especially in the calm dignity of the newly-built Senate House, but merit was evidently there, for in 1748 the printed sheets of the 'Tripos verses' were combined with those of the 'Tripos list', one on the back of the other. Not until 1894 did the custom die, and by then 'Mr Tripos' himself had long since vanished.

There is, however, the evidence of Weedon Butler, a Sidney man whose brother was senior wrangler in 1794, to suggest that levity was not always appreciated during a period when the University had advanced no further than requiring some written answers, and the whole system of examination was only beginning to take its present shape; for he, who suffered from no aspirations, wrote: 'It was remarked in the Senate House that I had more the appearance of an idle lounger than of a candidate for Academical Honours. Indeed I could scarcely avoid being of the same opinion when I beheld the ghastly looks of my competitors. One of them fainted away on the first morning of Examination; several declined the contest from mere debility; and most of those who did endure to the end looked more like worn-out rakes than men under three and twenty in the bloom of youth and in the prime of manhood.'

Although the written examination, when introduced, merely supplemented the act of disputation, it was not long in assuming the major role and as quickly made disputation unnecessary, but the act, with the unchallenged custom of many centuries behind it, lingered on until it became a mere formality with the pollmen. The Moderator, or presiding examiner, conducted the argument, two candidates at a time, one of whom as Respondent asserted that 'Recte statuit Newtonus', and the other, as Opponent, that 'Recte non statuit Newtonus'. They then changed sides, as it were, and repeated the formulae, thereby fulfilling statutory requirement to the letter if hardly according with intention. That the standard of Latin in the University was now sadly falling away, Arthur Gray, at one time Master of Jesus, reveals in his delightful story of a candidate who arrived in haste without his academic bands, the two short strips of white linen pendant from the throat that are lightly known as bibs, and met the Moderator's formal rebuke— 'Domine Opponens, non habes quod debes. Ubi sunt tui—Anglice— bands?'—with: 'Domine Moderator, sunt in meo—Anglice—pocket.'

The trivium and quadrivium, with their off-spring of philo-sophical, classical and religious studies, certainly had a long innings as a University education, but the curriculum was static whereas the bounds of knowledge are not, and increasing know-ledge demanded a new approach. Today, there are over a hundred professorships, and, apart from ceremonial, the Tripos is all that survives—as a name for an Honours examination in each of some twenty subjects, and in Natural Sciences alone there are fifteen sections, Physics, Chemistry, Zoology, Pathology, Metallurgy, Biochemistry, and so on. The modern undergraduate therefore tends to become a one-subject specialist rather than a broadly educated man in the old sense. Such specialists, however, are not new. None other than Macaulay showed how absurdly in-adequate the old examination was, with its single Tripos, mainly mathematical, when it offered the only path to an honours degree for a man of his attainments. Twice he had won the Chancellor's medal for English verse, and also a prize for Latin declamation, but he loathed mathematics, and had to face the academic world as a pollman, just one of the herd. But it did not preclude his election to a Trinity fellowship.

There has also been a notable adjustment—a democratic levelling, as it were—in the recognition of a candidate's worth by labelling it first class, second or third, with no order of merit within the class. Later, the second class itself was divided into parts known as 2(1) and 2(2). So, in 1910, the year of adjustment, the Mathematical Tripos not only lost its senior wrangler at the top of the Honours list, but also its 'wooden spoonist' at the bottom, and with him the boisterous finale to the admission ceremony in the Senate House. Here the pollmen lowered the wooden spoon from the gallery on to the junior optime at the bottom of the list, while he knelt before the Vice-Chancellor. As the spoon, perfectly proportioned and beautifully decorated with college crest and Greek inscription, often started life as an oar, and pollmen abounded then, the occasion was apt to lose some of its dignity.

Colourful and impressive though present-day ceremonies can be, with doctors in scarlet on high occasions, the past did not lack its moments. Apparently a candidate who had not completed the exercises required for his degree had first to make good the omission symbolically with 'some trifling and ludicrous' proceedings known as *huddling,* a name that is said to derive from a not so distant period when 'at a given signal *hooding* began, i.e., each man's bedmaker put the rabbit's fur hood over his head'.*

As bedmakers, or 'bedders', in early days were the only women allowed in students' rooms, and, by University law, they had to be *'senex et horrida ex aetate'*, the scene might well have been Hogarthian.

One result of the vast expansion of knowledge during the last hundred and fifty years is that the old 'learning of the clerks' as represented by Mathematics and Classics lost its dominance if not its importance. With it, too, vanished the tutor who, in earlier centuries, lived with his two or three pupils, privately coaching them in a little world apart. For external pressures were now at work, and the Schools again flourished, though not as first conceived. The Royal Commission of 1850 had recommended not only that the supervision of studies should be restored to the University, but also that academic honours should be given in the

---

* *Ceremonies of the University of Cambridge* by H. P. Stokes

new branches of knowledge. Among these, the Natural Sciences Tripos made a tentative appearance in the following year with three names on its list. That same year the Moral Sciences Tripos also appeared. Law followed in 1859, History in 1870, and others in steady succession. No less importantly, the Classical Tripos was freed of its Mathematical fetters. Although a separate Classical Tripos had been introduced in 1824, its candidate still had to obtain third-class honours in Mathematics before they could take it.

In 1872 a further Commission dealt with departments concerned with particular studies, and increased University funds with graded contributions from the colleges. Then came the Commission of 1926 to recognize that the colleges by themselves could never provide the huge facilities which Science alone demanded, and that the State would have to assist endowment. Furthermore, they required the colleges—again according to resources—to accommodate new professors with fellowships, and gave University status to all lectures.

Here, indeed, was also recognition that the turning of the colleges into teaching establishments, whatever their success with the *trivium* and *quadrivium* routine, was inadequate in the twentieth century. Never again would professorships be the nominal offices that some had been when Uffenbach expressed his amazement that 'no courses of lectures were delivered in the University', and that 'only in the winter three or four lectures are given by the professors to the bare walls, for no one comes in'. Gray, it will be recalled, never bothered to lecture, and even the forthright Sedgwick, who once remarked that 'when a man has his rump in the seat of a head, his whole moral nature becomes inverted', knew little about geology when he accepted the Chair in 1818. Then there was the Professor of Mineralogy who, ten years earlier when the Chair was established, had no place in which to lecture, and the Downing Professor of Medicine who was not unknown to rise from his bed and take his class of two at the breakfast table.

So, in the late-nineteenth century, the University threw off its medieval shackles and started in pursuit of the learning that was leaving it behind. Bacon had been some two hundred and fifty years ahead of his time when, in 1605, he wrote in his *Advancement of Learning* that 'there will hardly be any main proficience in the disclosing of nature except there be some allowance for expenses'.

XIV

LATE COMERS

AFTER the founding of Sidney Sussex in 1596, it might be said that the flow of benefactions into the University aimed at enhancing, and sustaining, the sixteen colleges that were already there, rather than the launching of new ones, and two centuries slipped by before the number was increased—then with some hesitation. Sir George Downing, Baronet, of Gamlingay Park in Cambridgeshire, and the sole founder of Downing College under his will of 1717, died in 1749. The Great Seal was not affixed to the Charter until 1800. Seven more years elapsed before the builders laid the foundation stone, and not until 1821 was the college in proper working order, by which time the first Master was dead. But the Downings were an odd family to whom odd things undoubtedly happened.

The first Downing to hold the title was at least a man of parts, having been a lecturer at Harvard, a Puritan preacher in Barbados, Cromwell's Resident at The Hague, and, according to Pepys, 'a perfidious rogue'. Nevertheless, he changed sides at the Restoration with sufficient skill, however deplorable the detail, for the King to reward him with title and estates. Nor, it seems, was grandson George cast in a different mould. The 'villainous fellow' who hit him on the head with a hammer alleged, before the magistrates, that he saw no wrong in killing a person 'who paid nobody, and was so ill a landlord and paymaster with so great an estate'. In his declining years Sir George may indeed have lived 'a most miserable, covetous and sordid existence', but there

must always be a spark of sympathy for an ageing man stricken
with gout, whose marriage collapsed on his wedding day,
especially when from that disaster came Downing College.

It is all a strange revelation of the times, for marriage was
thrust upon him at the age of fifteen, his wife being a girl of
thirteen, and with the completion of the ceremony they parted.
He was sent on his tour abroad, and when, yielding to parental
pressure as he had done, his wife graced the Court of Queen Anne
as one of her Maids of Honour, he never forgave her although she
waited ten years. Nor did he oppose the decree of nullity that
she finally sought. On his part he admitted that 'such disgusts and
aversions have arisen and continue between the two that there is
no possibility of any mutual agreement, and they are very
desirous of being set at liberty'. But the Bishops said 'no', em-
phatically, and Sir George and Lady Downing continued as they
had begun, married only in name.

Without a family of his own, he could do no more than leave
his property to his cousins on the condition that if they died
without issue, the estate should go to the founding of a college in
Cambridge; and as they so died, Downing College was born,
though not until a lawsuit between the Chancellor, Masters and
Scholars of Cambridge University and Dame Margaret Downing,
the widow of Sir Jacob, and his heirs-at-law, has lasted five years,
and another thirty elapsed in forcing Dame Margaret to hand over
the estate. It is therefore not inappropriate that today, in the
University, there should be a Downing Professor of Law.

With an endowment that proved to be woefully optimistic,
the trustees planned a society consisting of a Master, two Professors—the second devoted to Medicine—and sixteen Fellows
of whom fourteen were to be laymen, a stipulation that certainly
reflects the changing emphasis of the times. But, most striking of
all, in magnificence the college was to be second to none—a
masterpiece of Grecian revival entrusted to its expert practitioner,
William Wilkins. Space sufficient to permit the fulfilment of
these splendid ideas—and, in the outcome, provide a great court
larger than Trinity's—was found, at a second attempt, in the
thirty acres of St Thomas's Leys, the area, that is, between what

are now Regent Street and Trumpington Street to east and west,
and Downing Street and Lensfield Road to north and south. It
was also another enclosure of common land which Parliament
authorized in 1801. Nor even King's Chapel was to 'subject'
Downing, and nothing less than a Propylaeum should give access
to this temple of learning. That would have been from Downing
Street, had not the gates and posts that marked intention proved
to be no more than passing memorials to an early dream that was
soon to fade. By the turn of the century only two ranges—
undoubtedly Grecian though hardly as Wilkin intended—fore-
shadowed the court that one sees today by marking its western
and eastern sides; and after the college had sold the northern end
of its spacious grounds to the University, a less pretentious gateway opened on to Regent Street.

The University's swift and continuing development of the
land acquired throws an almost dazzling light on the strange
academic world into which the college had been born. Known as
the 'Downing Site', with the Sedgwick Museum of Geology
forming part of an impressive Edwardian façade along Downing
Street, it became an outward sign of the New Learning. For a
time the Law intruded its Library, but so ancient a symbol of the
static past soon made way for the litter of schools that marks the
urgent present: Geology, Mineralogy and Petrology, Biochemistry, Physiology, Psychology, Botany, Geography, the
Molteno Institute of Parasitology, the Low Temperature Station
... a vast complex of buildings that steadily increase the congestion. Nor is it alone. Across the street is 'The Cavendish' with
its own crowding neighbours, and already there is talk of expansion.

Meanwhile Cambridge itself began its nineteenth-century
sprawl which gives no sign of ending, and the early vision of
Downing as 'a principal feature in the view of Cambridge from
the London Road' faded with its shrinking acres. But it is still
spacious and impressive; and now that, in recent years, a northern
range has given the college its chapel, the resulting three-sided
court with its colonnades and Ionic pillars of Ketton stone is like
no other in Cambridge.

13

New Hall

Nor was Downing less interesting as a new foundation joining the community of the old—a college that had to establish its traditions in a period that saw the complete disruption of old ideas. A suggestion of precocity in its behaviour was therefore both inevitable and deplorable, though in retrospect delightful. One scandalized official of the University wrote, referring to Mrs Frere, the Master's wife: '(I vow my hand shakes so with horror at the very thought of it that I can hardly make my pen write down the awful profanation) she got up *The Rivals* and *The Critic* in the College Hall!' That being so, one could wish that he had been there to comment on Dr F. R. Leavis's powerful castigation of C. P. Snow as an author, made in the same hall only the other day.

That peace should come to Cambridge after some six hundred years of bickering between the Town and University, its 'unjust stepmother', was perhaps the least expected outcome of this expansion of learning. But change was not confined to the University. By mid-nineteenth century both sides were absorbed in their own affairs, for the corruption in the town, which was itself expanding rapidly, could no longer be overlooked, and, in effect, the University abrogated its privileges by neglecting them. Discords there were in the gathering harmony at the level of rowdy and student, and youth alone ensured that they continued for a while. Ten years after the great rapprochement, a police constable spent fourteen days in prison for assaulting a Trinity undergraduate during the 'Tom Thumb Riots', Tom Thumb being an American dwarf.

No doubt at the close of the eighteenth century, and for several decades to come, political malpractice in Cambridge was neither appreciably greater nor less than what it was elsewhere in the country. It was a legacy from the static past when authority was given to the few, and now that the community was expanding, the few were taking steps to ensure their own survival. One step resulted in the passing of thirty years, from 1788, without a contested election in the borough. Nor was it difficult to control these pseudo-elections in a community where its rulers had been able to do as they pleased after the revolution of 1688 had put an end to the Royal Prerogative in local affairs. The few aldermen set no problem. They chose themselves—for life—and could always be 'helped' with Corporation property. One is known to have paid two guineas for a building site worth over £100. Freemen, too, were created for the occasion, and they were not required even to live in Cambridge. Twenty of the seventy-three who were added to the voting-list in 1788 were tenants living on the Duke of Rutland's estates at Belvoir and Cheveley, near Newmarket, the Duke having recently purchased the 'influence' of Mr John Mortlock, the prosperous local draper who became a banker. Mortlock figured largely in the Cambridge scene at this period, not only as Mayor on thirteen occasions, but also as the master-mind who selected candidates and ensured their election. It mattered not that political reformation and commissions of enquiry lay ahead. For the moment the Corporation was unassailable, and in the days that preceded its downfall, it appears to have degenerated into a free, though select, dining club which met at the Eagle in Benet Street, 'with good wine and plenty of it', and 'the right to expend their income on themselves and their friends without being bound to apply any part of it to the good of the Town'.

That was the Rutland Club of the Tories. The Whigs, though increasingly vocal, had yet to rally.

Being able to have its own two representatives in Parliament— a right bestowed by James the First and not withdrawn till Hitler's war was over—the University was not deeply concerned with local manoeuvring, but in the Duke of Rutland it could point to a Trinity man who, as Charles Manners, had represented the University in the Commons until he succeeded to the title. That the Duke had no sympathy at all with Republican France in the throes of revolution can be accepted—aristocratic heads were falling—and it says much for the personal respect which he commanded that Cambridge produced the strange phenomenon of anti-Republican riots when other towns were rioting in favour of the Republicans. The Napoleonic wars, however, soon changed these cries to 'Give us bread!', and once invasion threatened,

politics were second to survival, with the further call 'To arms!'.
Cambridge then exceeded its quota of volunteers, and even in the
University, exempt though it was from the muster, a martial
stirring brought into existence a forerunner of the C.U.O.T.C.,
146 strong.*

So, until Napoleon's surrender, there was at least an uneasy
armistice if not political peace in Cambridge, and it might be said
that hostilities were resumed in 1815, a year that found the Duke
already established as High Steward and his brother the town's
Recorder. The battle of the cart-tolls followed—tolls, that is,
levied on loaded carts entering the town.

With no Parliamentary authority for this exaction—twopence
for a loaded cart—the Corporation had yet contrived to resist all
attempts at removing it. Only freemen were exempt, and Mr
S. P. Beales, who led the opposition and owned many carts, being
a well-to-do corn and coal merchant living in Newnham, could
never enjoy a freeman's privilege because he would not accept the
Rutland ticket. Instead, he flatly refused to pay. Sued by the
Corporation, he was tried at Westminster Hall in 1826, and won.
Sued again, on a technicality, he won again, and that was the end
of the cart-toll and the old Corporation as well.

By itself, the loss of revenue from these tolls was bad enough—
it roughly halved the Corporation's income—but legal expenses
of some £4,000 meant that money had to be borrowed; and
although the Rutland candidate's return to Parliament was
smoothly achieved in 1829, there was no telling what might
happen once the Reform Act of 1832 became effective, for that
vastly extended the franchise to bona-fide house-holders and, at
the same time, put a seven-mile limit on the residence of freemen.
Moreover, the Municipal Corporations Act of 1835 introduced
similar reforms, one of which removed half the aldermen from
office every three years, with the result that the old regime was
virtually swept away at the first local election. Meanwhile the

---

* Queen Elizabeth's statutes of 1570, under which the University was still
living, exempted all scholars and students and their servants, and the officers,
servants and ministers of the University, from musters and contributions
thereto, and from sending men to the wars.

Commission enquiring into the old Corporation's affairs had uncovered a state of negligence, if not worse, that is best instanced by a charge of maladministration which compelled the Corporation to refund £1,086 of money held in trust, and also pay £224 towards the informer's costs.

The first act of the new Council was to banish the Rutland brothers from office, and apart from an eagerness to convert the common land into building sites and to sell the Corporation maces, an eagerness that was happily thwarted, it carried out its task of restoring confidence and looking after Cambridge with reasonable success. But in the working of the Reform Act it was ineffective once the voters at large had discovered that the only significant difference between Whig and Tory at a Parliamentary election lay in their inducements: the Tories were more generous —so generous, indeed, that the Rutland candidate soon took his seat again. The Royal Commission that investigated these corrupt practices in 1853 found the electorate for the most part illiterate, a large number being unable to write their own names. The Tory agent who gave evidence before the commission, had been convicted and imprisoned for bribery after the 1839 election—a temporary embarrassment that, apparently, in no way damaged his career or his expertise and brought him £200 in compensation.

This opportunism, however, was soon to pass. A new and irresponsible electorate had merely found a profitable toy. Of far greater consequence was the adjustment in Town-and-Gown relations. By the second half of the nineteenth century, a rapidly growing community of some twenty thousand inhabitants, with street-lighting, a railway that was for ever extending, and a properly organized police force of twenty-four constables, produced a situation that the University was just as anxious to resolve as the Town. Wrapt in its own affairs, and also static in numbers, it was in no position to exercise its ancient privileges, and much can be said for the good-will and ultimate satisfaction of both Town and Gown that after a former judge of the King's Bench, Sir John Patteson, had arbitrated between them, they expressed appreciation with 'a handsome silver candelabrum of the value of 300 guineas in grateful acknowledgement of his services'.

The long 'war' was over.

This arbitration produced the Cambridge Award Act of 1856, and on its rulings it might be said, in brief, that the University from now on left the Town to look after its own affairs, and collaborated in matters concerning both. Away went the objectionable oaths and declarations of subservience that the early Mayors and officials had been called upon to make. With them, too, went the supervision of markets and fairs, and the old right of 'conusance' which had once made the Chancellor's Court 'the townsmen's scourge'. But the Proctors' authority and the Vice-Chancellor's powers relating to theatrical performances, wine licences and discommoning, remained with some modifications to which time has added others; and if there is a regretful glance from the Guildhall today, it must surely come from the Treasurer's office, for the University, while agreeing that its property should be rated in accordance with the Award Act, cannot forget that it enjoys the rebates of a charitable institution. Meanwhile Corpus Christi supplies the present Town Clerk whose immediate predecessors were from Sidney Sussex and St John's, and the University not only contributes eight councillors to the City Council, but also performs the supreme act of reconciliation by taking its turn in providing the Mayor himself.

After the founding of Sidney Sussex in 1596, Downing was the only college or approved foundation to appear in the next 273 years. Then Fitzwilliam Hall arrived—later to become Fitzwilliam House to avoid confusion with '*The* Hall' which is ever Trinity Hall in Cambridge—and it is probably significant of the University's new approach to scholarship that, in the last hundred years, the number of colleges and approved foundations which have come into being, has reached double figures.

Fitzwilliam College—for such it is today—started as an experiment, a deliberate throwback to the medieval hostel for non-collegiate students, but their 'admission, superintendence and regulation' rested with a Censor and his staff under the University's supervision. In due course the acquisition of the brewer's red-brick house in Trumpington Street provided something of a corporate life, but post-war expansion made a move inevitable, and in its new home off the Huntingdon Road it has settled down not only as a college in status but one of the larger foundations. Moreover, its buildings repeat the essentials, if not the design, of the old-fashioned college, condemned to the 'modern idiom' though they are; and if a suggestion of the Arabian Nights creeps in, it is not unpleasing.*

But Fitzwilliam did not alone ensure its natal year's significance. Already a movement was afoot to create, by public subscription, a women's college that would 'hold in relation to girls' schools and home teaching, a position analogous to that occupied by the Universities towards public schools for boys', and in October 1869 there was opened at Hitchin, in Benslow House, the 'College for Women' where Miss Emily Davies started her ride to fame as Mistress. It had five students. Nevertheless, only three years after this modest beginning, a large and pleasant site off the Huntingdon Road had been purchased—near enough to Cambridge for convenience but sufficiently remote for safety—and the purpose was to 'erect, maintain and conduct a College for the higher education of women', and ominously, 'to take such steps as from time to time may be thought most expedient and effectual to obtain for the students of the College admission to the examination for degrees at the University of Cambridge; and generally to place the College in connection with that University'. This declaration hardly accords with the Tenth Commandment, but it was at least an honest declaration of intent, and in the following year when Miss Davies and her invading army occupied the buildings of Alfred Waterhouse, the attack upon the masculine stronghold of Cambridge University had been mounted from Girton College.

* Cambridge has still to accept modern architecture with equanimity. Not long ago when the plans of an expensive memorial hall were displayed, its resemblance to the conventional African stockade was so striking that protest compelled a fresh design—duly likened to a trussed turkey in side elevation and a white-washed barn inside. But it is, one gathers, 'functional'—surprisingly so. A small part of what little ceiling there is, which had been sprung into position, suddenly threatened to spring out and had to be thwarted with scaffold poles— in the middle of a Tripos.

Nor was Girton lacking an ally—the society that today is Newnham College.

So many women, from far and near, wanted to attend the lectures which Henry Sidgwick started for them in 1870—he was the Moral Philosopher and Fellow of Trinity—that accommodation had to be found, and after the lapse of only a year, Miss Anne Jemima Clough, the poet's brother, followed the Girton recipe with five girls in a Cambridge house. To increase the scope of these lectures, an Association for the Higher Education of Women soon came into being, and the problem of financing a hall of residence for the growing body of students—building began in 1875 on a site in Sidgwick Avenue—was ingeniously solved by amalgamation with a commercial company. Like Girton in 1872, Newnham was incorporated by Board of Trade Licence in 1880, a sequence reversed by the Royal Charters granted to Newnham in 1917 and to Girton in 1924, but as far as seniority in the University is concerned, both were 'founded' in 1948, the year in which the last defences fell and women became full members of the University.

Inevitably Sidgwick himself played a large part in Newnham's development—he lends his name, with those of Pfeiffer, Clough, and Peile, to the buildings and halls that have added themselves to the one that is now called 'Old'—and it is possible that his philosophy at a time when both Oxford and Cambridge were breaking away from the thraldom of ancient religion, had some influence on the development of a college that has no chapel. But the whole design of Newnham is unusual because its expansion has taken the form of additions, separate and sufficient in themselves, that for the most part line a pleasant garden, and are connected by an arterial corridor. Girton's expansion, in contrast, has been less attenuated. With a single hall—and chapel—it follows the conventional college pattern in large and wooded grounds that are themselves delightful, and if it is remarkable for anything, apart from the Waterhouse family's passion for the reddest of red bricks, it is the most bewildering set of corridors in Cambridge.

Once established on the University's doorstep, with their

academic sympathisers within, the 'monstrous regiment' quickly gained a foothold—being allowed, by grace of the Senate in 1881, to take the Little-Go and the Triposes privately, without entitlement to an official degree. But this set-back merely spurred the defenders. When necessary, an enraged army of M.A.s from distant vicarages—all entitled to vote—now rallied in such numbers that even the railway companies ran special trains, suitably placarding their purpose, and the Kaiser's war had been fought and won when the local invaders achieved the title of a Cambridge degree. That was in 1921, and it was, in effect, the end. Admittance to the University Library, lecture-rooms and laboratories followed two years later. After three more, qualified members of Newnham and Girton became eligible for teaching offices and memberships of Faculty Boards, and but for the interruption of Hitler's War, it is probable that the formal admission of women on the same terms as the men would not have been delayed until 1948. Then it passed almost unnoticed in the University at large until, in a crowded Senate House, amid all the impressive formality reserved for these occasions, the University acknowledged the new era with a doctorate, *honoris causa,* bestowed upon her Majesty the Queen. But there was a short, and not unamusing, period of adjustment when the women found that they now had to adopt the dark and sober dress of formal occasions, and the Proctor concerned had to point out to the Head of one House that red and yellow polka dots the size of golf balls did not conform with the University's idea of subfusc.

For the University, compelled to expand westward, the direct route was for the most part that so recently followed by Mr Beales' historic carts—to and from Newnham and over the Silver Street Bridge. It is a sylvan and spacious corner of Cambridge, bearing no relation at all to development on the other side of the city, and today it is very much 'New University'. Beyond the curving sweep of Queens' transpontine block, built between the wars, there are traffic lights where Silver Street crosses Queen's Road and the famous Backs—sodium-lit at night. It continues as Sidgwick Avenue where Ridley Hall and Newnham share most

of the left-hand side, and the new Arts Precinct and Selwyn
College the other. As Ridley Hall is the Church of England
Theological College founded in 1879, and Selwyn arrived only
three years later with, according to its Charter, 'the expressed
object and intention of providing persons desirous of academical
education, and willing to live economically within a College
wherein sober living and high culture of mind may be combined
with Christian learning, based upon the principles of the Church
of England', it does appear that some agency was swift in meeting
Newnham's unorthodoxy with the powerful antidote of example.

Founded by public subscription in memory of George Augustus
Selwyn, Bishop of New Zealand for twenty-seven years from
1841, and then of Lichfield for another eleven, the new society
also commemorated a Johnian second classic who rowed in the
first race against Oxford in 1829, and, with reason, also disliked
Bishop Colenso's arithmetic. But Selwyn College, in 1882, a
definitely Anglican community seeking recognition in a University from which all religious restrictions had been abolished as
recently as 1871, was something of a problem, and although
recognized as a Public Hostel in 1883 and raised to an Approved
Foundation in 1926, it was not incorporated in the University
until 1958, after Newnham and Girton. Meanwhile it developed
and prospered as a normal Cambridge college, preferring the red
brick of the period and a pleasant court where even the chapel,
though prominent, does not offensively dominate.

In contrast, the adjoining Arts Precinct with its faculty accommodation and glossy new lecture rooms gives one a thoughtful
glimpse of what the future holds, for these flat-roofed, stilted,
brick-faced modern buildings with their shop-window glazing,
doubtless set the pattern of expansion yet to come. After the first
of the great wars, Clare built its Memorial Court in this inviting
refuge which was once the Cambridge Field, and in 1925 the
stately avenue of Queens' Road was the pride of its kind in
Cambridge. Now it is a motor highway and a by-pass for heavy
traffic. Sir Giles Gilbert Scott, architect of Liverpool's Anglican
cathedral, not only designed Clare's grey-bricked court, but also
created the University Library that stands in perfect symmetry

behind it. The façade alone of this huge building is 420 feet long, and its central tower rises 156 feet—at times startling the unsuspecting stranger by emitting smoke from the chimney which it conceals. Critics there are. One suggested that Sir Giles had confused his plans with those for a penitentiary. But it is still wonderfully impressive, and useful. King George the Fifth and Queen Mary opened it in 1934.

Not least among the problems of finding room to live in Cambridge since the war is that of dealing with the flood of postgraduate and research students—over two thousand and rising—for these amount to roughly a quarter of the entire University, and because segregation within an old foundation is often difficult, the 'College of the B.A.' is now appearing in the land of promise across the Cam. Most interesting among them is University College itself, for the Chancellor, Masters and Scholars of the University founded that by Trust Deed as recently as 1965, with the object of advancing 'education and research' especially among the graduate students of the University. In Bredon House, near Newnham, it has found a suitable haven rather as Peterhouse settled in Trumpington Street when the University was young, but there the analogy ends: women as well as men are admitted to the University's college, and one reads of such feminine touches as foam-rubber seats and non-slip carpets of misty-blue Irish wool, and finds no mention of *senex et horrida*.

Founded only a year before University College by the Masters and Fellows of Gonville and Caius, St John's and Trinity, also by Trust Deed, Darwin College is the oldest graduate foundation of its kind. It was conceived as such, and it takes its name from the old Darwin home—Newnham Grange—which it occupies with The Hermitage, built in the early nineteenth century, and The Granary, parts of which are several hundred years old. Additions and alterations have been 'designed to merge with the existing houses without aping them stylistically', but when a residential block is inserted and rounded off at one end with a dining hall, octagonal in shape and built on stilts with a carpark underneath, the shade of Sir Charles Darwin may well study the change with some perplexity if not regret. The new college lines one side of Silver Street—the other is open—between the old millpool and the traffic lights. Behind it, Coe Fen stretches away to the south, still recalling an earlier wilder age though long since tamed and denuded of Gunning's snipe; and to the north, the Backs are stretched in enfilade.

At the far end of this famous adjustment of Nature for man's delight, where Northampton Street connects Madingley Road with the Via Devana on its way up Castle Hill, are some of the oldest houses in Cambridge, and in two of them—not far from the School of Pythagoras—is the Lucy Cavendish Collegiate Society, the first graduate college for women. In its foundation, by Trust Deed in 1965, for the 'advancement of education, religion, learning and research among the graduate and research students in the University', there is nothing abnormal, yet in its origin one can detect a suggestion of protest, as well as challenge, for it sprang from the Society of Women Members of the Regent House who were not members of any college and, being 'homeless', dined together as a club—'a high table without a college', their President said. In its title the new college commemorates Lucy Cavendish who declined to be considered for the headship of Girton after the death of her brother, Lord Frederick, in the Dublin murders of 1882.

There is, too, Clare Hall, founded in 1966 by the Master and Fellows of Clare College as a graduate society for men and women; and housed in Herschel Road, beyond the University Library in this green and pleasant land, it is at the moment a Society of Fellows preceding the admission of Research Students.

After Girton and Newnham had presented the University with the 'problem of women', and Selwyn had shown its untimely religious bias, seven decades slipped by before the next colleges came into being—New Hall for women, and Churchill for men, both for undergraduate and postgraduate students; the one modestly 'to advance education, learning and research in the University', the other to devote itself mainly to Mathematics,

Engineering and Natural Science, and so ensure its reputation in advance. Founded by an association that was formed in 1953 to promote a third college for women, and recognized as an Institution of the University in the following year, New Hall prepared the way for Darwin College by warming the site in Silver Street before migrating to the heights of the Huntingdon Road. Here, close to Fitzwilliam, it has settled down as a normal college, complete with chapel, library, hall and lodge, though one of modern design, and apart from the attentions of some playful, and resourceful, undergraduates who contrived to give the impression that a giant with black paint on his feet had walked over the huge fibre-glass dome of the hall one night, its existence has so far been uneventful.

That can also be said of Churchill. But Churchill is not only a college for men: it is a mid-twentieth century and lay version of King's, designed to reflect the glory of the name it bears with comparable magnificence; and the idea of having a second giant among the colleges, rivalling if not exceeding Trinity, was not without critics in a University already overcrowded. From the Trust established in 1958, however, it was soon evident that the money was there for a country-wide subscription, as well as the determination to commemorate Sir Winston, and the project swept ahead. Madingley Road afforded an excellent site. Mr Richard Sheppard, the London architect, produced the winning design for Churchill College, and, no doubt, ensured a place with the honoured creators of ancient Cambridge. Sir John Cockcroft, one of the country's most eminent scientists, became the first Master and Prince Philip the first College Visitor, future appointments to these offices being reserved to the Crown. At High Table level the Fellows are described as Official, Professorial, Pensioner, Research (both Senior and Junior), Overseas and—fittingly perhaps—Extraordinary, and in 1967 those in occupation numbered seventy-five. There is, too, a chapel with a central altar beneath a suspended cross.

That Churchill should embody all the distinguishing features of the new age—flat roofs, stilts, and general expanses of plain brick—is no less inevitable than the lack of 'personality' which seems to be a characteristic of modern architecture. 'Gracious' is an adjective that does not apply. But whether or not Churchill College is successful as a national monument, its creation does give an idea of the cost of expansion today; for if its population settles at about 650, and rising costs do not leave the estimate of £4½ million too far behind, the initial outlay per head will be about £7,000.

XV

WIDER STILL AND WIDER

THERE is a story of a third-year man who, when asked what he intended to do on going down, morosely supposed that he would keep on going down, and it matters not whether Oxford or Cambridge is the summit referred to: the three undergraduate years that a young man spends at either can never occur again. All that is asked of him, apart from academic ability, is that he should have a soul, not an obsession—a humble appreciation of opportunity rather than a swollen head. It is not asking overmuch from one who is part of the University, probably at public expense. For an ancient University that has pioneered thought in a changing world and written a chapter in history, is more than a donor of B.A. degrees. It offers to its young men a way of life wherein the simple decencies of human conduct are still preserved, although one might not think so in these days of Student Councils. It knows, too, that the way ahead will be far from easy, the problem today being the cost of expansion that politics demand. Its good fortune, so far, has been the understanding of the Grants Committee.

When, in 1914, the Treasury made its first grant to the University—a yearly one for the Medical School—the sum was £5,873. Now, half a century later, the new science centre which responsible opinion considers necessary, would cost not less than £50 million and probably twice as much, an estimate sufficiently inflated to ensure that the 300 acres between the Backs and Coton's doorstep, bordering Madingley Road, are not wholly cluttered with 'monumental' buildings for a while, if at all in this century. In this far-sighted expansion, three times the area which sufficed for Cambridge itself when bounded by river and Ditch, the famous Cavendish Laboratory would occupy about nineteen acres of one of the 30-acre plots into which the site is divided—each far bigger than Parker's Piece. But any concentration of undergraduates in Cambridge means bicycles, and it is just as well that the City has time to solve its traffic problem—not least that of a western by-pass—before it has the further one of coping with the contribution of a new science centre, the flow from which, as the experts have ominously noted, would be against the main traffic streams in and out of Cambridge during rush hours. At present, the visitor in term has only to stand on King's Parade at one-o'clock, when lectures stop, to be reminded of the charge of the Light Brigade on bicycles.

Were it not for the older colleges and churches, Cambridge would have little to show for its antiquity, expansion having taken the form of a comparatively modern and eastern sprawl which has moved the centre of the populated area from the Market Hill to a point a mile away on the Newmarket Road; and with this transference has come, inevitably, the twin problems of access to the City's old shopping centre and the urgent need for creating a new one. Cambridge, in fact, had become a planner's paradise, and, it seems, nothing is safe. Not long ago acquisitive glances were cast at the City's particular and inviolate joy, Christ's Pieces, a delightful open space, ten acres of lawns and tree-lined paths that flank the garden wall of Christ's. Once it was Jesus land, and although, when acquiring it towards the end of the last century, the Town solemnly undertook to maintain it as a public amenity, already a bus-station has made a small encroachment. Yet here was the proposal that it should not only be a new shopping centre, but one so designed that 'in effect the various groups of shops would be large pavilions set in open spaces . . . more reminiscent of an exhibition than a normal shopping centre'. Recently, too, from the same imaginative source, came the idea of an underground track, a sort of Inner Circle for motor cars. But, fortunately for the ratepayer, the men of Cambridge remain

Fitzwilliam College

unmoved—a traditional posture. Against the victorious Danes at Ringmere in 1010, long before the University came, 'there stood Grantabrigg-shire fast only'; and today it seems likely that the new shopping centre will be purely functional, with no exciting pavilions, and, in spite of the devious paths of planning thought, near the new centre of population.

Nor is the routeing of traffic an easy task when the critical area is that once set by river and Ditch. How to develop the Lion Yard without making the chaos worse is itself a major problem. Only on two points is there certainty: new road-systems are necessary, and the four bridges that today carry the traffic over the river are insufficient. The outlook for the ratepayer is therefore bleak, whatever the solution. Meanwhile, as if the jesting gods were unable to resist the temptation to bedevil the problem completely, Magdalene Bridge—the Great Bridge itself—is sagging, like man, under the burden of his creation.

Being concerned with the part, rather than the whole, the University is less unhappily placed than the City, though still beset with problems. Soon the old Addenbrooke's Hospital will complete its reign of two hundred years in Trumpington Street, and, at the moment, the idea is to build a new home for the biochemists and generally improve the 'back-street thoroughfare' of Tennis Court Road behind it. Deferring to such venerable neighbours as Pembroke and Peterhouse, and to the classical architecture of the Fitzwilliam Museum in a street that is itself historic, the new building will not be 'monumental', but even so its presence sets a problem when the number of motor cars that will have to be accommodated, close by if not on the site, is estimated at nearly a thousand.

So the expansion goes on, striving to keep pace with the modern demand for education in general and science in particular. Over the Cavendish site a giant crane tells of clearances and new building in a space no less crowded than the Downing, and on the other side of a narrow street is the Red Lion's temporary car-park—a central problem if ever there was.

Faced with the task of housing the multitude, colleges have been steadily enlarging their own accommodation since the war,
14

Churchill College

within their bounds if possible, beyond—as hostels—if not. St John's has just brought into use the glass-and-concrete but still magnificent Cripp's Building, virtually a £1 million gift from the Cripp's Foundation which adds two courts to the college and accommodates some two hundred undergraduates, apart from Fellows. No less ambitious, Christ's is seeking to make the college a self-contained community within the bounds of its island site, and is proceeding by stages to add some 250 rooms for undergraduates and dons at a cost not far short of £1 million. Selwyn has plans for another court at a similar cost. And there is, it seems, no end. Meanwhile King's and St Catharine's, interlocking neighbours as it were, are working together on a scheme that will not only provide their domestic wants, such as a new hall for St Catharine's and kitchens for both, apart from normal accommodation and amenities, but will also straighten the old Plott and Nuts Lane, introduce a small 'stilted' court behind the Bull's cherished façade, provide an underground car-park and stowage for three hundred bicycles, also for St Catharine's, and cost something over £1 million. When completed, the new Lane will enter Trumpington Street through one of the old coach arches of the Bull. To that extent the whole scheme is an imaginative approach to an unavoidable problem, and St Catharine's, which pays the lion's share on benefits resulting, further conceived the idea of securing ready money by issuing its own mortgage debentures on the London Stock Exchange—a pattern for others to follow.

It says much for the hard thinking and good sense behind the recent development that Cambridge is still an ancient city, its architectural charm quite unimpaired, for 'glass and concrete' do not intrude. K.P. is still K.P. Unless one looks through the archway down the new King's Lane—the straightened Plott and Nuts—there is no direct indication from the street that an area the size of Trinity Great Court has been cleared, excavated and developed to meet the requirements of two colleges. The Cambridge that the visitor sees is still a garden in spring and summer. The gracious old buildings do not change.

The University's material expansion inevitably followed the widening bounds of learning. Hitler's war and the social revolution have merely increased the tempo, and in the University today there is little that is static—apart from its ancient monuments and ritual—and much that is revealing. Survivors of that Spartan age in University history when the undergraduate, having a bath, sat in a tin saucer before his sitting-room fire and poured a jug of warm water over his head, are not wholly amused to hear a young man complain that a bed-sitter is too box-like to allow him 'to express himself', when the amenities provided include central heating and a private bathroom.

That one generation of undergraduates should differ from another is inevitable: the times themselves change, and never more rapidly have they done so than in the twentieth century. Yet the extent to which the modern undergraduate differs from his predecessors is undoubtedly less than might be supposed. There is, for example, nothing original about a recent passion for luxuriant hair. As long ago as 1560, in the reign of Elizabeth the First, it was directed 'that no Scholler doe weare any long lockes of Hayre uppon his heade, but that he be polled, notted, or rounded after the accustomed manner of the gravest Schollers of the Universitie under payne of 6s. 8d.'; and since then the undergraduate hair seems to have risen and fallen with the monotony of the tide. Dr Caius, returning to his college two years earlier, after an absence of nineteen, recorded: 'Faces and things, manners and dress were new. I saw new looks. I heard a new pronunciation.' Were he alive at the moment, he would continue to do so. In the 1960s it is not unknown for High Table to speculate on the geographical origin of the scholar who read the Latin grace. Caius also wrote of students with 'frilled shirts, baggy trunk hose and tight nether stocks'. After the Kaiser's war he would have found baggy trunk hose not only in fashion but gloriously enlarged and known as 'Oxford bags'.

An estimate for 1965 gave the scholastic background of undergraduates in residence as eleven per cent 'working class', and the rest about equally divided between public schools and those grant-aided, including grammar. It therefore appears that the recent—and happily receding—eccentricity in dress and personal appearance was at least blessedly free of class distinction, especially as, at one period, the two leading exemplars were a Pauline and a Wykehamist; but this type of youthful nonsense is apt to steal the limelight and create a wrong impression. Nor is Cambridge free of that other product of the age, the 'professional student' who finds his vocation in ragged processions, carrying a banner.

Today it is inconceivable that Johnians should be called upon to thwart Trinity's assault on their gatehouse with burning torches, and do so by hurling down the brickbats kept on top of it for that purpose. But three hundred years ago, before strolling round Cambridge, young men armed themselves with swords, not slogans; and not so many years earlier one finds Robert Greene, of London's 'roaring boys' with Marlowe and Nash, recording in his *Repentance:* 'Being at the University, I light among wags as lewd as myself, with whom I consumed the flower of my youth.' Banner-bearing is at the worst an innocuous pastime.

But along with these passing and sometimes repetitious phases, there are the more sober adjustments of evolution, of breaks with custom that are final. One argument of the undergraduates who sought and achieved their release from the centuries-old inconvenience of wearing gowns after dark, was that it would enable them to avoid any taint of snobbish distinction from the local population; and the historic chaperon has disappeared completely, taking with her practically all the old prohibitions on women in men's colleges. Within the time limits imposed by authority, today's young women come and go as they please. Gone, too, is the Poppy Day rag with its collections—amounting to £10,000 in recent years—for the survivors and dependants from two world wars. Instead, the undergraduate body decided to hold a Camrag supporting charities of their own choosing, among which Earl Haig's Fund may or may not be numbered; for time has moved on: today's undergraduates were unborn in 1945, and 1918 is just as remote as 1066.

Some fifty years ago a cricketer of distinction played three times in the Varsity match—afterwards leading his county, taking an M.C.C. side to the West Indies, and succeeding to the family title—but never passed his Little-Go. Today that could not happen. He would first have to show a basic academic competence at school before being so much as considered by the college of his choice. This necessity also means that the only hope of finding a place in the University for a man of Churchill's calibre, is to found a college for him.

What is not always appreciated is that A-levels do no more than mark a standard attained at school. They carry no guarantee that the holder is suitably equipped to read for a Tripos. Too much may depend on the result. It is on record that one undergraduate so handicapped, an economist, suddenly leapt to his feet in the middle of his examination, scooped up his papers and flung them ceiling-wards—compelling, no doubt, a measure of sympathy— but he also let out a piercing shriek and fainted. Nor can one fail to hear dark mention of drugs, and even suicide, a revelation of instability almost unknown in the early years of the century, but now sufficiently intrusive for the Eastern Gas Board to promise non-toxic natural gas in Cambridge a year sooner than intended. Fortunately there is always the nonsense of normal young men to balance the Cambridge picture. Not long ago some ingenious sapper officers in residence suggested one way of solving the local traffic problem by parking an Austin van on top of the Senate House. It was a remarkable feat in every way; Cambridge had a good laugh; Civil Defence some useful practice; and no damage was done at all.

So the centuries have passed, and if the local wilderness hardly rejoiced when the University evolved in its midst, there is no doubt that an erstwhile morass duly blossomed as the rose. High-handed though it was, the University yet made a city known to the world. It is, indeed, so well known that even the laying of a simple flagstone path on the cobbled surround of a college court— cobbles being murder for women wearing stiletto heels—led a great London newspaper to refer to its 'popsification' in two-column headlines. Cambridge, in fact, is news on a number of counts, and however odd the actions of the earlier colleges may seem today, one should not forget that they alone, by jealously guarding their heritage from a more gracious age in architecture, have given the City its charm.

Much though there is for the visitor to see in Cambridge—the Fitzwilliam Museum is just as famous in its way as the University itself—there are still the private treasures that lie hidden, the small mementoes that colleges treasure, not for their value alone. Corpus Christi still has the magnificent fourteenth-century drinking horn that marked its foundation; Gonville and Caius, the small brass astrolabe, of like antiquity, that Caius himself is thought to have owned; Christ's, the silver-gilt Foundress's Cup of the sixteenth century, given by Lady Margaret; and Emmanuel, the Founder's Cup of Sir Walter Mildmay, also sixteenth century in silver-gilt. Of such is the private splendour of Cambridge— the gleam of silver and gold by candlelight, for colleges do not forget to commemorate their benefactors, in hall as well as chapel. Some two hundred years ago, a lady went so far as to direct in her will that the recipients of her wealth should spend £5 each year on an 'entertainment' at which one of the Fellows on her foundation should deliver a Latin speech in praise of education.

It may well be that the older colleges are sad memorials to a less urgent phase in man's evolution, never to return, and what the future holds for the human race may itself be alarmingly unsure; but there is little doubt that, while these monuments remain, men privileged to have passed from youth to manhood within the ancient walls one sees today, will return to them with pride and sober thankfulness for the privilege that was theirs. For them, Cambridge is ever a city of haunting memories. L. de G. Sieveking—a name once inseparable from the B.B.C.—has written: 'Cambridge is not only the vibrations of the youth of today, but the emanated emotions of a thousand yesterdays: of the love, happiness and gratitude of generations of those who have had in this place the richest experience in their lives.'

In that experience, Trinity men included the privilege of being lulled to sleep by their fountain's tinkling music in the Great Court.

Time, no doubt, adds enchantment, for even the high-minded

Richard Wilton who, in his second year, wrote to his mother that he had 'never entered on residence in Cambridge with so keen a sense of the peculiar dangers' to which undergraduates were exposed, some thirty years later, in his *Lyra Pastoralis,* yet recalled the days—

> When the dew
> Of youth was on us, and the unclouded blue
> Above us, and Hope waved her wings o'er all.
> The ancient elms, green Court, and tinkling call
> Of Chapel-bell; gowns flitting o'er the view
> To Hall or Lecture. . . .
> Nor time nor place nor circumstance can render
> Our hearts indifferent to those years long fled,
> With their rich store of recollections tender.

INDEX

A

Abdul Rahman, *Tunku*, 60n
Adams, John Couch, 118
Addenbrooke, John, 57–8
Addenbrooke's Hospital, 57–8, 85, 163, 209
Airy, Sir George, 158
Alcock, John, Bishop, 107
Anne Boleyn, 76
'Apostles, The', 159
Arms of the City, 13
 University, 96
Ascham, Roger, 183
Audley, Thomas, Lord, 137–8
Australes, 25

B

Backs, The, 21, 49, 53, 72, 123, 204
Bacon, Francis, 28, 110, 148, 150–1, 190
Badew, Richard de, 46
Baldwin, Stanley, 158
Balfour, Arthur James, 158
Balsham, Hugh de, Bishop, 34–5, 37, 42–3, 121
Barnes, Robert, 90
Barnwell Field, 53, 127, 133, 137
Barrow, Isaac, 148, 150, 152, 182
Bateman, William, 51, 53, 66–7
Beales, S. P., merchant, 196, 201
Beaufort, Lady Margaret, 44, 113–16, 120–21, 125
Benson, A. C., 141
Bentley, Richard, 147–8, 150, 152–7, 179
Besant, Sir Walter, 119–20
Bilney, Thomas, 52, 90–91
Bingham, William, 115
Birkenhead, Lord, 81
Boreales, 25–6
Botanic (Physic) Garden, 55, 85

Brooke, Rupert, 82
Browning, Oscar, 81–2
Brownrigge, Ralph, Bishop, 106
Bucer, Martin, 91
Buckmaster, William, 92
Burghley, Lord (William Cecil), 122
Butler, Wheedon, 186
Butts, Henry, 104
Bynge, Thomas, 69
Byron, Lord, 36, 148–9, 157–8

C

Caius, John, 67–8, 78, 152, 211
Calverley, C. S., 119–20
Cambridge Award Act, 1856, 20, 25, 130, 198
Cambridge Field, 53, 137, 202
Camden, Lord, 81
Campbell-Bannerman, Henry, 158
Cartwright, Thomas, 152
Catherine of Aragon, 92
'Cavendish, The', 56, 193, 208–9
Cecil, William, *see* Burghley, Lord
Chancellor's Court, 19, 198
Charles I, 171, 176
Charles II, 127, 139, 171, 177
Cheke, Sir John, 183
Chesterfield, Lord, 52
Chesterton, 13, 50, 96, 98, 110
Churches:
 'All Halowes in the Jury', 30
 Holy Sepulchre (Round Church), 27, 53, 178
 Holy Trinity, 81, 169
 Our Lady and the English Martyrs (R.C.), 163
 St Andrew the Great, 98
 St Benet, 18, 56, 62, 143–4
 St Botolph, 56–7, 59, 66, 86
 St Edward, 47, 90

St John Zachary, 30, 46–7, 73
St Mary the Great, 18, 30–31, 45, 55, 57, 63, 74, 77, 84, 91, 114, 123, 142, 144, 172–3, 186
St Mary the Less, 34, 37
St Michael, 43, 48, 91, 142
St Peter, *see* St Mary the Less
Cibber, Gabriel, 150
Clare, Countess of, 46, 47
Clarkson, Thomas, 123
Clough, Anne Jemima, 200
Cockcroft, Sir John, 205
Colenso, John, Bishop, 118–19, 202
Coleridge, S. T., 108–10
Colleges of the University:
Buckingham, 137, 146
Cavendish, 163
Christ's, 22, 43, 79, 85, 103, 114–20, 164, 169, 210, 214
Churchill, 98, 112, 138, 161, 205–6
Clare, 42, 46–51, 58, 74, 98, 106, 173, 202
Clare Hall, 204
Corpus Christi, 42, 50, 62–5, 104, 161n, 198, 214
Darwin, 203
Downing, 98, 169, 191–4, 198
Emmanuel, 84, 164, 166–9, 170, 214
Fitzwilliam, 56, 137, 161n, 198–9
Girton, 59, 137, 199, 200–1, 204
God's House, 73, 98, 113–15, 121
Gonville and Caius, 22, 27, 42, 57, 59, 66–9, 70, 98–9, 114, 203, 214
Jesus, 18, 64, 84, 107–9, 116, 133, 172, 175, 178
King's, 14, 22, 31, 38, 43, 45, 47–8, 57, 59, 66, 69, 73–82, 84–7, 90–92, 98, 113, 128, 132, 144, 146, 160, 171, 174, 181, 193, 205, 210
King's Hall, 42–5, 146
Lucy Cavendish, 204
Magdalene, 15, 84, 105, 109, 123, 137–41, 144–6, 161n, 172, 184
Michaelhouse, 42–3, 50, 62, 146, 151
New Hall, 204–5
Newnham, 200–1, 204
Pembroke, 39, 40, 42, 56, 58–62, 174, 209

Peterhouse, 34–40, 56–7, 79, 114, 121, 161n, 168, 175, 203, 209
Queens', 43, 48, 50, 85–90, 99, 105, 161n, 172, 175, 201
St Catharine's, 20n, 28, 48, 57–8, 60n, 77, 79, 93, 98–9, 102–3, 105–7, 125, 161n, 175, 210
St John's, 30, 43, 48–9, 69, 70, 84, 98, 105, 111, 114, 118, 121–5, 161n, 166, 172, 178, 198, 202, 210, 212
Selwyn, 138, 202, 210
Sidney Sussex, 21, 23, 43, 98, 103, 106, 111, 146, 161n, 169–73, 175, 191, 198
Trinity, 22, 27–8, 30, 36, 42–5, 48, 52, 67, 85–6, 98, 128, 132, 138, 146–61, 164, 171, 176, 179, 183–4, 192, 203, 205, 212
Trinity Hall, 20n, 42, 48, 51–4, 92, 98, 175, 198
University College, 203
Corporal Punishment, 30, 83, 116
Coverdale, Miles, 91
Cranmer, Thomas, 20, 92, 109
Crashaw, Richard, 39
Cromwell, Oliver (father), 38, 126, 140–41, 171–8, 191
Cromwell, Oliver (son), 175
Cromwell, Thomas, 183

D
Darwin, Sir Charles, 117, 204
Davies, Emily, 199
Devereux, Robert, 151–2
Doket, Andrew, 86–8
Downing, Sir George, 191–2
Dowsing, William, 38, 106, 174
Doyle, Sir Francis, 149, 152
Dunning family, 21, 35, 43, 204

E
Eachard, John, 56
Edward II, 19, 28, 43–4
Edward III, 23, 44, 149, 160
Edward IV, 99
Edward VI, 67, 93, 182

Elizabeth I, 50, 60, 77, 95, 108, 129, 147–8, 151, 166, 182, 184, 196*n*, 211
Elizabeth Woodville, 87
Ellys, Sir John, 143
Ely, Reginald, 75
Erasmus, Desiderius, 88–90, 114, 183
Essex, James, 105, 168, 170

F
Fagius, Paul, 91
Farman, Thomas, 90
Farmer, Richard, 132, 169
Fisher, John, 44, 61, 88–9, 114, 121–2, 138, 183
Fitzgerald, Edward, 158
Fox, George, 176–7
Frazer, Sir James, 158
Frith, John, 90

G
Gardiner, Stephen, 52
George III, 150
George IV, 74, 151
George V, 203
Gibbons, Grinling, 150
Gibbs, James, 76–7, 144
Glomerels, 29, 30
Gonville, Edmund, 66
Gray, Thomas, 39–41, 118, 189
Greene, Robert, 212
Grey, Lady Jane, 93
Grumbold, Robert, 105, 110, 150, 173

H
Hallam, Arthur Henry, 159
Harvard, John, 167–8
Harvey, William, 69
Henry III, 21, 25–6
Henry VI, 14, 22, 73–4, 76, 84, 113
Henry VII, 75, 113
Henry VIII, 44–5, 75, 77, 84, 92–3, 129, 146, 151, 160
Herschel, Sir John, 118
Hobson, Thomas, carrier, 24, 55, 90, 102, 164–6
Homerton College, 163
Housman, A. E., 32

Howard of Effingham, Lord, 52
Hullier, John, 91

J
James I, 51, 116, 127, 160, 195
Jebb, Sir Richard, 158
Jeffreys, George, 151
Jennings, Sir Ivor, 20
John, King, 21, 128–9, 133
Jones, W. H. S., 105*n*
Johnson, Samuel, 39, 116

K
King's Ditch, the, 21–4, 56, 85, 120, 126, 164
Kingsley, Charles, 140

L
Lambert, John, 90
Langton, John, 74
Latimer, Hugh, 60, 90–91, 141
Laud, William, 167, 181
Law, William, 168–9
Leavis, F. R., 194
Leys School, 55
Locke, John, 184–5
Long, Roger, 40
Luther, Martin, 90
Lutyens, Sir Edwin, 138
Lytton, Edward Bulwer, 52

M
Macaulay, Thomas Babington, 128, 148–9, 158, 187
Malcolm IV, King of Scotland, 107
Manners, Charles, 195–6
Mansel, William Lort, 157
Margaret of Anjou, 86
Marlowe, Christopher, 212
Mary I, 67, 91, 93–5
Maurice, F. D., 158–9
Mere, John, 144
Merton, Walter de, 35
Midsummer Fair, 133
Mildmay, Sir Walter, 84, 166–7
Milton, John, 38, 102, 116–17, 150
Montagu, Charles, Earl of Halifax, 151

Montagu, Edward, Earl of Manchester, 171, 174–6
Montagu, James, 23, 164
Morland, Samuel, 140
Mortlock, John, 195
'Mr Tripos', 185–6

N

Nash, Thomas, 212
Nevile, Thomas, 147–8, 150
Newton, Sir Isaac, 28, 131, 147, 149–150, 153, 155–6, 182, 184
Nicholson, Sygar, 27, 90
North, Roger, Lord, 96–7

O

Oates, Titus, 69, 70, 151
Oxford, 'Ad Eundem road', 179; Exodus of Clerks, 24; Lollardy, 84; Merton, 35; New College, 89; Ratcliffe Infirmary, 57; Reformation, 60, 91; 'University Hall', 46

P

Paley, William, 26, 117–18
Parker, Matthew, 65, 86
Parnell, Charles Stewart, 140
Parr, Katharine, 86
Parr, Samuel, 169
Patteson, Sir John, 197
Peckitt, William, 150
Pecock, Reginald, 74, 87
Pepys, Samuel, 139–41, 143–4, 191
Perne, Andrew, 23–4, 164
Perse, Stephen, 85
Pitt, William, 60–61, 118
Pitt Press (University), 57, 61, 150
Pollmen, 185, 188
Praed, Winthrop, 53, 158
Proctors, 19, 25, 27, 30–31, 33, 90, 95, 116, 130, 132, 142, 198, 201
Pythagoras, School of, see Dunning

Q

Quadrivium, see Trivium

R

Railway, coming of, 134–6

Ramsden, Mary, 99
Ray, John, 151
Regents, 31, 47
Religious Orders:
  Augustinian, 56, 85, 143
    Barnwell Priory, 18, 63–4, 84–5, 133
    Hospital of St John, 18, 34, 84, 113, 121–2
  Benedictine, 84
    St Rhadegund's, 18, 84, 107, 112
  Carmelite, 18, 84
  Dominican, 84, 99, 167
  Franciscan, 18, 84–5, 146–7, 170
  Gilbertine, 57
  Sack, Friars of the, 19
Richard II, 45, 93
Ridley, Nicholas, 60, 91, 141
Ridley Hall, 201–2
Rogation Fair, 133
Rogers, John, 91
Routh, Edward, 39
Ruskin, John, 14
Rutherford, Ernest, 28, 56, 150

S

'Saints, The', 141
Sancroft, William, 168
Sandys, Edwin, 93–5
Scott, Sir Gilbert, 122
Scott, Sir Giles, 202
Sedgwick, Adam, 158, 179–80, 189
Seeley, Sir John, 119
Selwyn, George, 202
Sheppard, Richard, 205
Shipley, Sir Arthur, 115
Sidgwick, Henry, 200
Sidney, Frances, Countess of Sussex, 146, 169
Sieveking, L. de G., 214
Simeon, Charles, 81, 169
Smith, Robert, 157
Spenser, Edmund, 60
Stanton, Hervey de, 43
Sterling, John, 159
Sterne, Lawrence, 108
Strafford, Thomas Wentworth, Earl of, 122

Stratford de Redcliffe, Lord, 81
Sturbridge Fair, 20, 104, 127, 129–33
Symons, Ralph, 121, 148–9, 170

T

Tait, Peter, 39
Taylor, Jeremy, 70
Tennyson, Alfred, 148, 150, 158–60
Thackeray, William, 149–50, 158–9
Thompson, William (Lord Kelvin), 39
Thompson, W. H., 158
Tripos, origin of, 185–7
Trivium, 29, 83, 182, 185, 187, 189
Tusser, Thomas, 52

U

Uffenbach, Zacharias, 38, 46, 61, 65, 70–72, 79, 87–8, 107, 139, 148, 150, 168, 189
Union Club, 53
University Press, see Pitt Press

V

Valence, Marie de, 58–9
Vermuyden, Cornelius, 14
Victoria, Queen, 160–61

W

Walker, Richard, 56, 156
Wallis, John, 182

Walpole, Horace, 39, 81
Walpole, Sir Robert, 81
Walsingham, Sir Francis, 81
Ward, Samuel, 173
Washtell, George, 75
Waterhouse, Alfred, and sons, 53, 59, 65–6, 199, 200
Watson, Richard, 28
Westcott, Brooke, 158
Whewell, William, 148–9, 151, 158, 160
Whiston, William, 184
Whitgift, John, 69, 152
Wilberforce, William, 123
Wilkins, William, 65, 76, 192
Willoughby, Francis, 151
Wilton, Richard, 25, 142, 179, 180, 215
Wolsey, Cardinal, 89, 90, 93
Woodlark, Robert, 99, 102, 105
Woods, R. Salisbury, 148
Wordsworth, Christopher, 157
Wordsworth, William, 15, 27, 41, 75, 110, 117, 123–5, 147, 159, 183
Wotton, William, 28
Wren, Sir Christopher, 37, 56, 150–51, 168
Wren, Matthew, 37, 59
Wright, Stephen, 144
Wyattville, Sir Jeffery, 170
Wycliffe, John, 74, 84, 87